Mrs. Willis L. Bontrager

D1234582

Mrs. Willis L. Bontrager

Right from the Start

. . . to release the creation and sustenance of life into the same realm of decision, struggle, surprise, imagination, and conscious intelligence as any other difficult but freely chosen work.

Adrienne Rich
Of Woman Born

Right from the Start

Meeting the Challenges of Mothering Your Unborn and Newborn Baby

by Gail Sforza Brewer

Author of *The Pregnancy-After-30 Workbook*

and Janice Presser Greene

Book design by Barbara Field
Photography by Suellen Perold
Illustrations by Jean Gardner

Rodale Press Emmaus, Pa.

Additional photography by Marjorie Pyle, R.N.C., pages 44, 76, 77 (bottom left and right), 78 (top left and right), 107, 111, 113, 114 (top), and 116 (top) and by Eric Brewer, page 75.
Additional illustrations by Mary K. West, pages 131, 133, 137, 167, and 180.
Copy editing by Felicia D. Knerr

Printed in the United States of America on recycled paper containing a high percentage of de-inked fiber.

Library of Congress Cataloging in Publication Data

Brewer, Gail Sforza.
    Right from the start.

    Bibliography: p.
    Includes index.
    1. Pregnancy.   2. Prenatal care.   3. Childbirth.
4. Infants (Newborn)—Care and hygiene. I. Greene,
Janice Presser, joint author. II. Title.
RG525.B664   618.2′4   80-27795

ISBN   0-87857-273-2   paperback
       6 8 10 9 7   paperback

Other books by Gail Sforza Brewer

The Pregnancy-After-30 Workbook: A Program for Safe Childbearing—No Matter What Your Age, (ed.), Emmaus, Pa.: Rodale Press, 1978.

What Every Pregnant Woman Should Know: The Truth About Diets and Drugs in Pregnancy, New York: Random House, 1977. Paperback ed.; New York: Penguin Books, 1979. Spanish ed., *Lo Que Toda Mujer Embarazada,* Mexico City: Diana Press, 1980.

The Italian Family Reunion Cookbook, New York: St. Martin's Press, 1981.

For Andrew
    Marni
    Marisa
    Ginevra
    Cornelia
    Thomas
. . . upon whom we learned

Contents

Contents

viii

Appendix

Acknowledgments

The photographic sequences in this book were made possible by the enthusiastic interest and cooperation of the staffs of the Departments of Obstetrics/Gynecology, Pediatrics, Midwifery, Nursing, and Public Information at:

    The Waltham Hospital, Waltham, Massachusetts

    Albert Einstein Hospital, Bronx, New York

    Cambridge City Hospital, Cambridge, Massachusetts

    St. Margaret's Hospital for Women, Dorcester, Massachusetts

and the office of:

    A. Y. Rathnam, M.D., Ossining, New York.

Additional photographs and original material for illustrations were loaned by:

Andrea's Baby Pack, Eugene, Oregon

Asoka Roy, C.N.M., Department of Midwifery, Beth Israel Hospital, New York, New York

Birth and the Family Journal, Berkeley, California

C/SEC, Boston, Massachusetts

Childbirth Education Association of Greater Philadelphia, Philadelphia, Pennsylvania

Lifecircle, Costa Mesa, California

NAPSAC, Marble Hill, Missouri

Resources in Human Nurturing, International, Denver, Colorado

We are also grateful to our editor, Charles Gerras, whose good will and good judgment have sustained us throughout.

Introduction

For the New Mother

There has never been a more challenging time to become a mother.

Controversies about pregnancy, birth, and child care, once reserved for the pages of medical journals, now make headlines on supermarket magazine racks and produce high ratings for television talk shows.

This generation, the first generation of women for whom having a child has been truly just one option among a wide variety of fulfilling life pursuits, couldn't be taking the choice more seriously. Debates about motherhood versus career, motherhood combined with career, and motherhood *as* a career are a hallmark of our time.

Much of the debate has turned on defining just what mothering is—"good" mothering. How to do it, yes, but also how to fix its value in a world dominated by the marketplace mentality. Inextricably joined to that question is one about the other half of the pregnancy equation, the baby. Just what does a baby need for normal development? Physical care, to be sure, but what of the capacity to form relationships, to trust, to enjoy, to love? How do babies develop these, and what, if anything, do mothers have to do with the process of development? How one answers these questions has profound bearing on the job description for today's mother.

Despite all the confusion and ambivalence, signs are everywhere that a mothering revival is underway. For the first time in years, having a baby is back in style!

- More babies were born in 1979 than in any previous year for a decade.
- Inaugural issues of magazines aimed at the new mother appear at an ever-quickening clip, while established publications rush to revamp their formats, adding pregnancy columns and features dealing with maternity.
- Chic maternity boutiques are popping up on fashionable avenues in the hearts of our American cities most noted as career centers for women.
- Even those feminists who once decried motherhood as the root of female oppression are having second thoughts. In an outpouring of recent articles and books, female biology—especially our unique ability to conceive and bring forth new life—is increasingly embraced as a wellspring of power, instead of being rejected as a millstone of defeat. Judged from this perspective, as Adrienne Rich has done so eloquently in her book, *Of Woman Born: Motherhood as Experience and Institution* (New York: Bantam, 1977), childbirth be-

comes an immensely significant way of coming to terms with our bodies, of discovering our physical and psychic resources.

In accordance with these heightened perceptions of both the needs of our babies and ourselves, mothering from conception onward turns out to require nearly every physical and psychic resource we can muster! The goal of this book is to provide you, the new mother, with one additional resource: the book of instructions that didn't come with your baby.

From the time you become pregnant until your baby is a month old, you'll be facing hundreds of new situations and be called upon to make many major decisions about your own care and that of your baby. This book echoes the good news emanating from the women's health movement on many other issues—taking the best care of yourself and your unborn/newborn baby is far easier and far more pleasurable than most of us have been led to believe. In the chapters that follow we present successful strategies for doing so, based on our 20 years' combined experience as counselors of thousands of expectant and new mothers, our day-to-day skills as mothers of our own six children, and, of course, the research background (much of it quite recent) that illuminates *why* certain practices work so much better than others.

Perhaps you, like so many of us these days, are beginning your mothering years far away from your own mother or other female relatives whose values you share, and you're finding that your former student friends or your work associates are unlikely to be of much help as you set about learning how to mother. We hope this book will go a long way toward filling in the information you lack and the support vacuum you're encountering.

The chapters that follow detail an approach to mother/infant care we wish we'd known about when we first became mothers, a set of principles our grandmothers took so completely for granted they would have thought it odd for anyone to write a book about it. But these basics are often at wide variance with the advice which has become standard over the past 50 years. How the "standard" advice came to differ so markedly from the nurturing norms of countless preceding generations, and how to avoid the pitfalls that can result from "standard" advice, are major themes throughout this book. It's clear to us that in many instances the advice we get about mothering from nonmother experts actually prevents us from doing a very good job of it. Unfortunately, forming a working partnership with a competent medical consultant is the number-one problem new mothers from coast-to-coast contact us about. So, whenever possible, we've included full information on the latest medical thinking on matters ranging from pregnancy nutrition to neonatal circumcision for you to use in evaluating the advice you're getting. It will also be helpful to you in gaining cooperation from professionals for your maternal and child care preferences.

It's important to say at the outset that many women before us have grappled with these crucial issues. All of us are indebted to those mothers who have managed to keep alive the tradition of human nurturing according to human norms—sometimes even in the face of strong disapproval from family, friends, and paid health consultants. Most often, women have found their way to this mothering style, not as the result of scholarly research into cross-cultural child-rearing practices, but as the result of personal experience—surviving one or two pregnancies and infancies conducted according to the dictates of standard advice. The stereotypical image of the new mother two weeks after her baby's birth—harried, haggard, and feeling helpless and hopeless after so many nights of lost sleep—is a classic case in point. Driven by sheer desperation to find a less exhausting, more enjoyable way of caring for a new baby, these women fashioned, mostly by trial and error, a nurturing style which fulfills both their baby's innate expectations and their own quest for increased physical well-being and peace of mind. The experience and hard-won expertise of these mothers are invaluable to those of us still mired in the contradictions born of today's standard mother/infant care. They rediscovered a more rational and more feeling way of doing things, and they and their families are the better for it. By using these care recommendations, you'll be able to look after your first baby as expertly as if it were your fourth. And, in the process, you will save numerous anxious calls to the doctor, to your local mothers' center hotline, and to the-woman-you-met-at-the-beach-last-summer-who's-your-neighbor-but-you-hardly-know-her-except-that-she's-got-three-kids-who-look-healthy-so-she-must-know-what-to-do-next!

This less-work, greater-reward approach to having a baby rests on a few fundamental premises, all of which we discuss more fully later on.

Introduction

- *Mothers decide* how to care for themselves and their children and are entitled to complete information in order to do a responsible job.
- Mother and infant are a *biological and social unit from conception through weaning* and the integrity of this unit must be respected at all levels of interaction with others.
- Human infants are born with an immutable *biological legacy of care expectations* that must be met for the infant to develop fully in body and spirit.
- The events of pregnancy, birth, and the early hours after birth *condition the events of the newborn period.*
- There is a pervasive, *commercialized concept of baby care* which undermines the mother-baby relationship in ways that are both obvious and subtle.
- Every baby has a *right to be well cared for by its own mother,* and every mother has a right to the social support that enables her to provide that care.

In our work with women and families we've found that asking a simple question usually resolves whether one way of doing something is better for you and your baby than some other way. Just ask:

Does this practice/object/individual serve the urgent need my baby and I have to stay together?

If the answer is yes, it's probably a fine thing to do, buy, or make an appointment with. If the answer is no, or if you are unsure of the answer, you need to take a closer look at what is being proposed, keeping in mind the six points above.

Consider for a moment the most primitive circumstances under which human beings have been born and you'll understand why we're convinced that this question is the right one to ask.

A woman and her mate have been living in the primeval forest of North America. She has noticed her middle swelling for a long time and has been by turns amused and awed by the flutters and blows she's been feeling there. She has followed her appetite, eating and drinking more than usual of the available food.

This day she has been walking slowly up and down the shore of the nearby mountain lake, stopping every so often to lean against the trunk of a mighty tree as she feels steadily increasing pressure and tension in her abdomen and between her legs. Her mate has walked with her some and now rejoins her on the path to their shelter. Soon, the woman begins grunting and bearing down. She senses enormous pressure on her rectum and assumes a squatting position over a bed of leaves with her mate supporting her from behind. A few more pushes and the mother feels a great release of pressure as the baby's head passes from her body. She feels the shoulders turn, then the rest of the baby's body tumbles out into her hands. The mother cries out with a mixture of relief, surprise, and exultation. She opens her eyes and beholds her wet, wiggling, and whimpering child for the first time.

She lifts the child to her breast for mutual comfort and reassurance and to inspect it closely. Because of the dangers of this place, the mother will not relinquish her child, nor will she leave it alone, even when she is occupied with daily work. She keeps the child bound to her person at all times in the early months, and within arm's reach until the child is sufficiently mature to recognize the dangers for itself. To do otherwise would be to risk the child's very life, to jeopardize the continuance of the group.

While we are not suggesting that a return to primeval conditions is necessary for good mothering, this vignette illustrates the essential pregnancy and infant care survival adaptations which have worked to the advantage of the human species over the millenia. Most striking is the extraordinarily close mothering that characterizes the child's early experience outside the womb. A strong bond of physical proximity and emotional attachment between mother and offspring has seemed to insure that the mother will take whatever steps are necessary to protect and nurture her young. Apparently, this has been the human way of nurturing for as long as we have inhabited the planet. Or at least up until the past 50 years.

When we consider these concepts in this remote, prehistoric context, their soundness is self-evident. But of what practical value are these survival mechanisms, so deeply rooted in our human essences, in a world in which few of us are threatened by predatory beasts, rampaging elements, and a food supply dependent on what we are able to gather and hunt? What can we who have access to decorator nurseries and Bo-Peep night lights, feeding bottles and baby nurses, college courses and other careers hope to learn from our prehistoric mothers?

First and foremost, a conviction that each of us is personally necessary to her own baby.

Second, an ever-watchful attitude toward environmental threats to our infant's welfare.

Erosion of these two precepts has created much of the confusion about mothering in contemporary life. For the past two generations women have been told that any number of other people are suitable substitutes for a given mother, and, subliminally in ads for baby paraphernalia, that the mother herself is a virtual incidental in the well-equipped nursery. Now the tide is beginning to turn, thanks in large part to exhaustive studies on every aspect of newborn life. Far from relegating personal mothering to the scrap heap of human behavior, the researchers are reaffirming its absolute necessity if children are to grow and develop normally.

There are direct and significant connections between the way a child is cared for and the kind of person s/he grows up to be. And the biological mother, especially in the early months, offers unrivaled advantages as her child's primary care giver.

No woman contemplating pregnancy today can escape the barrage of warnings about certain kinds of environmental hazards: poor nutrition, smoking, alcohol, drugs, radiation, viral infections, chemicals in the workplace, and chemicals in the food supply. They constitute the contemporary equivalent of the primitive person's confrontation with a mountain lion on the prowl. There are, however, other dangers in our everyday life which, though they don't directly imperil our physical health, still can deal a lethal blow to budding maternal-child attachment. Basically, anything or anyone who fosters mother-baby separation during the critical early period of mutual dependence is an environmental hazard. Scanning the current baby care scene with our prehistoric mother's eye, if you will, enables us to identify these hidden hazards and to steer clear of them in our own mothering.

Above all, we want this book to be a practical one. We remember so clearly the first days with our own babies—the mistakes we made, the needless money spent on items that proved to be dust-catchers, the puzzlement over how to fold a diaper and get it to stay on, the little things that are hard to figure out until you've been through it. These may not be earthshaking problems, but they can spell frustration and so much unnecessary work. They diminish the pleasure that should enrich the early weeks with our babies and, in many cases, cause us to waste our energy on tasks that don't need to be done at all. This book is dedicated to the idea that good mothering means less work and more joy than any of us ever thought possible.

GSB/JPG
Croton-on-Hudson, New York

Introduction

xiv

Chapter I

Pregnancy
Primary Care

Our babies are born expecting nothing less than the good life they enjoyed in the womb. Everything they associate with being alive—the sensations of being well fed, warm, closely enfolded, and pleasurably stimulated—they have learned from months of intimate contact with our bodies. This level of awareness and these specific needs remain for many months to come. Good mothering recognizes these facts and makes them the foundation for daily care of the unborn and newborn. Good mothering begins at conception.

Most of us have grown up with other assumptions. We are very likely to think of mother and baby as "one," as an integrated bio-social unit, only until the moment of birth. From then on, we typically behave as though each half of the unit has its own needs (often *competing* needs) and must be treated as an individual. We consider the mother's instinctive reach for her just-born child the start of their lifelong relationship, overlooking the obvious bond between mother and child that originates during pregnancy. All of these ideas are obstacles to implementing a style of mothering which generations of human experience and recent research tell us is essential for optimal growth and development of human children. Today's experienced mothers know this style to be time- and work-saving.

When a woman decides to bear a child she embarks on the most profound and intimate adventure of which her body is capable. Pregnancy embodies a yearning which has been expressed as a universal theme in literature, art, and music: the desire of lovers to experience the total environment of one another—to share not just the surfaces of one's body, but the very fluids, particles, and electrical impulses of which we are made, to merge with the beloved so completely that a new entity is created, an entity that is neither one nor the other, but both. The expectation that this ultimate intimacy will be pleasurable for both mother and child has been one of the most powerful organizing forces in human history.

All successful societies have recognized that these shared intimacies give rise to the most enduring of human bonds, the love of mother and child. In most of these societies, unlike our own, mother and child are viewed as indispensable to one another throughout the entire maternity cycle, from conception through weaning. It is seductive to romanticize this demonstrated concern for infants and their mothers, to discuss it in reverential or mystical terms. More likely, these societies found, after generations of experimentation and adaptation, that their very survival depended on promoting a close physical and emotional attachment between a mother and her infant. These essential attachments are most readily formed when mother and baby are healthy and available to one another on a continuous basis. A quick review of anthropological studies of mothering elsewhere in the world, particularly in those areas where industrialization has not occurred, supports the view that this is the norm for the human species. Many

Pregnancy: Primary Care

1

of our most "modern" care practices seem to have overridden our human biological imperatives, to the detriment of mothers, babies, and society as a whole.

Almost every mother will tell you that she experiences feelings of attachment and commitment to her baby long before it's born. She thinks about the baby, she hopes for the baby. But until recently, her drive to provide direct care to her unborn child was dismissed as mere wishful thinking. There isn't much you can do until the baby's born, she was told. Babies are preordained by genetics, heredity, or pure luck to attain a certain length, weight, and completeness at birth, no matter what the mother does during pregnancy, the experts agreed. A baby, they said, shares its mother's body for the first nine months of life, but emerges completely unaffected by that experience. The baby feels nothing, knows nothing, and can do nothing until separated from the mother. An unborn baby is a parasite.

Happily, the more we learn about the processes of earliest human growth and development, the more we find that our maternal impulses have been right all along. The way we care for ourselves during pregnancy *is* our earliest mothering. And it has dramatic and lifelong impact on our well-being and that of our children. People working in the field of maternal and child health increasingly target maintaining or improving the mother's health during pregnancy as the key to better pregnancy outcomes for individuals and the country as a whole. They are quick to point out that the things that make the most difference—our diets, our exercise programs, our choices in medical care—are the things over which each of us exerts absolute control. Willingness to act on the new information we receive is a chief feature of good mothering during pregnancy. In the most direct way imaginable, our first job as new mothers is to take the best care of our own bodies. We and our babies are the beneficiaries of any improvements we are able to make.

Nourishment: The Basis of Physical Health

If our babies don't grow automatically, exactly how do our bodies sustain them before birth? For centuries this question has captured the imagination of ordinary people and learned scholars. Fantastic theories have originated in each group, but the wisdom of ancient cultures in which women were encouraged to eat for two—and of the best foods available—has proved to be the soundest advice of all. Today it's clear that our babies' bodies and brains are formed solely out of what we eat during pregnancy.

The Chinese, for example, recognized this long ago and even have a list of foods traditionally recommended for pregnant women. Their historical experiences with the ravages of feudalism and famine are well documented. If you've read Pearl Buck's classic novel, *The Good Earth,* you probably remember how movingly the importance of a mother's access to enough good food during pregnancy was portrayed. It was quite literally the difference between life and death for mother and baby. It remains so for every pregnant woman today, no matter where she lives, no matter how wealthy or poor, no matter how many children she has borne.

The Chinese solved these problems by reorganizing their society in ways that eradicated malnutrition. They now boast a prematurity rate of under 3 percent, while in the United States today it is common for physicians with a middle-class practice to report infant prematurity/underweight statistics of 10 percent. In our public clinics the figure runs twice as high.

In other countries, the pregnant woman by custom and decree receives favored treatment when it comes to food. Portuguese families, even if very poor, try to provide extra eggs and chicken for pregnant women and encourage them to eat first at meals. In Poland, it is a matter of common courtesy to offer a pregnant guest in your home something to eat as soon as she arrives. If a pregnant woman in Greece expresses a desire for a certain food, people interpret this as a serious need of the baby and go to great lengths to obtain the item, no matter how frivolous it may seem. The French appropriate funds for a maternity grant to each expectant mother. The Scandinavians, with characteristic social vision, have written into their national charters that their future citizens are now in the womb, and therefore, insuring the nutrition of every mother is a matter of highest national priority. It's no coincidence that these countries lead the world in the excellence of their maternal and health statistics.

Meanwhile, here at home, most pregnant women are still advised to eat according to outdated principles that actually interfere with optimal nutrition. You've undoubtedly heard the ideas we list below from friends, family, or medical consultants—and they come with the warning that unless you follow them you place yourself and your baby at a higher risk for certain serious pregnancy and pediatric complications.

- Control your weight to a certain number of pounds.
- Control your weight to a certain pattern of gain (no more than so many pounds per month).
- Cut down or eliminate salt from your diet.
- Take measures to prevent swelling (especially of the face and hands), such as restricting fluids, salt, certain foods, and activity (bed rest) or take "water pills" (diuretics).

Not only are these pieces of dietary counsel incorrect, they are harmful, because they fail to take into account the unique changes in your body wrought by pregnancy. In fact, research done over the past 20 years conclusively shows that pregnancy imposes a nutritional stress on *every* expectant mother. More of all nutrients, including the accompanying calories, are needed.

Overwhelming evidence from the world medical literature indicates that even when undernutrition is not severe enough to cause serious illness in the mother, it may still compromise the growth and development of the unborn baby. The old idea that the baby is somehow favored over the mother's own tissues for available nutrients has not stood the test of scientific inquiry. One result of the officially accepted position in the United States that nutrition plays little role in the outcome of pregnancy has been the dramatic increase in the number of underweight, sickly newborns requiring intensive care at birth and for weeks or months afterwards at staggering costs, economic and social. Many of these babies manage to survive their ordeals, but grow up to have some form of learning disability, poor motor coordination, hyperactivity, or more serious neurological impairment such as mental retardation, cerebral palsy, or epilepsy. Depending on which medical journals you read, the percentages range from two in ten to seven in ten children who suffer with some measurable dysfunction. This is one of the major reasons why merely comparing countries' infant mortality rates is no longer an acceptable way to measure the quality of maternity care available there.

As mothers we are deeply concerned about the quality of life all our children can expect to enjoy. We want to do everything in our power to insure that they wind up on the healthy side of the "spectrum of reproductive casualty." Scientists now tell us that depends on our daily pregnancy diets.

An exhaustive review of this work, suitable for sharing with health professionals, is *Maternal Nutrition and Child Health* (Springfield, Ill.: C C Thomas, 1979), a book by Douglas Shanklin, M.D., professor of pathology and OB/GYN at Chicago Lying-In Hospital, and Jay Hodin, executive director of SPUN (Society for the Protection of the Unborn through Nutrition).

In 1963, Margaret Ramsey and her co-workers at the Carnegie Institute, Washington, D.C., were the first to explain the precise mechanism by which our babies are fed *in utero*. Focusing their attention on the placenta, the organ that permits transfer of nutrients and waste products between mother and baby, the Ramsey group was able to document in a striking series of radiographs how the mother's blood flows through the placenta, thereby laying to rest the idea that the baby could somehow extract nutrients from the mother's body even if they weren't provided by her daily food intake.

What Ramsey discovered is that blood circulates through the placenta in much the same way water is pumped through a pulsating fountain. The illustrations on the next page should help you visualize how this works in your own body.

Your baby begins an intimate acquaintance with your body weeks before your pregnancy is confirmed. As soon as the newly fertilized egg reaches the site on the uterine wall where it will implant, enzymes from its outer layer begin to dissolve the surface of the uterine lining, and with it the fine blood vessels called capillaries. These capillaries usually connect arteries and veins so that your blood remains inside a closed circulatory system. During pregnancy, as the capillary network in the uterine wall is broken down, arteries and veins there are left open-ended. This drawing illustrates, in a schematic way, what this looks like from the baby's point of view, looking at the uterine wall from the inside.

A cross-sectional view of what happens with each beat of the mother's heart is shown. Nutrient-laden blood spurts from the arteries at relatively

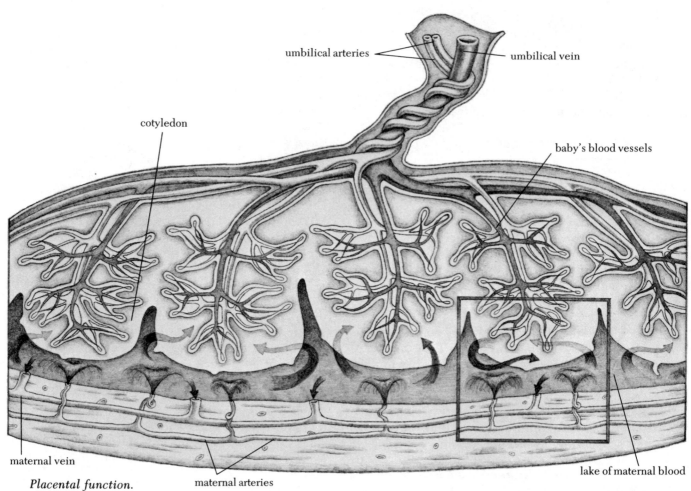

umbilical arteries — umbilical vein

cotyledon

baby's blood vessels

maternal vein

Placental function.

maternal arteries

lake of maternal blood

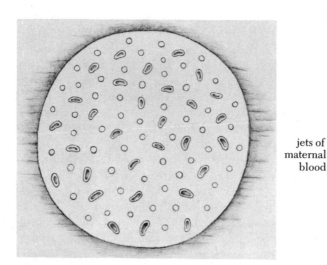

Maternal uterine wall (site of placenta).

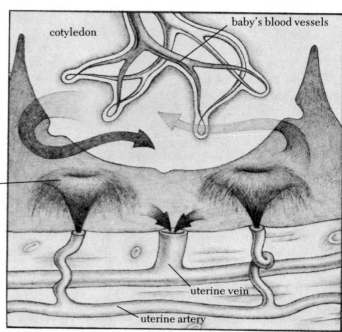

cotyledon

baby's blood vessels

jets of
maternal
blood

uterine vein

uterine artery

Detail of circulation of maternal blood in placenta.

Right from the Start

4

high pressure in funnel-shaped streams or jets. In response to this bounteous flow of blood, the embryo differentiates a new set of cells which eventually become the placenta. The placenta is a part of the baby which performs the functions of the baby's lungs, liver, and kidneys before birth. As you can see on the diagram, all the baby's placental blood vessels are encapsulated in membrane sacs called cotyledons, so there is never any direct mixing of mother's and baby's blood.

After the mother eats a meal, nutrients in her food are broken down in the process of digestion, then sent into the bloodstream via her liver. When the concentration of nutrients is higher in the mother's blood than in the baby's circulation, the nutrients pass through the thin membrane of the cotyledons and into the baby's bloodstream. There is no other way for the baby to be fed. Molecules that make up the cheese sandwich you eat for lunch wind up in the baby's bloodstream! This same basic mechanism also transports oxygen to the baby and, in reverse, allows carbon dioxide and other waste products to leave the baby's body through the mother's circulation.

As pregnancy advances, placental enzymes continue to erode large areas of the uterine capillary network.

To keep this system functioning optimally, your body must manufacture ever-increasing amounts of blood. By the eighth month of pregnancy you have approximately 60 percent more blood coursing through your blood vessels than you had before you became pregnant—most of it specifically needed to perfuse the placenta. Unfortunately, your blood volume does not expand automatically just because you are pregnant. There are two ways your body accomplishes this feat; both of them depend on what you eat.

The liver bears major responsibility for expanding your blood volume during pregnancy. All of the liver's 500 metabolic functions must be carried out at increased levels at this time, but the one that is crucial, in terms of sustaining the placenta and baby, is the liver's manufacture of a protein, albumin. The albumin molecule is large and requires the simultaneous presence of numerous nutrients to aid the liver in synthesizing it.

When the mother's diet is adequate in every way for her pregnancy, the liver manufactures increased amounts of albumin as the weeks pass. As the albumin circulates in the bloodstream, it exerts strong colloid osmotic pressure, acting to draw water into the circulation. Each gram of albumin has the capacity to mobilize 18 g of water, a powerful assist in expanding the plasma compartment of your blood to the levels necessary for a successful pregnancy.

A simple blood test, often performed routinely in early pregnancy for other reasons, can measure the amount of albumin circulating in your body and give firm indication of how well you're doing in terms of your nutrition. This test is well established in other medical specialties—pediatricians rely on it to judge how well a baby suffering from kwashiorkor or other protein-calorie deficiency diseases is responding to a therapeutic diet, for instance, and internists use it to monitor the recovery of patients with hepatitis or cirrhosis. However, its application to clinical obstetrics has been limited, primarily because few obstetricians have been trained to pay careful attention to these important hemodynamic relationships at every prenatal visit throughout pregnancy.

The standard blood work done primarily to detect anemia simply is not an adequate indicator of the mother's nutritional well-being. Indeed, some of the best-fed women may appear to be somewhat anemic toward the end of pregnancy because they have such expanded plasma volumes! Neither they nor their babies are threatened in the slightest way by this "dilutional anemia." In fact, according to Agnes Higgins, director of the Montreal Diet Dispensary, *when mothers are well fed, lower* hemoglobin concentration (the hematocrit measurement) is consistently associated with babies of *higher* birth weight. Higgins' findings, reported in an address to the spring 1978 meeting of the American Public Health Association, Southern Branch (Nashville, Tennessee), support the concept that larger blood volumes better service the placenta, resulting in more nutrients being transferred to the baby over the period of gestation. The result, of course, is a larger, healthier baby.

A way to prevent misdiagnosis of this "dilutional anemia" and avoid the standard prescription, large daily doses of unnecessary iron supplements, is to request that the physician or midwife order a blood test to determine your serum albumin value. Normally, albumin ranges between 3.5 and 5.5 g per 100 cc of serum. When your albumin level stays in this range during pregnancy, it's a good sign that your diet is adequate and your blood volume expansion and apparent "anemia" are normal. A reading of 3 g per 100 cc or lower calls

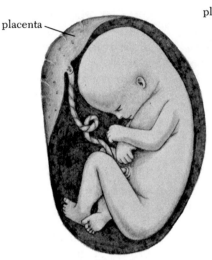

placenta

7 weeks

Actual size of baby and placenta at various stages of gestation.

placenta

10 weeks

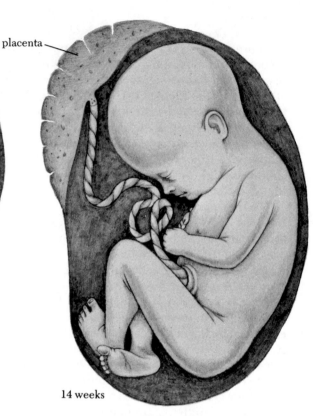

placenta

14 weeks

for prompt diet analysis and evaluation of other liver functions to see where the problem lies.

A second factor involved in maintaining the expanded blood volume in pregnancy is salt intake. Salt helps your body to retain the water it needs in the circulation and in the tissues. You have a need for extra salt during pregnancy because, in addition to keeping the blood volume expanded for placental perfusion, salt is also required to:

- assist in efficient functioning of muscles (the heart has to pump all that extra blood, for instance, and the legs carry extra weight, giving rise to leg cramps in women who lack adequate salt);
- provide the salt the baby's body needs (every cell in the human body must be bathed in a salt solution to remain healthy);
- continuously replenish the salty amniotic fluid which surrounds the baby;
- maintain a correct balance of electrolytes as the mother's body reacts to pregnancy hormone changes by retaining more fluid.

A few years ago we were in the midst of a cholesterol scare. Today it's salt that's the alleged culprit in ailments ranging from high blood pressure to obesity and other ailments. As a result, popular literature as well as some medical advisories now urge all of us to reduce our salt intake as a preventive measure. Almost never is the special situation in pregnancy exempted from these blanket prescriptions, as it certainly should be.

Regardless of what further research proves to be true about salt as a problem for men or nonpregnant women, it's well established that salt restriction during pregnancy poses a serious threat to the blood volume expansion we have seen is so essential for the baby's growth. So, except when the blood volume is overexpanded (above the needs of pregnancy) due to a disease process such as congestive heart failure or kidney failure, *pregnant women should salt their food to taste*. The American College of Obstetricians and Gynecologists (ACOG), in a major turnabout, now advises this in their *Standards for Ambulatory Obstetric Care* (revised 1977):

Sodium is required in pregnancy for the expanded maternal tissue and fluid compartments as well as to provide for fetal needs. The normal patient may use the level of sodium she prefers. Routine sodium restriction is not advised.

This statement reflects the earlier work of the ACOG Committee on Nutrition, which concluded in a 1974 publication, *Nutrition in Maternal Health Care:*

From a clinical point of view, however, it appears reasonable to permit the normal patient

Right from the Start

6

to use the level of sodium she prefers, *relying on the humoral interaction at the renal tubule to ensure that sodium balance is maintained.* [Emphasis added]

The point raised by this committee is that individual needs for sodium vary widely from day to day, and the body has compensating mechanisms for keeping the body level of sodium on an even keel. Anyone who works or exercises very strenuously, lives or works in high temperatures, or customarily eats foods that happen to contain small amounts of sodium (such as some vegetarian diets) may find herself needing to add more salt from the shaker than people who take little exercise, live and work in air-conditioned buildings or cold climates, or eat plenty of foods high in sodium. It's possible to lose 8 to 10 g of sodium just in perspiration on a hot day, for instance. All these individual variations explain why such bodies as the National Academy of Science/National Research Council have established no set Recommended Daily Allowance (RDA) for sodium, even though it is recognized as an essential nutrient in the diets of human beings.

The most important of the mechanisms governing the sodium balance in our bodies is the ability of the tubules in the kidney to respond to changes in the sodium level in the bloodstream. These mechanisms are studied in great detail in the basic physiology courses of medical schools, but this information, which could allay much of the fear pregnant women express about their salt intake, has not been communicated effectively to the general public. Walter Cannon, M.D., the noted Harvard physiologist, presents this information for general readers in his classic book, *The Wisdom of the Body* (originally published in 1939; reissued, New York: W.W. Norton, 1963). In brief, should you take in more salt over a given period of time than your body needs, the kidney tubule simply opens up and allows the excess to escape in your urine. On the other hand, if you take in less than you need, the tubule simply reabsorbs more from the bloodstream, thus maintaining the narrow range of normal. Numerous studies of pregnant women have shown that this mechanism is very efficient in pregnancy.

The easiest way to manage the salt question in your home is to refrain from salting foods while cooking them, then pass the shaker at mealtimes so each person can literally satisfy his or her own needs. When your food tastes flat, it's a signal from the salt sensors on your tongue and in your cheeks that you need more. If you eat a diet high in protein, you may find (since protein and sodium tend to occur together naturally in foods) that you seldom add salt—maybe only in the summertime or when you're pregnant or breastfeeding.

Except for the presence of a kidney problem which causes blood volume to expand above the body's needs, or congestive heart failure when the heart is unable to pump blood to vital organs, it's impossible to overdose on salt during pregnancy. To the contrary, during pregnancy the hazards arise from taking in too little salt, not too much.

The reduction in blood volume which follows a concerted effort to restrict salt and salty foods, many of which are high-protein foods as well, will also trigger a compensatory hormone-release mechanism in the kidney (the renin-angiotensin-aldosterone mechanism) which results in arteries throughout the body constricting. This is detected as a rise in blood pressure. Of course, blood pressure may rise during pregnancy for other causes (see *The Pregnancy-After-30 Workbook,* Emmaus, Pa.: Rodale Press, 1978, for a complete discussion of hypertension in pregnancy) with no appreciable ill effect on either mother or baby, *if the mother's diet is adequate.* Elevated blood pressure due to salt restriction (and the protein restriction that often inadvertently accompanies it) is hazardous—not because of the higher numbers on the medical chart, but because of the maternal undernutrition which is at the root of the problem.

We emphasize this salt issue because it's one of the questions we're asked about most often at conferences and on the Pregnancy Hotline we staff. If you are advised by anyone at any time in pregnancy to cut down on salt, or if you are prescribed a low-salt diet or "water pills" (diuretics, drugs which work directly on the kidney tubule to effect wholesale excretion of water, salt, and other water-soluble nutrients from the bloodstream), you need to ask whether your blood volume is pathologically expanded above the needs of pregnancy or if you are in heart failure. If the answer is no, you should continue to salt your food to taste and perhaps try to find a medical consultant whose practices are more in keeping with contemporary thinking on this subject.

Of course, important as protein and salt are, a baby doesn't grow on them alone! During pregnancy, you need more of all sorts of good-quality foods. To satisfy the nutritional stress of pregnancy for mother and baby, the basic diet plan

Eating for Three: Sample Daily Menu for Twin Pregnancy

For a complete discussion of twin pregnancy, including nutritional management, read *Having Twins* (Boston: Houghton Mifflin, 1980), by Elizabeth Noble, R.P.T.

Breakfast
4 oz. orange or grapefruit juice
2 eggs
2 slices whole grain bread or muffins
butter
8 oz. "super milk" (whole milk with 1 cup powdered nonfat milk mixed in to give extra protein)

Morning snack—you may feel like eating every couple of hours
2 oz. Swiss cheese
whole grain crackers
medium apple, peach, or other fresh fruit
4 oz. tomato juice or real lemonade

Lunch
4 oz. hamburger with lettuce, tomato, and mayonnaise
whole grain roll or 2 slices whole grain bread
8 oz. "super milk"
½ cup potato salad or beans
1 cup vegetable soup

Mid-afternoon snack
½ cup cottage cheese in a raw pepper or tomato
1 cup chicken or beef broth/boullion
whole grain croutons or bread sticks

Dinner
8 oz. "super milk"
½ cup fruit cocktail (variety of fresh or canned fruits)
6 oz. chicken (two breasts, three legs)
1 cup brown rice (cooked in chicken broth rather than water to absorb extra protein)
1 cup green salad with dressing
butter
½ cup broccoli or spinach
½ cup carrots or squash

Evening snack
1 cup pudding (made with "super milk") or egg custard
¼ cup salted nuts

Middle-of-the-night snack (when you have to get up to go to the bathroom)
choice of: milk, cheese, hard-boiled egg, yogurt, 2 oz. meat, nuts, peanut butter on whole wheat toast (focus: extra protein)

Salt to Taste, Drink to Thirst: your requirements are even greater because of the extra baby you're growing!

Goal: a minimum of 30 g additional protein (130 g total) and 500 extra calories above the basic pregnancy diet, plus all other vitamins and minerals; these needs could be met simply by adding a quart of milk a day to the basic SPUN diet.

---

of the United States Department of Agriculture (the Basic Four Food Groups) needs to be supplemented with extra calories and protein for most women. The diet plan that follows supplies at least 80 g of high-quality protein, approximately 2,600 calories, and all other essential nutrients in amounts sufficient for a single pregnancy. (If you're carrying twins, please see the accompanying chart for specifics of the extra nutrition you need.)

This diet should be regarded as a nutritional floor, not a ceiling, since it is designed to insure that your chances for certain pregnancy complications known to be nutritional in origin will be substantially reduced, or, in the case of metabolic toxemia and abruption of the placenta, prevented entirely. The diet does not attempt to deal with the issue of what is "the best diet" for humans; that is the realm of people doing research in metabolic units in academic departments of nutrition across the country and will probably remain a subject of debate for years to come.

If you are pregnant now, you don't have the luxury of waiting until speculations concerning your diet are resolved in every minute detail. You need an action plan that will be adequate for the amount of physical work or exercise you do, your individual metabolism, your prepregnancy weight, your lifestyle (relaxed or stressed), and your personal food likes and dislikes. These factors change dramatically from woman to woman. No two pregnancies are ever exactly the same for these reasons. Consequently, the most reliable indicator of your food intake needs is your appetite.

Right from the Start

Even in women who have been very overweight before pregnancy, the appetite can be trusted when the mother is encouraged to eat nutritiously. It is even possible for the overweight woman (and we mean *really* overweight, not just the extra five or ten pounds many people view with displeasure, but which do not constitute true obesity) to gain very little weight over the course of pregnancy and still give birth to a healthy, strong child. The key is *adequate daily nutrition*, not hounding about pounds.

This diet has been clinically tested as part of a metabolic toxemia prevention project conducted between 1963 and 1976 in the public prenatal clinics of the Contra Costa County, California, Medical Services by Thomas Brewer, M.D. Since then it has been used around the world in hundreds of thousands of pregnancies managed by medical personnel in clinics and in private practice. It was presented to the public in book form in 1977 (*What Every Pregnant Woman Should Know: The Truth About Diets and Drugs in Pregnancy*, New York: Random House, 1977. Paperback ed., New York: Penguin Books, 1979).

Practitioners using the diet consistently report impressive reductions in the number of low-birth-weight and small-for-gestational-age babies, which we have already noted are among the most ominous of conditions in the newborn. In a preliminary report published in the Swiss medical journal, *Gynaecologia*, in 1969, the Contra Costa project mothers gave birth to premature or underweight infants in less than 2 percent of the cases. The prevailing rate of prematurity at that time from other public clinics in the immediate area was 13.5 percent. All of the mothers were in low-income situations, and over 60 percent were from minority groups. The dietary counseling provided as a routine part of prenatal care by the physician was the only difference in care the women received.

The National Institutes of Health, in a 1976 summary report of their independent findings after studying the Contra Costa project patient records, also found a tenfold reduction in the incidence of hypertension (high blood pressure) in project participants, as compared to other mothers attending a different clinic in the county system. This was attributed to the likelihood that, in the mothers who were consciously trying to follow the doctor's advice to eat more and better food, to salt their food to taste, to drink to thirst, and to take no drugs except in life-threatening or exceedingly painful circumstances, their expanded blood volumes protected them from hypertension caused by malnutrition (previously discussed in this chapter).

One physician who has stressed the essentials of primary prevention of obstetrical and pediatric problems through sound pregnancy nutrition, Henry Davis, M.D., of Carson City, Nevada, shared his results with SPUN, an organization of professionals and parents working to have official practice standards for nutrition management incorporated into routine prenatal care. We include his report because it sums up just how many ways nutrition is of importance to you and your unborn baby:

I was fortunate enough to have had contact with Dr. Tom Brewer during my Family Practice residency at Contra Costa County Hospital. When I started my practice . . . eight years ago, I took these principles with me and put them into practice and have had a chance . . . to see the beautiful results of simply good nutrition on mothers. When I initially counsel patients with their first pregnancy visit, nutrition is strongly stressed. I do not mention limiting weight in any way. . . . I do not at any time, with any visit, tell the patients that they are gaining too much but instead stress only good nutrition. . . . The patients did need constant support from me since attitudes of others around them tended to express that they were gaining too much weight or that somehow weight gain was harmful in pregnancy. I do not use diuretics in pregnancy, nor any other medications other than a good prenatal vitamin.

During the time I have been in practice, I have managed approximately 500 obstetrical patients. I have had two patients with preeclampsia [a term that can include any hypertension, protein in the urine, or edema—EDITOR], both of whom had severe chronic diseases. One of these had systemic lupus erythematosus, the second a hereditary cholesterol problem. Both of these now have healthy babies. I have had six spontaneous premature infants. One of these was from a mother who had acute appendicitis in her sixth month of pregnancy. Three of the patients did not start prenatal care until their sixth month of pregnancy and were severely malnourished when I started with them, two of the patients had *placenta praevia*, and one patient was a total vegetarian whom I judged was on inadequate sources of vegetable protein. . . . The remainder of my patients have had normal, healthy children.

As an aside, there are a number of other phenomena which we accepted as "normal" in pregnancy which I have realized were nutritionally related and which I do not see in my practice anymore. . . . Mothers who are properly nourished do not get stretch marks, and they do not seem to have acceleration of dental caries or softening of the gums. I do not see loss of hair, splitting of nails, softening of bones, or postpartum hemorrhage. . . . We see very quick recoveries after pregnancy, and we do not see failures at breastfeeding because of nutritional problems in the mother.

(Reprinted, with permission, from SPUN's manual for their pregnancy nutrition counselors, *Preventing the Nutritional Complications of Pregnancy*, Suite 603, 17 North Wabash Avenue, Chicago, IL 60602, 1978.)

Since few physicians have had the benefit of applied nutrition education in their training, it falls to us, the mothers, to implement for ourselves the eating plan that insures the best care of ourselves and our developing babies. If you are pregnant and in tight financial circumstances, it's important that you begin to think of the food you eat as being "for the new baby," so you don't deny yourself food in order to feed others in your family. Even in middle-income families inflation is taking a terrible toll as food prices in the supermarkets skyrocket. Depending on the size of your family, your family income, and your health status, you may be eligible for a government-sponsored supplemental food program designed for pregnant and lactating women and their children, called W.I.C. (Women, Infants, and Children). Eligible mothers receive free coupons for use at regular retail markets. Items which can be purchased with W.I.C. coupons are staples such as milk, eggs, cereals, fruit juices, and cheese. All of these are included, along with other foods, in the SPUN (Contra Costa) diet. To find the W.I.C. program office in your area, contact your local health department or public prenatal clinic. In some areas, a physician may also write a prescription for a high-protein diet for patients who need it and are on public assistance. Any pregnant woman should automatically qualify for this special diet consideration wherever it is available. If you have trouble finding out about

W.I.C., food stamps, commodity food distribution programs, or public clinics where these programs are in effect, contact: The Children's Foundation, Suite 800, 1426 New York Avenue NW, Washington, DC 20005, (202) 347-3300, an information/advocacy organization concerned with all aspects of food programs for children.

Other ideas to cut your food bill while upgrading your nutrition:

- Join a food co-op to save money on produce, canned goods, cheese, and grains. (See *Food Co-ops: An Alternative to Shopping in Supermarkets*, by William Ronco, Boston: Beacon Press, 1974, or *The Food Conspiracy Cookbook*, by Lois Wickstrom, 101 Productions, 834 Mission Street, San Francisco, CA 94103.)
- Eat more beans, which can be fixed an amazing number of ways—especially soybeans. (See *The Farm Vegetarian Cookbook*, Louise Hagler, ed., revised 1979, The Book Publishing Company, 156 Drakes Lane, Summertown, TN 38483.)
- Stop buying soda, snack foods, pastries, candy, white bread, packaged dinners, flavored beverage mixes, soup powders, and frozen confections, and cook foods from scratch. (See *Nourishing Your Unborn Child*, by Phyllis S. Williams, R.N., New York: Avon, 1975.)

If you are following the SPUN diet and have questions about any aspect of it or any other pregnancy diet-related problem (weight gain, swelling, hypertension, diabetes, obesity, protein in the urine, nausea/vomiting), you may get a free consultation and referral to knowledgeable pregnancy nutrition specialists in your area from SPUN's Pregnancy Hotline (914) 271-6474, or by writing the national office: SPUN, Suite 603, 17 North Wabash Avenue, Chicago, IL 60602.

It is sobering to realize that only our daily diet—the foods we actually eat, digest, absorb, and metabolize—can insure the optimal development of body and brain that each of our babies deserves. We do, in fact, create the quality of the life we carry within us. This obligation, like so many others that affect the newborn period, starts long before we have traditionally assumed our mothering to begin. Fortunately, the dietary recommendations that lead to superior babies who are easier to get along with are simple to follow and enjoyable.

Right from the Start

The SPUN Diet

You must have, *every day*, at least:
1. Milk and milk products—4 choices
   1 cup milk: whole, skim, 99%, buttermilk
   ½ cup canned evaporated milk: whole or skim
   ⅓ cup powdered milk: whole or skim
   1 cup yogurt
   1 cup sour cream
   ¼ cup cottage cheese: creamed, uncreamed, pot style
   1 large slice cheese (1¼ oz.): cheddar, Swiss, other hard cheese
   1 cup ice milk
2. Eggs—2, any style
3. Meats and meat substitutes—8 choices
   1 oz. lean beef, lamb, veal, pork, liver, kidney
   1 oz. chicken or turkey
   1 oz. fish or shellfish
   ¼ cup canned salmon, tuna, mackerel
   3 sardines
   3½ oz. tofu (soybean curd)
   ¼ cup peanuts or peanut butter
   ⅛ cup beans + ¼ cup rice or wheat (measured before cooking)—beans: soybeans, peas, black beans, kidney beans, garbanzos; rice: preferably brown; wheat: preferably bulgur
   ⅛ cup brewer's yeast + ¼ cup rice
   ⅛ cup sesame or sunflower seeds + ½ cup rice
   ¼ cup rice + ⅓ cup milk
   ½ oz. cheese + 2 slices whole wheat bread or ⅓ cup (dry) macaroni or noodles or ⅛ cup beans
   ⅛ cup beans + ½ cup cornmeal
   ⅛ cup beans + ⅙ cup seeds (sesame, sunflower)
   ⅛ cup peanut butter or peanuts + ⅛ cup seeds (sesame, sunflower)
   ¼ cup milk + ¼ cup seeds (sesame, sunflower)
   ½ large potato + ¼ cup milk or ¼ oz. cheese
   1 oz. cheese: cheddar, Swiss, other hard cheese
   ¼ cup cottage cheese: creamed, uncreamed, pot style
4. Fresh, dark green vegetables—2 choices
   1 cup broccoli
   1 cup brussels sprouts
   ⅔ cup spinach
   ⅔ cup greens: collard, turnip, beet, mustard, dandelion, kale
   ½ cup lettuce (preferably romaine)
   ½ cup endive
   ½ cup asparagus

½ cup sprouts: bean, alfalfa
5. Whole grains—5 choices
   1 slice bread: whole wheat, rye, bran, other whole grain
   ½ roll, muffin, or bagel made from whole grain
   1 waffle or pancake made from whole grain
   1 corn tortilla
   ½ cup oatmeal or Wheatena
   ½ cup brown rice or bulgar wheat
   1 shredded wheat biscuit
   ½ cup bran flakes or granola
   ¼ cup wheat germ
6. Vitamin C group—2 choices
   ½ grapefruit
   ⅔ cup grapefruit juice
   1 orange
   ½ cup orange juice
   1 large tomato
   1 cup tomato juice
   ½ cantaloupe
   1 lemon or lime
   ½ cup papaya
   ½ cup strawberries
   1 large green pepper
   1 large potato, any style
7. Fats and oils—3 choices
   1 tablespoon butter or margarine
   1 tablespoon mayonnaise
   1 tablespoon vegetable oil
   ¼ avocado
   1 tablespoon peanut butter
8. Yellow or orange vegetable or fruit—1 choice
   3 apricots
   ½ cantaloupe
   ½ cup carrots (1 large)
   ½ cup pumpkin
   ½ cup winter squash
   1 sweet potato
9. Liver—at least once a week
   4 oz. liver: beef, calf, chicken, pork, turkey, liverwurst, liver sausage
10. Table salt—*Salt Your Food to Taste*
11. Water—*Drink to Thirst*
12. Other foods as desired from above lists, other fresh fruits and vegetables, nuts and seeds, dried fruits, and the like.

Remember, each food you eat may be counted for one group only—e.g., count ¼ cup cottage cheese as 1 milk choice *or* 1 meat and meat substitute choice, not both.

One aspect of nutrition we aren't accustomed to thinking of in those terms is all the nonfood substances that enter our bodies, cross the placenta, and, so, have a potential influence on the unborn. The placenta was once considered a barrier to harmful substances, selectively screening the molecules as they approached the placental membrane, so that the beneficial ones passed through and the harmful ones were repulsed. We now know that, as Robert Bradley, M.D., of Denver, Colorado, says, "anything smaller than your elbow" will pass through the membrane into the baby's circulation. Depending on the substance and the baby's stage of development the effects can range from catastrophic to nil.

Generally, it is advisable to avoid all chemical substances possible during pregnancy, including food additives, aerosol sprays, aromatic cleaning compounds, alcohol, marijuana and other street drugs, tobacco, industrial and heavy manufacturing discharges (air and water), over-the-counter drugs, exceedingly high doses of vitamins/minerals, purging preparations (whether administered by mouth or by rectum), insecticide/pesticide sprays, immunizations (your own shots should be up-to-date before you conceive), hormones, and, *most important*, drugs prescribed by physicians.

Prescription drugs are "by prescription only" because they are so potent and known to have potent side effects as well. It's not enough to inform the physician that you may be pregnant—studies show that pregnant women in the United States ingest 10 to 14 drugs per pregnancy, more than half being doctors' prescriptions for sleeping aids, antinausea compounds, constipation aids, and drugs to treat swelling (a normal condition in well-fed pregnant women). In almost all cases these conditions are better treated with other forms of intervention.

For complete information on what the drug companies tell the doctors about their products, consult the *Physicians' Desk Reference* (34th ed., Oradell, N.J.: Medical Economics Co., 1980), a compilation of drug industry package inserts. For *unbiased* reporting about drugs, how they work in your body, and their side effects and possible alternatives, you're better off plowing through *The Pharmacologic Basis of Therapeutics*, by Louis S. Goodman and Alfred Gilman (5th ed., New York: Macmillan, 1975), which your local library should have as a reference volume. If it's not there now, request it; the librarian may order a copy or obtain one for you on interlibrary loan.

The American Academy of Pediatrics (AAP) states that there is *no* drug that has been *proven safe* for the unborn child. The best policy is to refuse medication and other medical treatments/procedures (x-rays, ultrasound, amniocentesis) during pregnancy, birth, and breastfeeding, unless there is some urgent medical need for them.

One bright spot in all this is the foods we eat. The ability of our bodies to detoxify themselves (clear harmful substances from the bloodstream) is an indication of how well the liver is working. When our diets are adequate for pregnancy, the liver continues to handle this critical function very well. Work in this area, the interaction of nutrition and toxicology, is barely in its infancy, but promises to strengthen the claim that good nutrition is the body's first line of defense against harmful substances.

Choosing Pediatric Care: A Pregnancy Survey

Choosing your baby's medical care provider(s) is another important step you need to take during pregnancy to insure your baby's good health after birth. Many of the decisions made in the first few days after birth, about your baby's care in the hospital or at home, will be affected by the type of advice and support you get from these people. So, set aside time during pregnancy to investigate the options available in your area and settle in your own mind what particular attributes and services you will require.

A good person to start with is your childbirth educator. (Who does she take her children to for well-baby care and for treatment of illnesses?) Check with friends who share your views about child rearing. (What have their experiences been with medical personnel?) Ask at the Nursing Mothers Council meetings of your childbirth education group. (Are these new mothers satisfied with the care they are getting right now?) These contacts should provide you with a list with which to start working. As you conduct your survey, keep an open mind—your needs and preferences may be quite different from someone else's. Feeling a partnership with your baby's care provider(s) and maintaining good communication is essential, since it will be many years before your child can express his/her needs directly to the professional.

For an in-depth look at what pediatric care should include at every level from well-baby to

Pediatric Survey Checklist

1. What pediatric care choices are available in your community or within reasonable travel time? Request brochures.
   ____ well-baby clinic (usually sponsored by health department, organization, or agency)
   ____ federally funded clinic
   ____ privately endowed free clinic
   ____ hospital clinic
   ____ private clinic
   ____ pediatrician—solo practice
   ____ pediatrician—group practice
   ____ family practitioner—solo practice
   ____ family practitioner—group practice
   ____ pediatric nurse-practitioner—solo practice
   ____ pediatric nurse-practitioner—group practice
   ____ family nurse-practitioner—solo practice
   ____ family nurse-practitioner—group practice
   ____ health maintenance organization (HMO) prepaid plan
   ____ alternative health center (chiropractic, naturopathic, or other)

2. What is the availability of any service you choose from the list above?
   ____ 24-hour, 7-day coverage
   ____ limited hours—must see associate other times
   ____ limited hours—must use hospital emergency room other times (nights, weekends)
   ____ home visits made upon request
   ____ home visits made under special circumstances
   ____ home visits not made
   ____ will visit newborn in hospital to evaluate for discharge

3. What are the financial arrangements?
   ____ fee must be paid in full at time of service
   ____ bill sent monthly to be paid in full upon receipt
   ____ bill sent monthly—partial payments accepted
   ____ care refused with unpaid, overdue balance
   ____ free to all
   ____ sliding scale—fee set according to income
   ____ Medicaid/Medicare accepted
   ____ other insurance accepted
   ____ charge cards accepted

4. What does the fee include?
   ____ physical examination and consultation
   ____ laboratory work
   ____ immunizations—if indicated
   ____ medications—if indicated
   ____ counseling—if indicated
   ____ parents' classes

5. How are parent/professional communications facilitated?
   ____ "call hour" for routine questions
   ____ call any time directly to doctor/nurse practitioner
   ____ access by telephone only through office nurse
   ____ access by telephone through secretary/receptionist
   ____ access by telephone through answering service

[Continued on next page]

Pediatric Survey Checklist [*Continued*]

5. How are parent/professional communications facilitated? (Continued)
   ____ written report of child's health status at each visit
   ____ discussion period after each visit
   ____ reliance on printed matter (little opportunity for discussion)
   ____ reliance on printed matter supplied by commercial interests (such as breastfeeding information booklet provided by formula manufacturer)
   ____ free interview with parents during pregnancy

6. In an emergency, what are hospital affiliations and policies?
   ____ hospital within reasonable travel time
   ____ hospital with emergency room (how long a wait?)
   ____ hospital with pediatric unit
   ____ hospital with referral to pediatric specialists when needed
   ____ hospital with pediatric intensive care unit
   ____ hospital with emergency transport capability
   ____ rooming-in for newborns on postpartum unit
   ____ early discharge plan for healthy newborns
   ____ parents may room-in with sick child
   ____ children may visit sick parent
   ____ children may visit sick sibling

7. Which of the professional's attitudes and practices concerning baby care compare favorably with yours?
   ____ breastfeeding style (ad lib/schedule)
   ____ timing of addition of juices
   ____ timing of addition of solids
   ____ pacifiers, cribs, separate rooms
   ____ weaning
   ____ toilet "training"
   ____ discipline ("crying it out," "spoiling," scheduling)
   ____ family nutrition

8. What personal attributes make you feel comfortable with a medical care provider? We assume medical competence.
   ____ authoritarian
   ____ open to suggestions
   ____ restrained/objective
   ____ informal/sympathetic
   ____ older than you
   ____ about your age
   ____ younger than you
   ____ neatly groomed
   ____ healthy-looking him/herself
   ____ nonsmoker
   ____ position on social-ethical issues
   ____ respect for your lifestyle
   ____ where trained
   ____ a parent him/herself
   ____ attends professional continuing education courses
   ____ active in professional organizations
   ____ active in community organizations
   ____ same sex as you
   ____ same ethnic background as you
   ____ can converse in your primary language

Right from the Start

_____ punctual
_____ thorough
_____ gives understandable explanations
_____ employs courteous office staff
_____ works cooperatively with others in office/hospital
_____ schedules appointments at separate times for sick/well children

intensive care, you may wish to obtain a copy of the AAP's *Manual of Standards* (1801 Hinman Avenue, Evanston, IL 60201). Many of the more progressive positions taken in recent years by medical professionals on issues involving the welfare of unborn and newborn babies have been pioneered by the AAP. The circumcision controversy, the disputes about medications used in labor and birth, the impact of separation of mother and infant on bonding were all addressed by the AAP long before other professional bodies made any public remarks about them. This does not by any means insure that your local pediatricians are using the AAP recommendations as the basis for their own daily practice; however, it's always a good feeling to be able to quote the professional's own standards when a question arises about what should be done for your own baby.

Warmth, Enfoldment, Stimulation: The Basis of Mental Health

Ashley Montagu writes most eloquently in two of his books, *Touching: The Human Significance of the Skin* (New York: Columbia University Press, 1971) and *Life Before Birth* (revised ed., New York: New American Library, 1978), of the enormous importance of our babies' intrauterine sensory experiences in determining how they behave in the early weeks after birth. Noting that the skin is the largest sense organ of the body and the first to develop, he provides a stunning catalog of the ways in which skin stimulations are necessary for the healthy physical and behavioral development of the human organism, and he investigates the sad effects of the lack of particular kinds of skin stimulation in children and adults.

In an observation particularly interesting to us, he speculates that after birth the mother's need for continuous contact with her infant may be even greater than the baby's, since maternal behavior seems to arise *by stimulation she receives from the young.* We think this is an important concept to explore in terms of pregnancy, too, since the patterns of mothering we adopt before the baby's birth (in response to our ever-increasing awareness and acceptance of the baby's presence and vitality) are so likely to be carried over into the newborn period. In other words, we probably wouldn't be treating ourselves this well if we weren't pregnant, so our most elementary forms of maternal behavior also develop in response to "stimulations" we receive from the baby.

- We're probably hungrier than before, so we respond by eating more or more often or both (unless someone tells us not to).
- We probably tire more easily than before, so we respond by napping more often or going to bed earlier or sleeping later or cutting down on work schedules or all of these (unless someone tells us not to).
- We're probably more limber than before, but may have backache due to the softening and loosening effects of hormones (manufactured by the placenta, a part of the baby!), so our exercise patterns should respond to our "new bodies" (jogging may be temporarily replaced with swimming, for instance).
- We're usually having a slowdown in digestion, so we add more fiber to our diets, eat more fresh fruits, drink more fluids, take more gentle exercise (walking a mile or two a day is especially helpful) and eat smaller meals more frequently as pregnancy comes to term.
- We feel the baby's vigorous or languorous movements and respond oftentimes by stopping everything we're doing to enjoy and record every sensation in the depths of our innermost body memory or playfully respond to that foot making the cute little bulge next to our rib cage by massaging it until the baby withdraws it. Is this not contact?
- We feel the baby's weight and form as an outward pressure and downward pull on our frame, so we try to tuck our buttocks

under and straighten our shoulders to compensate; we often catch ourselves standing with our hands clasped under our bellies—already holding and protecting our babies.

- Our breasts feel fuller, firmer, warmer, so we make an effort to wear a supporting bra so the upper back doesn't get fatigued; we do a few simple massages in preparation for breastfeeding when our nipples need to be very elastic (see chapter 8 for specifics); we may notice droplets of sweet colostrum as our love partners nuzzle our breasts; we spend minutes gazing into the mirror tracing the network of brilliant blue veins appearing across our chests; we anticipate how the tuggings of the newborn's mouth will feel on our full breasts—and we can hardly wait for the baby to be born.

All of pregnancy, then, is an adaptation on your part (in body and spirit) to your developing baby. The contacts with and connections to your baby you feel now set the groundwork for your future relationship. Many of the things we take for granted about pregnancy really offer us sterling opportunities to gain a perspective on our babies' needs and presence. Each time you associate a pregnancy-related activity with your baby's existence you add a new dimension to your growing affectional bond to that child. The old-fashioned way of expressing this is to talk about love.

If pleasurable stimulation and continuous contact do indeed engender loving feelings, then our babies must be born in a truly rapturous condition. Their experiences inside healthy women prepare them for a life of the most exquisite intimacy. According to psychiatrist James Clark Moloney, M.D., these experiences insure that babies are born mentally healthy, that is, with a full capacity to give and receive love.

In an unpublished 1964 paper, "The Outward Directed Self and the Inward Directed Self," Maloney and Joan Gould talk about the cycle of tenderness between mother and infant that begins before birth. They emphasize that the criterion for good mental health is good mothering, which they define as *unconditional* mothering—mothering which responds immediately to the biologic needs and signals of the baby. They stress that human infants are nowhere near ready for complete physical separation from their mothers at birth and that the conditions of warmth, enfoldment, and continuous body contact that exist prior to birth need

to be maintained for some months after birth in order for the child to complete a normal pattern of development.

Montagu mentions the figure of 266 days as the period after birth when infants still have intense needs for body contact with parents and siblings. He terms this the period of extrauterine *gestation*—noting that our infants are very immature at birth, much more so than other mammals, and suggesting that we should adopt a time frame of 18 months as the duration of pregnancy, with birth the midway point.

Jean Liedloff, author of *The Continuum Concept* (New York: Warner Books, 1979), calls this period the "in arms" phase of human development, and she agrees it is essential for humans to have these experiences in order to mature fully. She writes of the "expectations" our infants enter the world with, carefully describing how, on the most basic biological level, the fact that we have ears means we "expect" to hear, that we have eyes means we "expect" to see, and that we have skin and organs of balance means we "expect" to be touched and moved. Given this set of biologic expectations, it seems unspeakably cruel to separate mothers and babies after birth and to enforce solitary confinement in a stationary box for the infant.

All these investigators present convincing evidence that challenges our stereotypical notion of life *in utero*. Far from being a sensory limbo—quiet, dark, motionless—life before birth for all of us appears to consist of warm encounters with every aspect of our mothers. We hear her beating heart and the rhythmic rush of her blood against the placenta; in bright light we peer through a rosy glow cast by her skin and blood vessels (perhaps this is the origin of the lyric "looking at the world through rose-colored glasses"); we feel amniotic fluid swirling around us (the waters are freshened every three hours); we feel the fluid enter our mouths and travel to our stomachs as we swallow; we feel the pressure of her touch as she massages her abdomen; we feel the gentle resistance of her organs, skin, and bones as we move our limbs; we feel the motion, the swaying and the purposeful striding, the bending and the stretching as she goes about her daily activities; and, in the night, we also sense the absence of motion (rest) and the absence of tension (relaxation) as she sleeps. That human infants require this sort of care as their biological birthright seems an inescapable conclusion; otherwise, one could speculate, conditions before birth would be different than they are.

Our babies are not born blank slates. They

have months of human sensory experience behind them at birth. They expect to continue to be treated as a human being needs to be from birth on. Pregnancy is the time given to us and to our babies to begin to know one another and to grow in appreciation of our unique human natures. The continuous flow of feedback you receive from your baby's body and your baby receives from yours during pregnancy is the primary way those ends are accomplished.

The Last Month: A Prelude to Birth

It's unlikely that babies know beforehand that they are about to be born. It is also unlikely that if they knew it would make much difference in their outlook. From the baby's point of view, birth is merely one step in a long developmental process, a transition from gestation within the womb to gestation outside it. Granted, it's the sensory equivalent of a day at an amusement park and a night on the town, but by the end of pregnancy your baby might willingly volunteer to run that gamut in order to wind up in more comfortable circumstances.

If you're eating well enough, your baby gains an ounce a day during the last month of pregnancy. While the baby does add inches in length during these weeks, much of that weight takes the form of a protective layer of fat beneath the baby's delicate skin. This fat layer, as we shall see later, proves to be very important in the baby's self-regulation of body temperature after birth. Absence or reduction in thickness of this essential fat layer is one reason premature babies must usually spend some time in an incubator after birth. The fat layer also contributes to a baby's characteristic "cuddliness," a look which researchers say increases a mother's attraction to her baby.

Far more important than these considerations, though, is the amazing development of the baby's brain which undergoes an unparalleled growth spurt in the weeks just before and after birth. The brain is at the same time making new cells and differentiating those cells into the intricate pathways that regulate every aspect of our physical and emotional existence. Capacity for learning, coordinated movement, speech, and sociability are the higher cerebral functions made possible by this additional development of our brains above that of

other mammals. Many writers have speculated that this larger brain mass (which makes our babies' heads proportionately so much larger than other mammalian offspring) is the reason human infants are born midway through their gestation. Otherwise, the theory goes, if labor commenced only when the brain was fully formed, the child's head would always be too large to fit through the mother's pelvis.

The likelihood is that, as the head becomes ever larger and heavier in the later weeks of pregnancy, it obeys the law of gravity. The baby's body gradually turns inside the uterus until the head settles into the pelvic basin, ready to serve as the lead point in labor. This accounts for the fact that, in 96 percent of births occurring at term, the head is the first part of the baby's body to emerge. Of course, within the category of head down there are numerous positions the baby can assume. The accompanying illustration shows several variations of the birth position, including breech when the buttocks or feet come first (3.5 percent of all

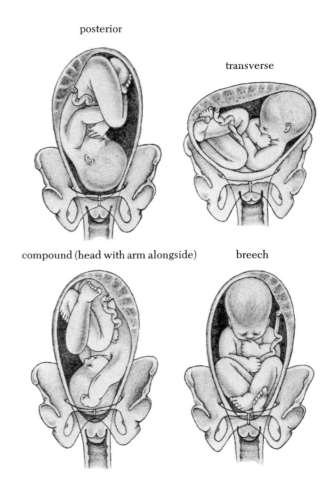

Variations in baby's position before birth.

births) and transverse when the baby is lodged crosswise (0.5 percent). It is also possible to have a compound presentation, such as a head with an arm tucked up next to it. These are exceedingly rare, however. The relationships between the position and size of the baby, the particular spatial relationships in your pelvis, and the strength of your uterus in working through labor determine how efficient your labor will be.

There will be much more about this in the next chapter. The point here is that the baby is getting heavier, larger, and settled into position for birth. All these factors mean that the baby may be less comfortable than before. And, because of the increased brain function, perhaps more aware of discomfort.

Other factors which create pressure and which the baby now may find somewhat displeasing:

- There is less of a cushion of amniotic fluid around the baby—particularly in front of the head as it descends further into the pelvis—so the baby's head may have more contact with the mother's bones than before.
- The baby fills the mother's abdominal cavity and then some, so enfoldment within her body in the last weeks may begin to resemble confinement instead, as baby's freedom of movement is increasingly restricted.
- The baby may begin to feel the effects of gravity (weight) and have limited means of adjusting its body to the stress—a clue that this may occur is the kicking all mothers have felt upon arising or reclining or rolling over in the later stages of pregnancy.

There is no way to interview babies before birth to substantiate these possibilities, but a quick survey of women waiting for labor to begin usually brings a chorus of confirmations that *they* are ready to give birth. Pregnancy is wonderful, they say, but it would be even greater if it only lasted eight months! The pressure on bladder and lower back from the baby's weight and position is tolerated less well later on, because joints and ligaments have been softened to a remarkable degree by placental hormones. Here is another example of a maternal response to a stimulation from the baby *in utero*. This relaxation of body hinge points permits the pelvic bones to be parted a bit during progress of labor if need be to allow the baby to emerge (another accommodation of the mother's body to the baby's need).

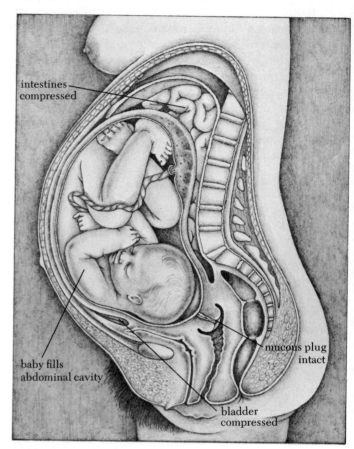

intestines compressed

baby fills abdominal cavity

mucous plug intact

bladder compressed

Baby settling into birth position.

The placenta begins to manufacture these hormones in the early weeks of pregnancy. By the eighth month, if the mother's diet has been adequate and her blood volume expanded so the placenta is optimally perfused (as discussed previously in this chapter), the placenta makes the equivalent of 100 birth control pills a day in hormones. These hormones influence the connective tissue *throughout your body* (not just your ankles) to retain fluid, just as the monthly buildup of hormones causes many women to retain water a few days before their periods.

This swelling, termed edema, is a sign of health in the well-fed pregnant woman—it's a sign of adequate diet, of a liver that is manufacturing enough albumin to keep the blood volume expanded, and, so, the placenta is well supplied with nutrient-rich blood and working fine. The swelling may mean that your face looks a bit puffy or rounder, that your rings may be tight on your fingers, or that your feet are too swollen for your regular shoes. When you know how important this stored fluid is for you and your baby during the labor to come, you won't worry about being a bit swollen for a few weeks. To make yourself more comfortable, remove those rings, put your feet up a few times a day, and make sure you're getting enough protein and salt. Especially in the summertime, when many people feel less like eating because of high temperatures and humidity, it's important to keep a diet record, checking off each day's food requirements as you go so you don't fall behind on the protective foods you need. (See sample chart.)

Why is the swelling on a good diet something to be happy about? It insures that you and your baby are safeguarded from some common complications during labor and immediately after birth.

- The expanded blood volume provides two to three pints of extra blood, just in case you should lose extra blood during delivery (in the event of a tear that opens a large blood

SPUN Diet Food Record (Basic Requirements)

	Sunday	Monday	Tuesday	Wednesday	Thursday	Friday	Saturday
Milk							
Milk							
Milk							
Milk							
Egg							
Egg							
Protein							
Protein							
Protein							
Protein							
Protein							
Protein							
Protein							
Protein							
Green vegetable							
Green vegetable							
Whole grains							
Whole grains							
Whole grains							
Whole grains							
Whole grains							
Vitamin C source							
Vitamin C source							
Fats and oils							
Fats and oils							
Fats and oils							
Yellow fruit or vegetable							
Liver (at least once a week)							
Other snacks (Specify)							

Check each box as you meet that requirement each day. Note special locations for meals (for example, at a restaurant, while commuting, while watching television).

vessel, for instance, or should you require a Cesarean)—it's insurance that you won't go into shock under these circumstances.

- The stored tissue fluid can be mobilized and drawn back into the circulation over the course of labor so, in case you don't feel like eating or drinking (many women feel nauseated and may actually vomit during the intense phase of labor), you won't become dehydrated—nature didn't foresee intravenous fluids being served up to everyone in labor!

- The stored fluid also protects against failures at breastfeeding, because there will be plenty of fluid to initiate and sustain a good milk flow—breastfeeding ad lib from birth onward is the best protection against postpartum hemorrhage ever designed. As the baby suckles, hormones are released which cause the uterus to contract, clamping off those open arteries and veins at the placental site which we discussed earlier.

The swelling in your legs may be increased toward the end of the day, due to the pressure of your baby's head on the veins in your pelvis that return blood from your legs to your heart. After the head is engaged in the pelvis (so the head can no longer be moved from its position by palpating your abdomen), this dependent edema may stay with you all the time. It is still not a cause for concern if you are eating well—it's a purely mechanical slowdown of blood flow which the birth of your baby will correct. If you find it unsightly, wear slacks and, of course, flat, open sandals or soft slippers for your tender feet.

This situation usually lasts no more than a few days, since the pressure from the baby's head and the rising levels of hormones also begin to soften your cervix—one of the first signs that labor is imminent. You may also notice considerably heavier vaginal secretions during the last few days of pregnancy for the same reason. All in all, you are in a very juicy (what doctors call "ripe") state, physically ready to give birth.

Your uterus has been preparing for labor ever since you became pregnant. Your good diet has provided all the nutrients needed to form collagen, the connective tissue between muscle fibers that strengthens the uterus as it grows larger. The uterus has been tightening and relaxing automatically a few times each hour as a way of exercising. In this way, the uterus is like your heart—you have

no conscious control over either; they function according to their own natures. However, it is possible to increase the efficiency of your heart by undertaking a properly graduated series of aerobic exercise (such as strenuous walking, running, or swimming).

The way you can increase the efficiency of your uterus is to eat well and keep up an active love life during pregnancy. Orgasm results in a strong tightening and then deep release of the uterine muscles and is the only way you can consciously exercise your uterus. If you seldom experience orgasm or if your partner is reluctant to make love during pregnancy (a problem many women report), or if your doctor has told you that you must refrain from sex during the last six weeks of pregnancy just because he tells everyone that (i.e., you have no medical reason to avoid sexual relations), you might want to read further. Highly recommended are:

For Yourself: The Fulfillment of Female Sexuality, by Lonnie Garfield Barbach (New York: Doubleday, 1975). A guide to achieving orgasm that you might want to share with your love partner, too.

Making Love During Pregnancy, by Elisabeth Bing and Libby Colman (New York: Bantam, 1977). A discussion with several hundred women and their partners about their feelings and needs during pregnancy—and why doctors have traditionally advised abstinence. This book has beautiful drawings of lovemaking during pregnancy.

"Pregnancy Means Parenting," by Jane and Jim Pittenger in *The Pregnancy-After-30 Workbook* (Emmaus, Pa.: Rodale Press, 1978). This chapter details massage and other forms of sexual expression as part of pregnancy. Illustrated.

If you feel uncomfortable touching your own genitals, now's the time to remedy the situation. Your feelings are very likely to be transferred to your baby as you care for him or her and feelings of shame or displeasure about their bodies is one problem children should not have. They are born, after all, with nothing but good feelings about their physical selves and it's unfortunate when they grow up thinking otherwise.

In the last few weeks of pregnancy, the uterine tightenings and releasings, called Braxton-Hicks contractions after the doctor who wrote about

Right from the Start

them, may become more pronounced. You may even have a few stretches of time in which the contractions seem to settle into a fairly regular pattern, mimicking labor. Because these episodes do not accomplish dilation (opening up) of the cervix, they are called false labor. It's helpful to view these experiences as "tune-ups" by your uterus for real labor, so you don't feel disappointed when they cease. Your baby probably also benefits from these trial contractions—a sort of gradual introduction to the sensations that will be sustained for several hours during labor.

Chapter 2

Birth
Individualized Care

During the birth process the sensory aspects of pregnancy are intensified to the limits of our ability to feel and respond. The friendly relationship established in pregnancy is flamed by the passion of birth into a love affair that lasts a lifetime. The reality of the existence of each other is indelibly imprinted into the physical and emotional memory of both as the baby is propelled through the mother's birth canal. The sheer power of these sensations makes it virtually impossible for a human mother to overlook the fact that her baby has been born. It guarantees that she will pay close attention to her child. They have shared and have survived the most ecstatic and most awe-inspiring of human experiences, birth. Quite literally, they will never be the same. They are comrades in body and spirit forever.

We've noticed that, after giving birth, women often talk about labor as something that happened to them and their babies *completely independent of their will or conscious control.* Everyone has always assumed this to be the baby's point of view. We are impressed with the fact that mothers feel the same way. As we shall see, these maternal observations are borne out when we learn how our bodies work in labor and, so, provide us with reliable guidelines for making our birth plans. In order to strengthen the continuum of attachment that began at conception, we need to know how labor affects us and our babies and how to apply

the test for togetherness as the standard for selecting birth places, birth attendants, and birth practices.

Labor Begins

Nobody knows for sure what triggers the sequence of uterine contractions that result in the birth of your baby. It seems clear to everyone, though, that these contractions work remarkable changes in you and your baby in a matter of hours. Most obvious is that after birth your baby is no longer sheltered within your body. However, from the very beginning of labor and long before the moment of birth you and your baby make amazing physical accommodations to one another.

The chief agent in this intense process is the uterine contraction, the involuntary pulling together and subsequent relaxation of the muscle fibres that comprise your uterus. By the end of pregnancy you've probably become quite aware of these contractions. You've been having them approximately every 15 minutes during your pregnancy; it's the way your uterus maintains its tone and strength while rapidly growing 30 times larger than usual to hold your baby, placenta, and amniotic fluid. Just because the uterus is so much larger by the end of pregnancy, its cyclical tightening and releasing is more noticeable. You may find that these contractions are made even stronger while you make love or breastfeed your older baby.

These prelabor contractions are viewed by some as an integral part of the birth process, since they often accomplish some effacement (thinning) of the cervix. In *Human Labor and Birth* (3d ed., New York: Appleton-Century-Crofts, 1976), Oxorn and Foote comment, "Prelabor merges into clinically recognizable labor by such small degrees that the exact point at which so-called true labor begins is difficult to determine."

Some midwives and physicians try to assess how close you may be to the onset of true labor by feeling the cervix during an office visit close to your expected due date. If the cervix is long, still firm (like your earlobe), and admits only the tip of the examiner's finger, you may be told that birth is a few days or weeks off yet. If the cervix is beginning to shorten, soften (like your lips), and admits one or two fingers, then you will be termed "ripe" and ready to give birth at any time. Of course, many women have been told not to expect to go into labor for two weeks and had their babies later that night, while others have walked around for a week or two halfway dilated, so there's no 100 percent foolproof way to determine what will happen in your own case. Best to avoid fixing on a given due date. Instead, earmark your last weeks for resting as much as possible, eating well, and addressing those birth announcements. When your body is ready, labor will ensue.

For the sake of having some way to chart progress in labor, most obstetricians regard true labor as the presence of contractions that result in dilatation (opening up) of the cervix. Only when the cervix is "ripe," the presenting part (usually the baby's head) well applied to the cervix, and the contractions strong enough and frequent enough to move the presenting part down into the pelvis, does dilatation occur. This is why, even though you may have episodes of contractions that mimic true labor toward the end of pregnancy, dilatation does not result. In most cases, your cervix simply wasn't ready to be opened up by the contractions. This also explains why, when labor is induced merely on the basis of a date (often ten days "over" is the cutoff), the induction often fails and the mother and baby wind up with a Cesarean, a procedure which interferes in numerous and serious ways with the continuum of care they should receive during and after birth.

When you've been eating enough good food every day throughout pregnancy, your uterus grows optimally and is far more likely to work in a coordinated fashion during labor and bring forth your baby in an efficient manner. John Ebbs, M.D., a Toronto pediatrician, observed in 1941 that mothers in a study group who were on the most nutritious diets during pregnancy (even though they had been undernourished prior to pregnancy) had labors that were *five hours shorter,* on the average, than mothers whose diets were known to be less good. This was so even though the better-fed mothers had babies that were, on the average, a full pound heavier than babies born to the less well fed mothers. And as anyone who has ever been in labor will attest, five hours is a considerable difference!

What actually happens during a normal contraction? Work done at the Hospital de Clinicas, Montevideo, Uruguay, shows that each contraction moves in a wavelike pattern and that different parts of the uterus behave differently as the contraction progresses. (See the accompanying illustration.) The uterine muscle fibres are arranged in three layers:

- an outer layer, most of whose fibres run longitudinally;
- a middle layer with fibres in a whorl pattern through which the uterine blood vessels pass; and
- the inner layer, consisting mostly of circular fibres, the bulk of which are concentrated in the lower segment of the uterus (near the cervix).

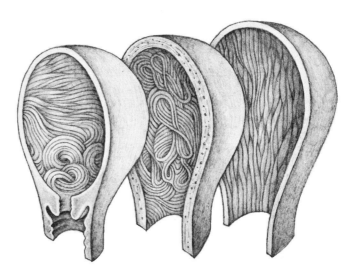

Muscle layers of the uterus.

Birth: Individualized Care

The Montevideo researchers point out that coordination of these layers and segments is absolutely essential to normal labor. While all parts of the uterus contract, the upper segment does so much more strongly than the lower and the cervix least of all. This is the major factor allowing for gradual dilatation of the cervix. During each contraction wave:

- One of the two "pacemakers" located at either side of the uterus near the Fallopian tubes initiates the contraction.
- The wave travels from the pacemaker downward toward the cervix, gradually losing strength the lower it extends.
- All parts of the uterus attain their maximum possible tension at the same time, with the upper segment, the fundus, being in action for a longer period of time with a more gradual ascent toward peak intensity than the lower segment.
- Relaxation begins at the same time in all parts of the uterus; however, the longitudinal fibres retract after each contraction, gradually becoming shorter and thicker in the upper segment of the uterus and longer and thinner in the lower segment, thus pulling the cervix farther and farther apart and higher into the body of the uterus.
- The baby is moved downward with each normal contraction wave and fixed at the lower station by virtue of the retraction of the longitudinal fibres; otherwise, the baby would be pushed into the pelvis during a contraction only to return upward after it ceased, making no progress toward being born.
- Normal resting tension exerted by muscle fibres is 8 to 12 mm of mercury; during a normal contraction the intensity increases to 30 to 50 mm of mercury (just about the maximum grip strength of an adult male).
- During a contraction, blood flow through the middle layer of muscle fibre is cut off both to the uterus and to the placenta (baby); the resting phase of each contraction, then, is just as important as the tension phase. Without sufficient relaxation between contractions, blood flow through the uterus and to the baby is reduced; waste products of muscular activity (chiefly lactic acid) are carried away less efficiently, leading to painful spasms in the fibres them-

selves; and the baby may begin to suffer distress due to an inadequate supply of oxygen—this series of unfortunate events occurs all too frequently when labor is artificially stimulated with oxytocics to "speed things up," and unnecessary Cesareans can be the result.

Since the uterus has become the largest muscle in your body by the time you go into labor, planning to cope with contractions by doing something else while they are occurring is likely to be self-defeating. Better to attend a class where the working uterus is respected during labor and you learn simple techniques of muscular release you can use during contractions to allow the uterus to work most efficiently. Classes in the Bradley method or cooperative childbirth, we feel, are far superior to others in helping you achieve this objective. (For referral to a certified Bradley instructor in your area, write: Bradley Method, P. O. Box 5224, Sherman Oaks, CA 91413.)

Ashley Montagu writes, in *Touching: The Human Significance of the Skin* (New York: Columbia University Press, 1971), that labor contractions are important for stimulating the baby's sustaining systems—that, in fact, improper contractions may lead to failure of the principal organ systems after birth. In a rather curious way, contractions happen to both birth partners, mother and baby, but the sensory effects of labor are markedly different for each.

The baby, Montagu observes, receives stimulation of the sensory nerves in the skin from the intrauterine pressure caused by the contracting uterus. These nerves stimulate the baby's central nervous system which activates the autonomic nervous system which then triggers the organ systems. No system escapes excitement; the respiratory, circulatory, digestive, eliminative, nervous, and endocrine systems all benefit from labor and are made ready for the new functional demands that will be made of them in the immediate neonatal period.

Montagu likens human labor to the period of licking and grooming of the birthling that other mammals do immediately after birth. If the mother is unable to perform these acts, mammalian offspring languish and die. Without genital stimulation by the mother, for instance, puppies are unable to eliminate waste. This system simply does not function until the proper trigger mechanisms have set it in motion. It may be, ac-

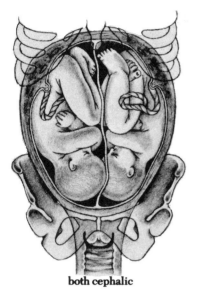 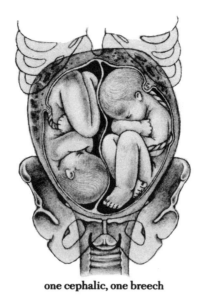 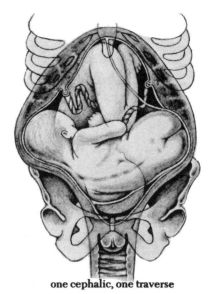

| both cephalic | one cephalic, one breech | one cephalic, one traverse |

Some of the possible positions of twins before birth (note marked crowding of abdomen).

cording to Montagu, that the process of coming through the birth canal provides the considerable head and facial stimulation human babies need to activate their respiratory centers. Studies of babies born by Cesarean seem to support this view, since many of them, even when born at term and of normal birth weight, initially have problems with breathing.

The events of normal labor are illustrated and charted below, emphasizing the sensory experiences of mother and baby. If birth marks a midpoint on the continuum of mother-child attachment, then, clearly, there should be no interference with the birth process unless medical urgency requires it. Otherwise, severe and long-

lasting disturbances of maternal-child attachment may occur. In other words, mother and baby lose important stepping-stones to their new life together.

The process of uterine activity is exactly the same in a multiple birth, although it is much more likely that twins will present in a variety of positions. (See illustration above.) This may necessitate a bit more assistance from the attendant than in the relatively uncomplicated birth of a single baby coming head first. Elizabeth Noble's *Having Twins* (Boston: Houghton Mifflin, 1980), the complete, up-to-date book about multiple pregnancy, explains the differences in management for twin births step by step. However, as she remarks, only

[*Continued on page 36*]

Things That Might Make You Think You're Having Twins:

1. Voracious appetite.

2. Feeling fetal movements everywhere and most of the day and night—some describe this as the "basket of puppies" sensation.

3. You're eating everything on the basic pregnancy diet every day and you start to swell dramatically in the sixth or seventh month of pregnancy (two placentas put out a double dose of hormones to sustain your multiple pregnancy).

4. Your uterus is growing much faster than what is usual with a single fetus (one of the things checked at your monthly prenatal checkup).

5. Palpation of your abdomen by the doctor or midwife leads them to suspect twins because of the "extra" body parts they feel.

Confirmation is possible by sonogram, x-ray, or waiting it out. (See chapter 2.)

Birth: Individualized Care

Sensory Experiences of Labor and Birth

Event of Normal Labor	What Mother Feels
1. Contraction, relaxation, and retraction of uterus—intermittent	Hardening of fundus Backache Groin ache Pressure on bladder Release of pressure and ache

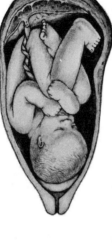

Contraction and retraction of uterus.

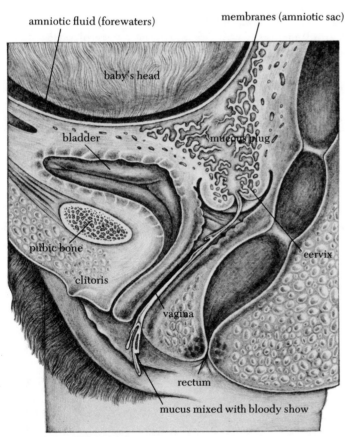

amniotic fluid (forewaters)

membranes (amniotic sac)

baby's head

bladder

mucous plug

pubic bone

clitoris

cervix

vagina

rectum

mucus mixed with bloody show

Expelling of mucous plug.

Event of Normal Labor	What Mother Feels
2. Expelling of mucous plug, bloody show, increased vaginal secretions, diarrhea	Wetness and stickiness in vagina, and on perineum and inner thighs Smell of body secretions specific to birth Stroking of genitals in cleansing

Right from the Start

Mother's Response	What Baby Feels	Baby's Response
Moving about, pausing during contraction and leaning forward Sitting upright, leaning forward during contraction	Being pushed from behind Pressure on rump Being moved downward into pelvis Increased pressure on head Increased pressure on skin Need for oxygen at peak of contraction?	Stimulation of respiratory center May signal onset of contraction with movement May cease movement during contraction Draws chin down toward chest as protective measure? Drop in rate of heartbeats at peak of contraction
Resumption of activities	Some release of pressure, but not total because of retraction which keeps head down into pelvis	May signal end of contraction with movement Heart rate returns to normal
Wipes area from front to back Wears sanitary napkin if in early phase Places underpad under body if in bed	Unknown	Unknown

[*Continued on next page*]

Birth: Individualized Care

	Event of Normal Labor	What Mother Feels

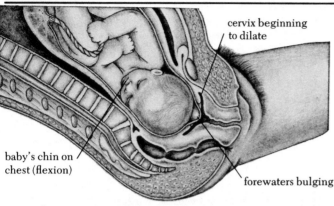

cervix beginning to dilate

baby's chin on chest (flexion)

forewaters bulging

Flexion and dilation.

3. Flexion of baby's head and dilation of cervix

Sensations stronger

Thirst caused by muscular effort (work)

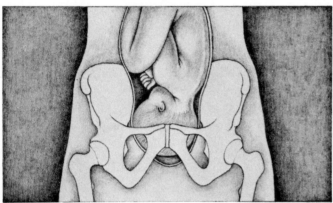

Engagement of head.

4. Descent of head into engaged position

Intense pressure on bladder
Weighty sensation in pelvis

Increased backache (sometimes)

Being held and stroked kindly (if desired)

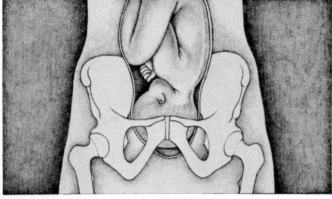

cervix fully dilated

amniotic fluid escaping

Breaking of membrane.

5. Full dilatation of cervix and rupture of amniotic sac; head approaching pubic bone and coccyx

Gush of warm fluid

Increased breathing rate as body works much harder
Legs trembling

Nausea (perhaps)

Sweating/Chills/Hot flashes
Urge to empty bowels

Sensations at their strongest, may be approaching sensory overload

A lack of awareness of events outside her body or an extreme sensitivity to them
Possible fatigue

Mother's Response	What Baby Feels	Baby's Response
Practicing relaxation techniques during contractions Drinks, chews ice	Release of some resistance to downward progress	Unknown
Urinating often Requests pillows to support legs and back (if in bed) May request backrub or walk about Pelvic rock Improved relaxation	Constant pressure on head Contact with bones of pelvic basin Contact with vertebrae of mother's spine	Molding of head Possible formation of *caput succedenum* and/or cephalhematoma Possible facial bruising if in posterior position
Changes underpad Skin flushes May request leg massage Vomiting (perhaps) Adding or throwing off covers Requests assistance to bathroom or for use of bedpan May request not to be touched, moved, or spoken to, and may want others present to remain silent May groan, hum, or moan during contraction May sleep between contractions	Loss of cushion for head Reduction of oxygen Head well into vagina (soft tissue on face) Mother's abdomen moving spasmodically Unknown May feel some release of head pressure as more room in pelvis if rectum empty May also be approaching sensory overload	Additional molding of head Possible hemorrhage into conjunctivae of eye Temporary duskiness Stimulus to initiate breathing efforts? Unknown Unknown Unknown May trigger hormonal/enzyme tranquilizing agents to lessen pain/stress perception

[*Continued on next page*]

Birth: Individualized Care

Sensory Experiences of Labor and Birth [*Continued*]

	Event of Normal Labor	What Mother Feels

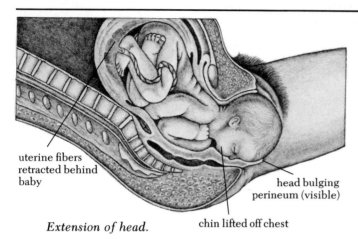

uterine fibers retracted behind baby

head bulging perineum (visible)

chin lifted off chest

Extension of head.

6. Extension of the head

Involuntary bearing-down efforts with rest periods in between

Breath being held briefly, then released (may cry out)

Spreading of the pelvis (movement apart of hips)

Spreading of vaginal lips
Tightness and distension of perineum to the point of numbness
Intense pressure on rectum
Gushes of water and blood with each push—keeps vagina lubricated
Genitals being cleansed
Possible involuntary urination
Profuse sweating
Possible dry throat

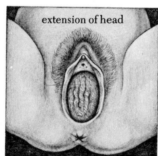

caput visible

extension of head

7. Crowning of the head—largest circumference coming through vaginal outlet

Burning sensation as skin around vaginal outlet stretches to utmost

crowning

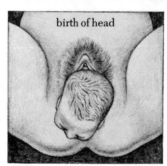

birth of head

8. Birth of head

Partial release of pressure on perineum
Head between legs

Sees head (shape, color, hair, vernix)

Passing through vagina stimulates baby's skin and internal organs and structures.

Mother's Response	What Baby Feels	Baby's Response
Releases air in work-grunt (like weight lifter) at peak of contraction to prevent excessive increase in abdominal pressure—gradual bulging of perineum gives skin a chance to stretch, reducing tears	Head coming in contact with perineum	Unknown
	Body being elongated for first time in months	Unknown
	Muffled sounds of mother, attendants (ears blocked only by thin layer of mother's perineum)	Unknown
Finds comfortable birth position—legs spread, upper body supported		
Looks in mirror to see progress		
Touches perineum to feel head and degree of skin tension		
May ask to be wiped off or for clean underpad		
May request cool cloth on forehead		
May request ice chips		
May cry out	Cool air felt on scalp for first time	Unknown
Reduces expulsive effort so head slips through slowly		
May cry out, start talking to baby	Mother's taut skin passing over face and resting around neck	Cue to open eyes and mouth?
		May cry
Reaches to support head	Release of intense pressure on head	Relief?
Looks in mirror or peeks over abdomen to see directly	Clearly hears sounds of mother, other people, and surroundings	Curiosity?
	Cool air on face	Fear?
	Touch of another's hand supporting head as it emerges	Cannot integrate?
	Smells amniotic fluid, blood, maternal secretions, pubic hair, air, bedding, skin of person supporting head	Stimulate adrenals and heart for temperature change?

[*Continued on next page*]

Birth: Individualized Care

Event of Normal Labor	What Mother Feels
8. Birth of head [*Continued*]	
9. Rotation of body—shoulders pass under pubic arch with uterine contraction propelling them	Turning of baby inside vagina Head brushing against perineum Urge to bear down again
10. Restitution of body—baby turns back into face-downward position as shoulders approach the vaginal outlet with push from behind	As above
11. Birth of body	Shoulders distending perineum (usually not as much as did the head) Body slipping out all at once following shoulders Gush of remaining fluid Complete release of pressure on perineum Sees baby change color (gray to pink) Hears baby cry/whimper Softness of baby's skin, wetness and crinkliness of head, weakness of neck Tininess of hands and feet, minute details

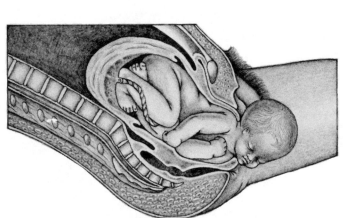

External rotation.

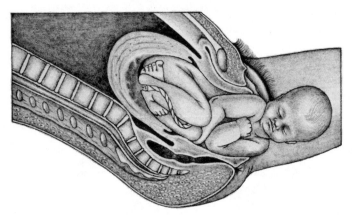

Birth of body.

Mother's Response	What Baby Feels	Baby's Response
	Direct light entering eyes	Open them if light dim; shut tightly if harsh
	Rest of body still squeezed in vagina, torso extended, legs being stretched out behind	Unknown
	Mucus and fluid from lungs being expressed by vaginal pressure and draining through baby's nose and mouth	May sneeze or cough
	Shoulders at pubic bone	Unknown
May cry out, groan, or grunt with expulsive effort as above	Being rotated and thrust downward in close-fitting chamber	Unknown
	Hears sounds of mother, other people, and surroundings	Unknown
	More mucus drains out	Preparation for first breath
As above	As above	As above
May cry out	Mother's taut skin passing over shoulders and entire length of body	First breath
Reaches to pick up baby almost immediately		Cry, whimper on exhalation
Stroking baby	Release of pressure on abdomen	Opportunity for chest to expand as air enters
Talking to baby	Air entering nose, mouth, lungs—chest expanding, falling	May clear away membranes so skin can function?
Looking at baby		
Embracing baby		Cue to begin unfurling process?
Kissing baby	Body fully extended briefly, then legs and arms drawn back into prebirth positions	
May be oblivious to all others for a short time	Cool air on all skin surfaces	Evaporation of water may cause trembling of chin, shivering, urination
	Senses body weight as lifted onto mother's abdomen	Return to status of enfoldment and warmth in mother's arms —reassuring?
	Smells mother's skin and breath	
	Senses mother's skin texture and warmth	
	Sees mother	Grasps mother's finger

[*Continued on next page*]

Birth: Individualized Care

Event of Normal Labor	What Mother Feels
11. Birth of body [*Continued*]	Smell of amniotic fluid, vernix, baby's skin, blood (perhaps)—smells specific to human birth Eye-to-eye contact
12. Cutting of umbilical cord	Slight movement of cord against perineum as it is moved to be cut
13. Separation of placenta from uterine wall—placenta settles into bottom of uterus	Series of small contractions (may not be felt) Small gush of blood from vagina as placenta separates/settles Cord pushed out further from vagina Baby licking and gumming nipple Nipples become erect Baby suckles strongly
14. Birth of placenta	One last push to expel placenta and membranes and empty uterus Small distension of perineum compared to distension caused by baby Globular, spongy mass passing through vaginal outlet Strong uterine contractions to hold shut blood vessels at placenta site

Placenta separates.

Placenta settling into vaginal canal.

Mother's Response	What Baby Feels	Baby's Response
	Hears mother	Gazes fixedly Orients toward sound
Watches to see that baby is safe Keeps baby held close May offer breast	Freedom from sense of cord tugging or pulling on abdominal skin Nipple near lips	Unknown Roots for nipple, latches on, begins suckling
May be too absorbed in baby to notice		
Pleasurable sensations mother wants to repeat	Texture of nipple in mouth Feel of breast against lips Tongue licking and thrusting up against nipple Smell of mother Being closely held Sweet taste of colostrum	Satisfaction of rooting reflex—pleasure Warmth and enfoldment—pleasure Good taste makes baby want more—pleasure
May want to see placenta and membranes	As above	As above
Continues to nurse baby—initiates rhythmic contractions which continue whenever mother nurses		
Reduces flow of blood Prevents postpartum hemorrhage		

about half the twin pregnancies are diagnosed, so only half of the twin labors are managed according to the specialized plan of management.

In *Human Labor and Birth* (3d ed., New York: Appleton-Century-Crofts, 1976), Oxorn and Foote comment drily on the difficulty of making a conclusive diagnosis of twin gestation: "At birth the delivery of more than one child is positive evidence." They outline their plan of management when multiples are anticipated.

- Make an accurate diagnosis of the presentations (x-ray may be indicated).
- Obstetrical medications must be held to the absolute minimum. (Their reasoning is that twins are usually smaller than a singleton and, so, more susceptible to drug-induced central nervous system [CNS] depression, but with proper maternal nutrition each baby can weigh as much as a singleton. See chapter 1.)
- Have cross-matched blood available, in case the overdistended uterus is slow to clamp down after birth of the second baby. (It's also important to put the babies to breast as a prophylactic measure for this same reason.)
- *Watchful expectancy is the procedure of choice during labor; the best results are obtained when interference is minimal.*
- Intravenous fluids are started just prior to the birth of the first baby in case medications to stimulate the uterus (oxytocin) to deliver the second baby are required.
- After the birth of the first baby, clamp the umbilical cord to prevent possible loss of blood from the second baby through a shared placenta.
- The position of the second baby may change dramatically after the first baby is born—the attendant may have to guide the presenting part (head or buttocks) into position manually, or a baby with a compound presentation or transverse lie will have to be turned before being delivered. Often a light inhalation anesthesia will be offered to the mother at this time if she wishes it (she may be asleep for two or three minutes), since these procedures can be painful.
- In 80 percent of cases the second twin is born within 30 minutes of the first.
- The placenta(s) deliver after the two babies.
- The presence of twins is never justification in and of itself for a Cesarean delivery.

One of the common misconceptions new mothers have is that all doctors practice obstetrics the same way. As controversy over the "new obstetrics" (aggressive management of every aspect of labor and birth by the physician, usually with considerable technological hardware) rages, the range of obstetric practice widens. The responsibility of being fully informed in our choices falls more and more to us, the parents. We've found that a few direct questions asked of personnel at hospitals and birth centers and of those who attend births at home can be enormously helpful in narrowing your own range of acceptable alternatives to the standard hospital delivery.

Probably the foremost consideration is under what circumstances are you and your baby most likely to have all your needs, physical and emotional, met? The answer to this question is not the same for everyone, but the process of seeking an answer is applicable to each of us. What follows is a Birth Considerations Questionnaire, with our comments about the questions. By carefully interviewing prospective attendants and mothers who have used their services it is possible to gain a fairly accurate picture of their actual practices. Don't feel shy about asking questions. In almost every case the individual will be well paid for services to you and your family. Remember, too, that the answers to these questions can make or break your earliest weeks with your new baby.

Birth Considerations Questionnaire

Part 1

Questions to ask the prospective care giver:

1. What percentage of babies born to the mothers you've cared for are born too early (before 37 weeks) or underweight at term (less than 6½ pounds)?

This is a strong indicator of the person's nutrition practices. The premature rate should be under 3 percent, and there should be very few underweight infants. If the person can't tell you these figures, it means s/he isn't paying attention to one of his or her most important critical functions. In effect, s/he is practicing without "quality control"! Ask for a copy of his or her diet sheet.

2. What kind of childbirth preparation do you favor? Are classes part of the practice package (included in the fee)? Have you attended a complete series of classes so you are familiar with their content?
In the best of all possible worlds, childbirth preparation will be an integral part of prenatal care. It will start as soon as you know you're pregnant and continue at regular intervals until your baby is born and, in many cases, will become a support group for new mothers. The doctor or midwife will work in a team practice—with all members of the team (other health workers, educators, social service counselors) working by the same protocols, with respect and full knowledge of the work of other team members. Very few places today operate in this manner.
The next-best course is for the doctor or midwife to refer everyone to classes sponsored by a nonprofit, independent, community-based childbirth education organization, whose instructors have completed a careful period of education and training. These classes should also be addressed to all the concerns of the entire maternity cycle, not just labor and birth. The instructors should be committed to improving the health of women during the childbearing year, and they should be competent in individualized nutrition counseling, teaching progressive relaxation for labor, introduction to breastfeeding (how to as well as why), and dealing with medical care providers and institutions, and acquainted with medical complications of pregnancy and their management.
Mercifully, the days of a few classes late in pregnancy geared strictly to getting through labor are ending. Classes which rely on exhausting breathing techniques as a major form of coping with labor are outdated. Why should you be burdened with extra work to do while your body is caught up already in the strenuous work of giving birth? Patterned breathing techniques seldom work throughout the entire labor anyway, since most mothers find out that fighting your body is much more tiring than cooperating with it. Nothing less than comprehensive childbirth education is good enough for you and your baby. You don't need to settle for less. To find out about quality childbirth education in your area, consult the organizations profiled in the Directory at the end of this book.
Beware of doctors or midwives who are noncommital or who discourage you from attending comprehensive classes. An educated, prepared patient is always a better patient, from the enlightened doctor's or midwife's point of view. Many care providers are unfamiliar with class content or, when parents have only had access to classes that offer too little, too late, the doctor or midwife may have become disillusioned about the value of *all* classes. Try to share with these individuals the information covered in your comprehensive class so their ideas about childbirth preparation can be refocused. The worst situation is when someone tells you that s/he "will tell you everything you need to know when you get a little closer to delivery," or when you hear that "all you need to have a super birth is lots of good energy." Both are hazardous forms of know-nothingism and don't bode well for the kind of open communication and mutual respect with the care giver you're entitled to.

3. What percentage of your clients require medication during labor and birth? Electronic monitoring? Cesareans?
In well-prepared, well-nourished mothers with supportive attendants during labor, medication should be needed less than 10 percent of the time. The unavoidable Cesarean rate (due to "no-fits," difficult presentations, or maternal disease) is approximately 3 or 4 percent.
Unfortunately, among parents who have attended classes which emphasize breathing techniques and who have had no continuous nutrition counseling during pregnancy, the medication rate is approximately 75 percent. Cesareans have skyrocketed to 30 to 50 percent in many hospitals, often due to unnecessary electronic monitoring (which the hospital childbirth classes present as de rigueur for every woman in labor). The answers to these questions merely inform you about the doctor's or midwife's frame of reference for birth. You are not necessarily doomed to be included in their disappointing statistics if you take the proper precautions on your own—i.e., learn everything you possibly can about birth and how to arrange your birth according to your preferences. (See the

Cooperative Childbirth Preferences sheet in *The Pregnancy-After-30 Workbook* [Emmaus, Pa.: Rodale Press, 1978] for starters.) After many years' experience, we are convinced that it is better not to take classes at all (prepare yourself through study and practice) than to take classes in which misinformation masquerades as fact and women are socialized to accept whatever the prevailing hospitals' routines call for.

4. How accessible are you?

   When you need to consult with this person, can you reach him or her? The most competent individual does you little good if his or her office is perpetually running late, so you always feel rushed during your appointments and wind up putting off important (to you) questions. Suppose you were to have a complication and the person were overcommitted to too many deliveries and couldn't make it to see you—a very important consideration for those having babies at home. Is s/he the kind who, in lieu of personal attention during labor, still relies on "standing orders" at the hospital for all clients, so you have to haggle with a floor nurse about your labor preferences at a time when you need to be devoting your full attention to your contractions? When this individual must be out of town, is the "back-up" associate an absolute stranger who shares few of this person's attitudes about childbirth (but who may be an exceptionally well qualified surgeon)? Is the office staff lax in relaying your messages and getting the physician or midwife to return your calls? (In some practices, a "call hour" is established so you can talk directly to the care giver without having to be put on hold or first recite your problem to a "screener".) All of these situations represent barriers to communication and may jeopardize your well-being and that of your baby. It's hard to get straight answers to this question without talking to others who have used this person's service.

5. What percentage of women in your care breastfeed their babies for six months or more?

   The higher the number the better. Since breastfeeding has become fashionable once again, the figures may be pretty high in the newborn period, but tend to drop off sharply after the third month. This is still a token breastfeeding society and women need much better information from professionals than is currently provided in order to plan for the normal human nursing period—suckling ad lib according to the child's needs, in some cases for three or four years. (See discussion in chapter 8.) Assistance is also available from local comprehensive childbirth education groups who perceive the entire maternity cycle as their area of expertise. The caring professional maintains an open referral network with these groups and recommends them to every new mother.

6. Can you provide me with a list of five to ten women who have used your services in the past year?

   Would you hire someone to build an addition onto your house without checking the contractor's performance with some past customers first? Just because a doctor or midwife is still in practice doesn't necessarily mean s/he has performed to your standards. Past patients who were willing to discuss their experiences could register with the office helper, so there would be no problem with violating the "doctor-patient relationship" and "professional ethics."

   If this proves impossible directly through the care giver's office, your childbirth education group usually keeps on file reports of prenatal and birth experiences according to doctor's or midwife's name. People who give permission for their reports to be used in this way are usually open to a call from another expectant mother about any aspect of the care they received. This is one way to find out whether the "dream doctor" or the "perfect midwife" really comes through with things s/he promises in the office during pregnancy—or whether the person who seems somewhat cool or distant in the office turns out to be very kind and helpful during delivery. Here, probably more than in any other category we've discussed, the force of individual personalities comes into play. There's no accounting for people's reactions to one another, so we've learned that the doctor one woman swears by may be considered totally hopeless by another.

   Assuming that questions 1 through 5 above are answered the same way by two people you're considering, you have the luxury of fine discrimination in lifestyles or other criteria of importance to you. Talking with more than one person before you decide about a certain care giver is also important for this reason. Your childbirth educator can help fill in the picture with her observations if she's ever worked with the individual in the past. Her job is to help you toward the birth you want by providing as much information as possible to help you make your decisions. Open discussion of doctors' and midwives' practices is part of her professional responsibility to you, her client. When questioning others about their impressions of an individual's practice, try to be as specific as possible in your questions. Avoid such general questions as, "Did you like Dr. X?" You'll get a much better idea of what to expect if you make a list of your own preferences and see if the person you're talking with valued the same things—and how well the midwife or doctor cooperated.

Part II

Questions to ask about the birth place:

7. Are there circumstances under which trained support people of the mother's choosing would be required to abandon her during labor, birth, or the early postpartum hours?

   About the only legitimate time this might happen is if the mother were to need general anesthesia, and even then someone she knows ought to be present as she awakens in the recovery room. Institutions which persist in interrupting the progress of labor by interfering with the mother's access to her chosen support people are best not patronized by the childbearing population. A letter explaining why you have taken your business elsewhere (let's not forget that hospitals are, in most cases, business enterprises) addressed to the administrator is often quite effective in getting policies changed.

8. Are there circumstances under which mothers would be required to surrender their babies to a third party for care?

   Except in cases where the baby or the mother is suffering some malady and requires medical attention due to the abnormality, routine baby care should be carried on by the mother. When the baby is ill, s/he needs close mothering even more. (See chapters 4 and 5.) Progressive hospitals recognize this and respect it in practice. This means that parents are welcome in intensive care nurseries just as they are in standard care units. If the baby is healthy, nursing care should be oriented to teaching the mother to care for her own child, rather than to nurses doing the mothering. Cesarean mothers, of course, require special help in the first few days after surgery, but most are eager to care for their own babies as soon as possible.

   In cases where the mother is incapacitated, the father or another family member should be encouraged to come to the hospital to care for the baby in the mother's room. This promotes closer family ties and insures that the baby receives the one-to-one personal parenting each child needs for optimal development. This is almost never the case when babies are placed in a central nursery (see chapter 4), no matter how kind or competent the nursery staff may be.

9. Are there provisions for early discharge (6 to 12 hours after birth) of healthy mothers and babies?
   Healthy people do not require hospitalization.

10. How many times in the past year have the obstetric staff and the pediatric staff had in-service presentations dealing with aspects of family-centered maternity care? Were these programs made available to workers on all shifts? What were the topics covered? What was the response of the staff?

    There is high turnover in hospital staff, so continuing education and sharing of information needs to be done on a more or less continuous basis in cooperation with the local childbirth educators (those from independent organizations as well as those who teach for the hospital). Labor, delivery, postpartum, and nursery nursing are professions distinct from parent education, but all these individuals need to be able to work together in the best interest of mother, baby, and family. Parents should not be placed in the position of having to conduct in-service education programs while they are busy having their babies. Hospital staffs should have complete knowledge of what is being done in parent education in the community, just as childbirth educators should know how various hospitals conduct their services. Parents need to know everything.

11. For birth in your own home, do you feel comfortable assuming responsibility for all the necessary arrangements? Can you determine the competence of prospective attendants? Do you know what to do in case your attendants miss the birth? Do you have an emergency back-up plan for all contingencies? Have you visited the closest hospital to familiarize yourself with it in case you or your baby must be transported there during or after birth? Do you have access to classes to prepare you for home birth?

As mothers who have had children in hospitals and at home, and as health professionals deeply involved in childbirth, we support the concept of individualized care based on individual circumstances and needs of the expectant mother and her family. There are women for whom childbirth at home is the best choice. There are those for whom birth centers are appropriate. There are those who will prefer to use hospitals for childbirth. *If the mother is well nourished, has an adequate pelvis, has no medical problem which would make her a high risk, is carrying the baby in a favorable position for uncomplicated birth, and wants to give birth at home, she should have the support of family, friends, and medical care providers that will enable her to do so.*

The American College of Obstetricians and Gynecologists (ACOG), in a most regrettable position paper, has termed childbirth at home "the earliest form of child abuse." Not only does this statement reflect an incredibly insular point of view in a world where the vast majority of human infants are born in the dwellings of their families, it also fails to recognize that the *place* of birth is a matter of relative insignificance when compared to the proper nourishment of pregnant women to insure that they are removed from most high-risk categories, no matter where they decide to give birth!

The United States, which has the highest rate of birth in hospitals anywhere in the world, still ranks only sixteenth in infant mortality—far behind many other countries where birth at home is still the rule, not the exception. The idea that countries with better maternal and infant outcomes should pattern their maternity care after ours is a curious one indeed. But because many doctors from abroad come to the United States for specialty training, then return to their countries as senior administrators and professors, the tendency toward universal hospitalization for childbirth is spreading—and with it, the increased use of America's electronic gadgetry and pharmacological armamentarium.

As this trend becomes more widespread, we can expect to see other countries following the sad path of England where, in just the past ten years, the independent and highly esteemed profession of midwifery has been brought to heel as physicians have campaigned to hospitalize all women for birth and to bring midwives under their command in hospital-based practice. We view these forces with alarm, because the ancient profession of midwifery is being reduced to the status of physician's helper (and a vital area over which women have traditionally exerted independent personal and professional discretion is now being usurped by men). But more than that, the great amount of attention, time, and money lavished on aggressive technological management of childbirth is just that much less attention, time, and money being devoted by policy makers to solving the problem of truly *preventing* so many obstetric and pediatric emergencies in the first place!

In the United States, the historical problems resulting from slavery, the displacement of large numbers of agricultural workers by machinery in the South, and the waves of immigration early in this century (all factors which meant extreme poverty and malnutrition) were overlooked by the medical system, except where these poor people found their way into large cities and became "teaching material" for medical centers. The diseases and disabilities so many of these women experienced during pregnancy and childbirth (and continue to experience today) provided excellent opportunities to physicians to learn how to manage the most dire of complications.

The circumstances of these women's lives that made them subject to so many problems during the maternity cycle were seldom recognized, particularly their sorry nutritional status. Many times, these women were blamed for "not seeking prenatal care" or for "having too many babies too close together" or were dismissed as being "bad breeders," so their problems were attributed to their own personal failings rather than to a medical system that was insensitive to their needs. When these poorly nourished women chose to deliver their babies at home because of financial difficulties or because they were from cultures where women attended other women in childbirth (and doctors were associated with illness) or where they were excluded from medical care on the basis of race or inability to pay, their higher rates of infant and maternal mortality were blamed, not on their profound malnutrition, but on the fact that they gave birth at home with midwives. The drive to force all women into the hospital during childbirth arose from this error. And today, there is still no distinction made between healthy women who are good candidates for home birth and poorly nourished and poorly cared for women who are *not* good candidates.

We recount this history because if you are interested in having your baby at home, you need to understand where the intense resistance to the idea came from in medical circles—so that you can decide how you feel about going ahead with your decision in the face of such hostility. Unless you live in an area where there are groups of family practitioners who do attend birth at home as part of their general practice, or a few other locations around the country where midwives are enjoying a resurgence and more home births are occurring under safe conditions, you face the prospect of arranging a birth at home more or less on your own. Most doctors, when advised of your plans to deliver at home, refuse to see you any more, a practice condoned by ACOG and one which can hardly be expected to make birth at home safer. It also deters virtually no one who truly wants a birth at home from going ahead, anyway.

Fundamental to this whole dispute about the place of birth, and an idea unfortunately shared by some home birth proponents as well as by their opponents from ACOG, is that *management of birth itself* is the primary factor in such terrible problems as stillbirth, brain damage, cerebral palsy, respiratory distress of the newborn, and mental retardation. Advocates of home birth typically point to routine hospital interventions as the major cause for these disabling conditions and assert their right not to be exposed to these unnecessary dangers during birth. So, they prefer to give birth at home in surroundings and with people they perceive as being oriented toward nonintervention in normal childbirth. ACOG, on the other hand, views birth as "the most hazardous journey any of us ever take" and uteri as potentially treacherous organs upon which no one should rely to perform ably in childbirth (hence, the *need* for all the gear and interventions that have become standard operating procedure in today's obstetrics; see chapter 3). To ACOG, birth at home increases the risks of damage to mother and baby primarily because they are "denied" these "proven (sic) advances of modern obstetrics."

Both sides commonly lose sight of the fact that *birth itself is not usually the time when devastating damage to the baby takes place.* Millions of women have been subjected to inhumane childbirth practices and have *not* produced defective children. It goes without saying that the health of the baby is not the only criterion for success in childbearing (for example, the mother's lifelong memory of rude handling during a period of stress may do incalculable damage to her self-esteem for years afterward). However, the health of the baby is the concern mothers and ACOG both place foremost in the debate.

We believe it essential for both sides to recognize officially that most damage to babies is caused by inappropriate circumstances during gestation (particularly poor nutrition of the mother). It seems to us that harangues about the place of birth serve no purpose but to further distract well-meaning people from the major work at hand: improvement of prenatal care to incorporate protective standards of nutrition management for all mothers. When this is accomplished, it will be more readily apparent to all that birth at home is a logical and safe choice for the well-fed, normal mother and baby and the standards for screening risk will be more precise than is currently the case. When all mothers are well fed throughout gestation, it will become clear which complications of pregnancy and childbirth are caused or aggravated by poor maternal nutrition. Then ACOG and others primarily interested in disease diagnosis and treatment will be able to devote their full attention and research efforts to solving those problems—free of the question of malnutrition of the subjects, which holds up to question the results of virtually all research and experimentation in the field today.

Where does this leave you, the pregnant woman who wants to investigate home birth options in your area? How can you decide where to place your trust? The Association for Childbirth at Home, International (ACHI), publishes comprehensive suggestions in their manual for prospective home birth families, *Giving Birth at Home* (ACHI, P. O. Box 2232, Buena Park, CA 90621, 1976), which we have adapted here. Informed Homebirth, Inc., of Boulder, Colorado, has published a very detailed, illustrated book, *Special Delivery,* which is available through retail and mail-order bookstores and mail-order birth and health care supply services. (See Directory.)

Birth: Individualized Care

Checklist for Competent Birth Attendants

The parents deserve assurance of the birth attendant's ability to:

Provide comprehensive prenatal care, including laboratory work, either on his or her own in close association with other qualified individuals. ————

Properly interpret tests (urine, blood, diagnostic) given during pregnancy. ————

Counsel re: nutrition/malnutrition and do clinical follow-up. ————

Identify and handle failure to progress in labor. ————

Identify which problems s/he can handle at home and which require hospitalization (may vary with experience of attendant). ————

Monitor labor:
    baby's heartbeat ————
    mother's blood pressure ————
    mother's pulse ————
    check dilation of cervix ————
    check baby's position ————
    check baby's descent ————
    assure adequate fluid intake ————
    assure urinary output ————

Reduce or prevent perineal, vaginal, and cervical tearing. ————

Check placenta, cord, and membranes. ————

Identify and give immediate care for time-is-of-the-essence emergencies:
    hemorrhage ————
    shock ————
    cardiac arrest ————
    shoulder dystocia ————
    resuscitation ————

Arrange for the mother's admission as a "booked" client at a hospital on his or her own or in close association with a doctor who has delivery privileges. ————

Examine and assess condition of baby. ————

Provide immediate care of newborn. ————

Examine and provide immediate postpartum care of the mother:
    contracted uterus ————
    suturing of tears ————
    care of episiotomy (if performed) ————
    hygiene ————

Assist in initial breastfeeding. ————

Provide clear instructions for postpartum care of mother and baby. ————

Right from the Start

Make at least one postpartum visit in the first two or three days after birth—or where distance makes this unfeasible, schedule a telephone conference.   _____

Communicate with mother, associates, and other family members in an effective manner.   _____

Identify and accept the range of his or her practice abilities.   _____

Provide the names of others who have employed him or her in the past year, or, if s/he is just beginning in practice, the names of those who have trained him or her.   _____

Provide a back-up attendant who is similarly qualified in case s/he is unable to attend the birth due to illness or unforeseen commitment at another birth. (Even with optimum scheduling, birth can occur at times other than that expected; however, repeated failure to attend births to which one is committed should be a warning signal to parents.)   _____

Parents need to know that home obstetrics is a specialty distinct from hospital-based obstetrics, and physicians without experience in attending birth at home are unlikely to have the special skills required in the home setting. On the other hand, there are, unfortunately, many individuals attending births now and calling themselves midwives who lack many of the essential skills listed above. In either case the welfare of mother and baby are needlessly jeopardized. *Each prospective attendant must be judged on the same basis.* Don't assume that just because someone has an M.D. degree or an R.N. or C.N.M. (certified nurse-midwife) that s/he is qualifed to assist you at home. Such attendants should have specific training *in the home.*

In some circles there is also the feeling that midwives are automatically "better" (that is, less likely to intervene in a normal birth) than doctors. Unfortunately, this is not true. Too many midwifery programs turn out graduates who think like orthodox doctors, behave like them, and expect to wield their authority in the same way. Such an individual (who may be male or female, incidentally) is not the sort of attendant most home birth families would knowingly choose.

It's also important to say that there is nothing which prevents any doctor from being humane and thinking and acting like a midwife when it comes to birth, so s/he may be an exceptionally fine birth attendant in the home. Again, the people you interview must be evaluated according to your needs—and without any hidden assumptions either on your part or theirs.

ACHI and Informed Homebirth offer referrals to classes for home birth and qualified home birth attendants who have completed their training programs. The class series is also available on cassette tapes for people living in an area where there is no instructor/attendant.

Discussion and support groups for home birth parents, but *no* classes to prepare you or training programs for attendants, are offered through: Home Oriented Maternity Experience (H.O.M.E.), 511 New York Avenue, Takoma Park, Washington, DC 20012.

12. What options are open to me if I don't want or am not a good candidate for home birth, but I also don't want the routine treatment provided by a standard hospital OB service?
   Keeping in mind everything that's been said before about birth attendants and how to choose one, you might be happy with a birth center, a birthing room, or a midwifery service that functions as an integral part of a standard OB department.
   A *birth center* is usually a free-standing unit apart from, but near to, a hospital. Many physicians and midwives practice jointly in birth centers (their offices often are expanded to include one or two labor/birth units). Most adhere strictly to the principles of nonintervention in normal birth and transport women to the hospital whenever medication must be used during labor or birth. Sadly, some do not. You must investigate this point thoroughly, as drugs should not be administered to laboring women outside a hospital setting.
   The advantages of a birth center are that you will be in homelike surroundings with people you know well (all family members, including children, are usually welcome at birth centers, if the parents so

Birth: Individualized Care

desire), but you will have immediate access to a hospital should you require it. This is the main feature which someone living more than a half-hour from a hospital might appreciate, since living farther away than that is generally considered a contraindication for delivery at home.

At a well-planned birth center, you will not be separated from your baby after birth, you will be fed and observed for a few hours after birth before you return to your own home, and you will have close contact with the doctor or midwife throughout your postpartum weeks. Often, a visit two or three weeks after birth will be scheduled if you feel ready to resume intercourse and want contraceptive counseling. Also, many birth centers include pediatric nurse-practitioners on their staff, so you can bring your baby back for well-baby checkups.

Birth centers are increasing in popularity across the country, although they often encounter a great deal of antagonism from the medical community when they open and may even be subject to harassment by health departments and medical societies afterward. One reason is clear: if birth centers do a good job for normal patients, the hospital is going to have empty maternity beds. Two outstanding examples of birth centers are: Maternity Center Association's Childbearing Center, 48 East 92d Street, New York, NY 10028, and NACHIS (*Na*tural *Ch*ildbirth *I*nstitute), 10862 Washington Boulevard, Culver City, CA 90230. For referral to similar services outside the New York City and Los Angeles areas, contact: NAPSAC (National Association of Parents and Professionals for Safe Alternatives in Childbirth), P. O. Box 267, Marble Hill, MO 63764, a national organization seeking to establish medically safe, family-oriented birth programs in out-of-hospital as well as hospital settings.

Alternative birthing room at Los Alamitos General Hospital, California.

A *birthing room* is a private room set aside in conventional hospital labor and delivery units where the mother can labor and deliver in the same bed, usually with but one support person of her choice (in addition, of course, to the medical staff). Since this is an in-hospital facility, children are rarely allowed to be present. Typically, a birthing room features home-style furnishings (curtains, pillows, couch, rocking chair, TV, private bathroom), often with a double bed so parents can snuggle during and after the birth, or one of the very expensive labor-delivery beds manufactured by hospital outfitting companies. Equipment for emergencies (oxygen, monitor, IV apparatus, and the like) is usually stored out of sight since in theory it will be used only if necessary.

Most hospitals with birthing rooms have provided them in response to consumer demands. The drawback is that often, even where the birthing rooms exist, some doctors never use them! On your hospital tour, ask if there is one available; then at your appointment ask the physician whether s/he uses it.

The question that comes to our minds every time we see a nicely appointed birthing room is why all the other labor rooms must be so cheerless and institutional-looking. If homelike surroundings truly make a mother more relaxed, then shouldn't everyone have access to such surroundings? If women do better when they are not forced to move during the most intense phase of labor, why aren't all women delivered in the same bed in which they have labored? If most healthy women can give birth under their own power, why are the overwhelming majority of births still conducted under sedation and anesthesia when the harmful effects of these substances are so well documented and so commonly acknowledged? All too often the birthing room represents no change whatever in birth

Right from the Start

practices. The same rigid routines are adhered to, just carried out in more cozy surroundings. So evaluate your local birthing room with a cautious eye, too. Try to talk to other women who have used it (check with your local childbirth organization for reports) and see what happened to them. One other pitfall: in many hospitals if the birthing room is in use when you arrive, you will have to follow standard procedures.

A *midwifery service,* usually staffed by certified nurse-midwives, may function as a part of your hospital's obstetric department. Depending on the protocols (written agreements listing the duties and chain of responsibility for practitioners in the unit) which govern the way your local midwives work, the midwives may have quite a wide latitude in their prenatal and delivery care. At the Albert Einstein Medical Center in the Bronx, New York, for instance, midwives have private clients whom they see throughout pregnancy and attend at delivery in the hospital. Unless there is some complication requiring the supervision of one of the obstetricians (who are the teaching faculty at Einstein College of Medicine in this case) the midwives handle all aspects of the maternity cycle, including well-women gynecology (routine Pap tests and family planning).

For women who get nervous at the thought of having to be examined by the doctor, the midwife is a godsend. And, since their practice is devoted to well women, they don't have to rush off to surgery in the middle of your list of questions.

At Einstein, the midwives' clients are not routinely shaved, enemaed, monitored, or IV'd, though these procedures are still the routine for most of the attending physicians' patients. The mother is encouraged by the midwives to come to the hospital when she feels the need, to walk around as much as she wants during labor, and to assume the most comfortable position for birth. If the parents desire, the father can catch the baby and cut the umbilical cord under the midwife's supervision. Mother and baby do not have to be separated after birth (the baby is examined at the mother's bedside), and the parents may bathe the baby and be present at any other procedures that become necessary. If all is well and the parents desire it, the new family is discharged after 12 hours, and the midwife customarily schedules a home visit two or three days later to see that everyone is progressing normally.

Midwives work in many settings where things are not so well arranged. Their deliveries may be interrupted and taken over by young doctors in training, for no reason other than that the doctor wants to practice. They may have arbitrary rules about who may use their services (in many communities midwives are only allowed to take clients through the public prenatal clinic thus insuring that mothers with the financial ability to obtain private obstetrical care from physicians will not flock to the midwifery service in order to obtain more woman-centered care). They may not be able to take clients on a personal basis at all—getting assigned only to the evening shifts or weekends when doctors would prefer not to be disturbed by having to attend normal deliveries. They may have to refer large numbers of their clients to "high-risk" clinics in teaching hospitals where protocols are so skewed that 70 percent of all pregnant women are classified as "high-risk," and, so, mandated to be under the care of a physician. In many areas, the midwife has no delivery privileges at all—she is used to provide prenatal care and postpartum checkups, jobs which, as sociologist Diana Scully reports in her new book, *Men Who Control Women's Health: The Miseducation of Obstetrician-Gynecologists* (Boston: Houghton-Mifflin, 1980), physicians may find time-consuming and "not where the action is." The births are managed by residents completing their training.

So, as you investigate your hospitals, ask whether there are midwives on the staff and in what capacity. Many hospitals do not volunteer information about the midwifery service when prospective parents call to inquire about the hospital's policies or take the hospital tour. Get the midwife's name and telephone number so you can discuss things with her personally before you decide on a birth place. To find out where there are midwives working in your area, contact: American College of Nurse-Midwives, 100 Vermont Avenue NW, Washington, DC 20005, and NAPSAC, P. O. Box 267, Marble Hill, MO 63764, (314) 238-2010.

Working toward an independent midwifery service as part of your area's health services may be a high-priority project of your childbirth education organization. If so, you could contribute a great deal to women's health care in your area by becoming involved and sharing the wealth of information you will have accumulated about birth places and practices by the time you finish your personal search.

Birth: Individualized Care

Chapter 3

Intervention

Routine Care

Routine obstetrical practices in the United States have come to deviate markedly from the physiological norms for our species. In fact, numerous investigators now identify unnecessary intervention in pregnancy and birth as one of our culture's chief environmental hazards to mothers and babies. These deviations alter the childbearing experience by substituting other stimuli for those which normally occur. (See the Sensory Experiences of Labor and Birth chart in chapter 2.) In the process, childbirth as a woman-centered, biologically satisfying adventure is distorted into a traumatizing, alienating surgical procedure which engenders far-reaching defects in maternal-infant attachment.

A review of widely employed obstetrical practices, how they originated, and why they persist even when in most cases their reputed contributions to the health and safety of mothers and babies have been demonstrated to be otherwise, is essential information for fledgling mothers. It should come as no surprise to women who have lived through the disclosures about DES, the Pill, the IUD, involuntary sterilization, radical mastectomy for breast cancer, estrogen replacement therapy, soaring rates of hysterectomy, and the tranquilizing of large segments of society with powerful psychoactive, addicting drugs, that the prevailing medical approach to childbirth follows along the same lines.

The fault lies with a system of medical training which rewards aggressive treatment of disease, often to the exclusion of consideration of the patient as a human being. How women's normal reproductive and nurturing functions came to be classified as disease states is the subject for another book, but those of us having babies today must do so with complete, if uncomfortable, awareness that pregnancy, birth, and lactation are viewed by many medical professionals as deviations from a model of normality for humans—a model based on a view of the world that originates from men's bodies and minds.

So many excellent, thought-provoking books on these matters have appeared in the past decade that we are hard put to limit our recommendations to just these few:

Of Woman Born: Motherhood as Experience and Institution, by Adrienne Rich (New York: Norton, 1976. Bantam paperback, 1977)

Immaculate Deception: A New Look at Women and Childbirth in America, by Suzanne Arms (Boston: Houghton Mifflin, 1975)

The Hidden Malpractice: How American Medicine Treats Women as Patients and Professionals, by Gena Corea (Jove ed., New York: Harcourt Brace Jovanovich, 1978)

Forced Labor: Maternity Care in the

United States, by Nancy Stoller Shaw, Ph.D. (Elmsford, N.Y.: Pergamon Press, 1974)

Labor and Delivery: An Observer's Diary, What You Should Know About Today's Childbirth, by Constance Bean (New York: Doubleday, 1977)

Men Who Control Women's Health: The Miseducation of Obstetrician-Gynecologists, by Diana Scully, Ph.D. (Boston: Houghton Mifflin, 1980)

For Her Own Good: 150 Years of Expert's Advice to Women, by Barbara Ehrenreich, Ph.D., and Deirdre English (Anchor ed., New York: Doubleday, 1979).

Our Bodies, Ourselves, by the Boston Women's Health Book Collective (4th ed., New York: Simon and Schuster, 1979): the grandmother of them all.

In discussing these obstetrical practices we do not intend to issue an unqualified condemnation of them. There are bona fide indications for the use of each of them—situations in which one or more of these practices might be medically warranted, even lifesaving, for an individual mother or baby. The problem today is that such practices are *not* employed on a selective basis according to medical necessity, but enforced indiscriminately as hospital policy in the vast majority of maternity institutions in this country. One has only to take a few hospital tours intended to acquaint prospective parents with the obstetrical unit to verify that this is the case. Since over 96 percent of us will give birth in hospitals, forming realistic expectations about the care there—and learning how to circumvent aspects of it that are not in our best interests—are important mothering skills in today's world.

Doris Haire, president of the American Foundation for Maternal and Child Health and consumer representative to the Federal Drug Administration Bureau of Drugs, was one of the early critics of the interventions that have been introduced to American obstetrics. Her monograph, *The Cultural Warping of Childbirth*, a 1972 special report of the International Childbirth Education Association, laid the groundwork for many others in the field by pointing out that many of the maternity care practices that have become standard procedure are not supported by scientific research and appear to be rooted more in hospital and medical tradition than in human physiology. In the foreword to *Cultural Warping*, Jerold

Lucey, M.D., past chairman of the Committee on Fetus and Newborn of the American Academy of Pediatrics, commented:

> There is still a great deal we do not know about the consequences of various obstetrical practices and aspects of maternity care.... [This report] will be particularly useful if it causes parents and professionals alike to re-evaluate American maternity practices and their effects on the mother, the infant, and the family.... There is increasing evidence that parents want to become involved in those decisions which possibly will influence their future relationships with their children and with each other.

The catalog of interventions in childbirth presented in *Cultural Warping* has, unfortunately, grown, not diminished, since 1972. Despite the best efforts of a multitude of childbirth activists and the findings of a host of dispassionate researchers, many procedures which in 1972 were reserved for use in "high-risk" centers in major teaching hospitals have now been adopted for universal application to pregnant and laboring women.

Much of the hardware has been promoted on the flimsiest of evidence that it has anything to do with reducing obstetrical or pediatric complications, using the same techniques of "hard sell" we have become accustomed to in advertisements for automobiles, laundry detergents, and fast-food restaurants. At medical conventions, booth after booth displays the latest electronic gadgetry. The programs of these meetings feature speakers who are representatives or "research" grantees of the firms that manufacture the machines. Such observations soon begin to shake one's confidence in the presumed scientific basis of many of our doctors' medical judgments. The medical journals we receive at our offices and the continual mailings and calls from manufacturers' representatives for both drugs and electronics companies do little to dispel the impression.

Whether we like it or not, childbearing women and their families *do* comprise a "market" these days and a most lucrative one at that. Consider carefully whether you are willing to have your pregnancy and birth manipulated to someone else's economic advantage. It does not have to be so. Getting as much information as possible about the types of obstetrics being practiced in your area

Intervention: Routine Care

should help you formulate your own pregnancy and birth priorities. The following summary of routine obstetrical interventions is offered as a framework for your decision-making, not the last word on every issue you will encounter.

Interventions: Information and Implications

Ultrasound

Ultrasound is an application of the "pulse-echo" principle, first used in the navy's sonar equipment, to medical diagnosis involving internal body structures (particularly soft tissues which conventional x-rays cannot capture). Used in internal medicine to pinpoint difficulties with such organs as the liver, gallbladder, spleen, pancreas, kidneys, thyroid, and heart, and the circulatory system, the use of ultrasound imaging has become a mainstay of hospital-based and private office obstetrics and gynecology in a few short years. Technologic improvements resulting in the reduction in size of the machines themselves as well as introducing the capacity for continuous display of electronic impulses on the machine's screen (the same way your television set works), now make having an ultrasound scanner a distinct convenience and unsurpassed diagnostic tool in the doctor's office. The scanning equipment consists of a transmitter, known as a transducer, which sends out a short, aimed pulse of high frequency sound into the subject's body and then acts as a receiver of the reflected sound waves. As the echoes return, they are converted to electric current by the transducer and displayed as dots of light on the screen—in exact relation to the points in the body where each echo was produced. The most common applications in obstetrics are:

- to confirm pregnancy by viewing enlarged gestational sac with embryo present (a beating heart can be detected as early as seven weeks into pregnancy);
- to detect multiple pregnancy (important because of the extra nutritional stress involved—only half the twins in the United States are diagnosed before delivery);
- to locate the placenta in cases where amniocentesis is necessary (see Amniocentesis, below) or where bleeding is occurring and a low-lying placenta (*placenta praevia*) must

be ruled out or plans made for Cesarean delivery;
- to *estimate* gestational age and diagnose intrauterine growth retardation (IUGR) by measuring baby's length and head size— (This is far from an exact science, particularly since the scales used as measurements of "normal" development are heavily weighted by babies from mothers who are not as well nourished as they might be. In other words, if you're really eating well you may be told that your pregnancy is two to four weeks ahead of where you know it is, strictly on the basis of the fetal growth chart the sonographer consulted. If you are unsure of when you conceived, and this is true of many women, you may be assigned a "due date" far too soon for your baby's true maturity, leading to strong pressures on you to be induced when you are a week over the erroneous date, but in fact still have three weeks until your pregnancy would terminate naturally. Obviously, if the induction is begun, the dangers of premature birth under these circumstances are considerable.);
- to identify location and size of fibroid tumors, ectopic (tubal) pregnancy, certain fetal abnormalities, other growths that could jeopardize pregnancy, and locate "lost" IUDs prior to attempts at retrieval.

Any drawbacks to having an ultrasound examination during pregnancy? Nobody knows for sure. The technology is just too new. Some Japanese studies on animal embryos have raised the concern that ultrasonic bombardment of the female embryo may lead to changes in *her* egg supply that might result in infertility or the birth of deformed babies in subsequent generations. This would tend to put a damper on the overenthusiastic rush to use ultrasound for every pregnant woman at every prenatal visit, even without a specific important purpose. Termed "family-centered" ultrasound in some promotional brochures sent to physicians' offices, the idea is that the whole family can accompany Mom to the doctor's office every month and "see the baby before it's born," simply out of curiosity rather than for any legitimate medical indication.

Oxytocin Challenge Test (OCT)

The OCT, also termed a "stress test," is an attempt

to predict how well an individual baby will withstand the stress of labor when, in the mind of the doctor or midwife, there appears to be a chance that the baby will have some difficulty (cases of supposed toxemia, maternal diabetes, hypertension, prolonged pregnancy [more than 42 weeks], previous stillbirth, and intrauterine growth retardation are prime candidates). The mother enters the hospital, usually as an outpatient, is attached to an external fetal monitor (see Electronic Monitoring, later in this chapter) and an intravenous infusion of oxytocin which starts very slowly and gradually builds up in strength until the mother is having at least three uterine contractions every ten minutes. The monitor records the baby's response to the contractions. Any abnormalities in the response pattern may be indication enough to stop the test and proceed directly to Cesarean delivery, since the baby, according to the test, will be unable to withstand labor.

The problem? The test is wrong 25 percent of the time; that is, out of every 100 babies born in normal labor even when the stress test is positive, 25 do fine. That amounts to 25 unnecessary Cesareans, with all the attendant risks of that procedure for mother and baby (see Cesarean Delivery, later in this chapter), for every 100 positive stress tests. Also, women have reported that their doctors advised them to have an OCT on the ground of postmaturity, then once the test was underway tried to persuade them to allow the test to become a full-fledged induction of labor ("You're already on your way!") by continuing the administration of oxytocin and rupturing membranes.

Because of the difficulty of ascertaining with absolute certainty the date of conception in any given case, recommending OCT on the basis of the calendar alone seems unjustifiable. Challenging a baby at 32 weeks gestation may turn out to be a self-fulfilling prophecy, since at two months before term, who would expect any baby—even the healthiest—to test out "ready to be born"? And a baby who is suffering intrauterine growth retardation needs to have a mother whose diet is improved, not one who is slated for immediate Cesarean delivery.

Non-Stress Test (NST)

An NST is like the above, but without the oxytocin infusion. Everyone just waits for a normally occurring uterine contraction, and the machine charts the baby's response to it. Typically, a 30-minute monitor strip is run. What's gained? Assur-

ance that the "overdue" baby, in particular, isn't being threatened with oxygen deprivation due to "placental insufficiency" (the theory that a mother's placenta just automatically starts to degenerate and malfunction after 40 weeks gestation, irrespective of her diet or general health status). With the NST, far fewer positives result, since the baby is not being suddenly subjected to strong contractions. However, the well-nourished mother has nothing to gain by running in for an NST every week until she delivers. "Placental insufficiency" is simply an artifact of a reduced blood volume caused by undernutrition. Many studies have shown that when a woman's diet is improved, even in the last month of pregnancy, her placental function improves due to the increased blood flow through it. An appropriate therapeutic intervention in cases of "placental insufficiency," therefore, is not scheduling the mother for more tests to determine whether her baby could survive delivery at this time (see Amniocentesis, below), but intensive efforts to improve her food intake, both in terms of food choices and amount of food consumed. In clinics where this point of view is taken seriously, a mother may often be hospitalized on the pregnancy "high risk" unit, not for drug therapy, but for closely supervised feeding until her malnutrition is eradicated. This plan of management stands in direct contradistinction to the current thinking of the neonatologist (specialist in caring for "high risk" newborns, mostly premature and/or underweight at birth—see chapter 6) whose standard response to this sort of problem is to get the baby out of that "sick uterus" as soon as possible (usually by Cesarean) and place the infant in the neonatal intensive care unit for as long as it takes to get the baby functioning on its own (days, weeks, months). The advantages of trying to improve the maternal health situation—and so, the baby's environment *in utero*—are obvious.

Amniocentesis

Amniocentesis is widely publicized as a way of detecting certain chromosomal abnormalities of the unborn baby early in pregnancy; this procedure is also employed to determine a baby's functional lung maturity in situations such as those outlined above where labor will be induced or surgical delivery carried out prior to the end of the period of gestation. A needle is inserted through the mother's abdominal wall and into the amniotic sac (presumably with the assistance of an ultrasound scanner to localize the placenta and baby's body parts and avoid accidental puncture). Amniotic fluid is withdrawn and analyzed in the laboratory for the presence of a substance, surfactant, manufactured by the mature fetal lung. Without enough surfactant, babies born too soon have a very high rate of serious respiratory problems, since the lungs have trouble staying properly inflated. Many women who have had a previous Cesarean and are planning another due to a recurring indication (such as a very small pelvis) are routinely scheduled for amniocentesis as part of their preoperative workup. A wiser course, many doctors feel, given the potential hazards of amniocentesis, is to wait for the spontaneous onset of labor, when it is known that the mother is well nourished. Following this protocol, instances of neonatal lung malfunction are reduced to the barest minimum. At $300 to $500 each, an amniocentesis is not equivalent to a blood test. Many people today are underinsured for medical care, and an unnecessary expenditure of that magnitude can be worrisome for months after the baby is finally born.

Bed Rest

Bed rest is the current "in" treatment for everything from multiple pregnancy to high blood pressure, despite its deleterious effects on anyone, not just pregnant women, put to bed for prolonged periods of time. A classic review article, "The Hazards of Immobility," published in the April 1967 issue of the *American Journal of Nursing,* discusses the effects of bed rest on cardiovascular function, respiratory function, gastrointestinal function, motor function, urinary function, metabolic equilibrium, and psychosocial equilibrium. Awareness of just a few of the drastic alterations in body processes brought about by bed rest should make anyone for whom it is casually prescribed think twice about following the doctor's or midwife's order:

- reduced metabolic rate;
- tissue atrophy;
- protein catabolism and negative nitrogen balance;
- bone demineralization;
- fluid and electrolyte imbalance;
- formation of ulcers;
- formation of urinary tract stones;
- formation of blood clots;
- increased sweating and excess fluid loss;

- psychologic and physiologic stress reactions, including a *rise in blood pressure* due to anxiety (worry over one's condition, rather than getting the "rest" one supposedly needs);
- reduction in hormone production;
- increased need to urinate at first, then urinary retention;
- decreased motivation to participate in social encounters (talking, taking meals, pastimes);
- depression/anger/aggression/apathy;
- exaggerated emotional responses;
- decreased perceptual abilities;
- loss of sociocultural and economic status;
- *loss of appetite resulting in malnutrition;*
- constipation and complete bowel obstruction;
- muscle spasm;
- increase in systemic infection due to malnutrition;
- *fall in serum proteins due to malnutrition;*
- upon arising, weakness, dizziness, falling in a faint due to a falling off in the body's ability to equalize the blood supply (this can happen in as little as a week on absolute bed rest and, where the rest has been imposed for three weeks, the ability of the body to respond effectively to the upright posture is not regained for five weeks or more);
- *increased* work load on the heart;
- decreased respiratory movement and decrease of the movement of normal secretions, leading to bronchitis, tracheitis, or pneumonia;
- diminished exchange of oxygen and carbon dioxide, resulting in respiratory acidosis and *reduction in oxygen supply to the unborn baby*—just what the doctor did not mean to order!

A reprint of the article, appropriate for sharing with medical professionals, is available from: *American Journal of Nursing* Company, Educational Services Division, 10 Columbus Circle, New York, NY 10019.

Hospitalization

The hospital itself is probably the most significant intervention in the birth process in human history. At the turn of the century, instead of the comforts of her own home and family, the hospital originally offered "painless childbirth" via drugs for women willing to accept patienthood. In an era when 6 women out of every 100 delivered died in childbirth, and deformed pelvises due to nutritional deprivation and childhood illness were commonplace, the idea of reducing maternal mortality by caring for all laboring women in hospitals was very appealing.

Prior to this time, we must recall, hospitals were viewed by the public at large as places to die; only those whose living conditions were deemed hazardous to the health of mother and baby sought hospitalization for childbirth. Only with the advent of antiseptics (to control the ever-present hospital infections), blood banks, and improved surgical technique, and the increasing sophistication of anesthesia, were hospitals able to shake their bad image.

The smell of the hospital upsets many people. The noises, especially the cries of other women on the labor and delivery floor, the scratchy, loud paging system that always seems to be located directly opposite your door, the myriad discussions in the hall and at the nurses' station, the screaming of ambulances coming to the emergency room, the crinkles of the rubber sheet on your bed—any of these may distract you from the work at hand.

Add to this the good chance that you or your baby will come into contact with virulent, drug-resistant strains of bacteria and viruses (the people who clean up, clean up throughout the hospital; the air circulates from floor to floor; dietitians, lab technicians, nurses, doctors, and numerous other workers visit patients in all stages of health and disease), and the idea that the hospital is automatically the most desirable place for birth becomes open to question.

Reading in hospital administration journals about the problems of infection control adds to the concern. For example, the June 1978 issue of *Hospital Tribune* reported in its own survey that only a few states, such as New York, require comprehensive preemployment physicals for hospital workers and that hospitals are often reluctant to invest in comprehensive employee health services, despite the proven long-term benefits of such programs in identifying and treating contagious disease. Rubella (German measles), venereal disease, viral hepatitis, and parasite screening tend to be overlooked almost everywhere, and the Joint Commission on the Accreditation of Hospitals has no specific guidelines or enforcement mechanisms dealing with this issue.

The December 1, 1977, issue of *Ob. Gyn. News* contained remarks by Leslie Iffy, M.D., director of perinatology at New Jersey Medical School, who has observed that many teaching hospitals in the United States do not strictly adhere to aseptic techniques, and this has undoubtedly contributed to the high rates of infection in obstetrics and gynecology services. Among the offenses are the lack of sterile vaginal exams during labor, not assigning special nurses to patients with infections, and no washing of hands by the medical staff between patients.

This last rule is considered so important by infection control experts that they recommend patients request that doctors, nurses, and all others who deliver "hands-on care" wash their hands in the patient's presence before the procedure is undertaken, or request that they wear a sterile glove.

Enema

Enemas, a standard part of obstetrical admitting procedure, are supposed to clean out the mother's bowel so she won't worry about passing feces as she bears down in giving birth. Typically, the mother has very loose bowel movements the day or so before labor begins, anyway—nature's method of accomplishing the same objective. It's true that a full bowel can impede progress in labor by creating an obstruction to descent of the head; however, a mother who's been eating correctly and taking regular, mild exercise is unlikely to suffer from constipation.

Women who want to feel cleansed can take a Fleet's enema at home (a very small packet of fluid which comes with its own inserter). The advantages of this in sensory terms are readily understandable; the hospital enema is usually a quart of very warm, soapy water which can take up to 45 minutes to expel completely, often while you are left alone teetering on a bedpan, coping with regular labor contractions. It's enough to make even the most relaxed woman wind up demanding drugs. As if this weren't disruptive enough of the mother's body feedback, the irritation of the bowel caused by the soapy water may persist for days after.

By the way, when women are in an upright or semireclining position for labor, the spurts of amniotic fluid accompanying contractions toward the end of labor flow across the perineum and automatically cleanse the anal area, too, so there's really no need to worry even if you do pass a bit of fecal matter during a push.

Intervention: Routine Care

Shaving

Shaving the pubic hair, a practice introduced when routines used in preparing a patient for surgery were adopted in obstetrics, is supposed to reduce the chances of infection for mother and baby by eliminating a site where bacteria might thrive. Study after study has associated this practice with *increased incidence* of maternal infection (presumably from tiny nicks in the skin which make an open passage for pathogens), but still hospitals cling to the practice fervidly. The vast majority of women having first babies say they fear the "prep" more than any other single procedure. Women are justifiably reluctant to permit anyone to shave them in their most sensitive and vulnerable location—especially when they are likely to have a contraction at any time during the shaving process, making it very difficult for them to resist the impulse to move to a more comfortable position. (Shaving is commonly carried out with the mother flat on her back with feet flat and knees pointing toward the ceiling.) Shaving of the pubic hair, many women have told us, is loaded with negative associations (up to and including genital mutilation as the result of an accidental slip of the blade).

These psychological effects alone should constitute basis enough to refrain from the practice. Midwives rarely insist on shaving, and elsewhere in the world this practice is looked upon as a curiosity. For example, by eliminating routine shaving of all surgery patients and instituting an infection surveillance program, the Foothills Hospital in Calgary, Canada, has been able to achieve what is probably the lowest infection rate of any hospital in the world, according to Hiram C. Polk, Jr., M.D., chairman of the Department of Surgery at the University of Louisville. "Shaving is a nuisance, a waste of time, and it is not necessary for most patients," he commented in an interview with the *Chicago Tribune*.

Peter Cruse, M.D., director of a large-scale study at the hospital which followed infection after surgery, found that patients who were shaved had an infection rate of 2.7 percent. Those whose hair was clipped had a 1.7 percent infection rate, while those who were neither shaved nor clipped had the lowest infection rate of all, 0.9 percent. A hospital-based infection forces the average patient to stay in the hospital an additional ten days, he noted, adding a cost of $3.18 billion a year to spiraling disease care figures.

When mother and baby must stay in the hospital for treatment of an infection, numerous barriers to their close contact with one another are raised. In fact, mothers who are running a temperature may be completely forbidden to handle their infants, a situation which imposes hardship on everyone concerned.

Intravenous Fluids

Intravenous fluids, a relatively new addition to the "must" list for hospital birth, are prized on obstetric units because:

- they provide a direct route to the circulation in case drugs are to be administered;
- they prevent dehydration during labor (a common consequence of hospital policy that denies liquids or anything else by mouth to women in labor);
- they reduce the concern about treating hemorrhage or shock, since a vein is already accessible in case of circulatory collapse.

Since the current obstetrical view is that any woman, no matter how normal she seems to be, may develop any complication at any time, starting an IV for everyone as part of the admitting process seems logical. However, this line of reasoning fails to distinguish between the physical state of healthy, well-fed pregnant women during labor and those who have been spontaneously malnourished or managed with low-salt, low-calorie diets and/or diuretics during pregnancy. In the well-fed woman, there is ample water in the circulation so that even if a mother tears during delivery, or requires a Cesarean, she has two to three extra pints of blood available to cover the loss *without going into shock*. She does not experience vascular collapse due to a reduction of fluid inside her blood vessels, nor does she become dehydrated over the course of labor, since she is able to mobilize stored tissue fluid as needed for use in the bloodstream. Also, if she is well nourished throughout pregnancy, she is less likely to need drugs to stimulate her uterus into efficient action during labor since the well-nourished uterus works in a coordinated fashion and labor is easier.

All these considerations are lost on hospital workers who tend to view all women who walk through the doors as being in the same state of health. Failure to attach dietary histories to prenatal charts denies hospital workers a basis for judgment or for screening those who are likely to develop labor difficulties. Consequently, all are treated as though they're in danger.

Infusion of intravenous fluids over an extended period of time has produced serious disturbances in some patients' electrolyte balance and water intoxication. Most women report that they worried about the needle in their arm or hand while it was in place and that they limited their range of movement to avoid placing stress on the part of their body where the needle was inserted. Oftentimes, women stay in bed out of fear of dislodging the IV. Needles occasionally do become dislodged from the vein and fluids then seep out into the surrounding tissues. Usually this is not harmful to the mother or the baby, but it can be very upsetting when the mother notices that her arm is swelling.

All of this means that some of her attention is being redirected from her labor to her IV apparatus, with attendant anxiety. It may make it much more difficult for her to relax.

One additional consideration, once the IV is in place, is that it's difficult to keep track of what is going through the needle. Hundreds of women have told us of childbirth experiences in which they were given drugs they did not want or need because the drugs via IV were part of their doctors' "standing orders." Only upon obtaining their medical records at a later time did they discover that the medications had been administered.

Obviously, if a woman has been in labor a long time and is becoming tired, has been vomiting a lot, or hasn't felt like taking fluids, an IV might be in order. But routine IVs are an example of a patch-up procedure at the end of pregnancy to handle situations that should not routinely occur.

Confinement to Bed

Confinement to bed was considered a necessity when everyone was heavily sedated for labor and all laboring women were clustered together in a large ward under the supervision of one or two nurses. But it is obvious that this practice interferes with the awake mother's ability to adopt the most comfortable and efficient positions for labor—standing up and moving about. Definitive studies in this field have been conducted by Roberto Caldeyro-Barcia, M.D., of the University of Uruguay, Montevideo, who is director of the Latin American Center of Perinatology and Human Development. As past president of the International Federation of Obstetricians and Gynecologists, he presented the 1978 clinical meeting of the American College of Obstetricians and Gynecologists with inescapable evidence against

bed confinement during labor. A cooperative study involving 11 maternity hospitals in seven countries showed that when mothers remained vertical throughout the first stage of labor, labor was 25 percent shorter, and the mothers experienced a significantly reduced amount of discomfort.

A pioneer in the application of electronic monitoring to problem-solving in human labor management, Caldeyro-Barcia used monitors to compare the duration, intensity, and effect on the baby of labor in 324 women closely matched for their health status, pregnancy backgrounds, and parity (number of children born). Research confirmed that uterine contractions are less frequent but much stronger when the mother is upright; therefore, labor is more efficient.

Noting that a French obstetrician, in 1783, was the first to advance a supine, in-bed position for labor and birth in order to facilitate obstetrical examinations and the use of forceps and to afford the *accoucheur* a better view of progress in labor, Caldeyro-Barcia pointed out that these are benefits to the attendant, not to mother or baby. All of the mothers in the study agreed that they preferred to be standing, sitting, or walking as women have always done.

Failure to encourage mothers to remain ambulatory in labor is a major intervention in human labor which increases painful sensations, increases the need for analgesia and anesthesia, prolongs labor up to 36 percent in first-time mothers, and intensifies the aura of debility we have seen emerging as the hospital norm for childbirth. There is no justification for this practice except when the mother herself chooses to go to bed—and then she should lie on her side, or be propped up, not on her back, to avoid compressing the veins that return blood from the lower half of the body to the heart and compromising the baby's supply of oxygen. These precepts should be followed regardless of where the birth takes place.

Induction

Induction, augmentation or stimulation of labor, is labor started or made more vigorous by means of drugs (e.g., Pitocin, a synthetic form of oxytocin) and/or artificial rupture of the membranes. (See Amniotomy, below.) Originally used by conservative practitioners only in cases of medical necessity (such as severe metabolic toxemia, uncontrolled diabetes, Rh sensitization of the baby), in recent years induction has been carried out as an elective procedure, strictly for the convenience of the mother and/or the obstetrician. Everybody except the baby agrees on a date; the mother enters the hospital and an attempt to initiate labor is begun.

The result is often contractions of overwhelming intensity, increased use of pharmacologic pain relief (which often paradoxically reduces the efficiency of the uterine contractions, necessitating more Pitocin, and so on—a classic vicious cycle), and use of instruments or resorting to Cesarean to accomplish delivery if the baby should respond to all this by going into distress (usually detected by the heartbeat's falling to dangerously low levels with too little time between the overly strong contractions to return to normal).

Induction or stimulation of labor, even when serious medical complications of mother or baby demand it, imposes potentially life-threatening risks on both. Among them: an increased chance that the baby will be premature or underweight—nobody can be absolutely sure of when they conceived no matter how closely they've been monitoring mucus levels, temperature charts, or time of intercourse. Unless your doctor is willing to sign a document assuming all financial responsibility for short-term intensive care and possible long-term special care if the baby is neurologically damaged as a result of the induction, there is no good reason for you and your family to assume such risks, either. Why take chances during birth that might compromise your baby's precious brain after you've been so careful all through pregnancy to make sure the child has had optimal growing conditions? Incidentally, we've noticed that better-nourished mothers seem to hold their pregnancies a bit longer than women who haven't had the best advice about their diets.

You need to know that there is indeed such a condition as the "postmature syndrome" in some babies who are born late; however, these babies are not the products of well-nourished pregnancies. On the contrary, these babies typically have loose, wrinkled skin which the obstetrician will probably attribute to "placental insufficiency" (their underlying fat layer has been used up *in utero* due to the mother's undernutrition) and are underweight for gestational age.

Amniotomy

This artificial rupture of the bag of waters has been practiced during early or mid-labor as a routine procedure with the aim of shortening the duration of the birth process. According to Caldeyro-Barcia and co-workers who published a major review article on amniotomy in *Modern Perinatal Medicine,* edited by Louis Gluck (Chicago: Year Book Medical Publishers, 1975), it is responsible for numerous undesirable consequences for the unborn and the newborn and, so, should be reserved for cases when detailed information on the condition of the baby is required during labor—information which cannot be obtained by external means. (See Electronic Monitoring, below.) Membranes usually stay intact during normal labor until the cervix reaches full dilatation. Thirty-four percent rupture at this time, with another 20 percent breaking during the pushing stage of labor. In normal mothers, 12 percent will have intact membranes at delivery. Intact membranes preserve the amniotic fluid which cushions the baby's head and equalizes pressure during the peaks of contractions (many exert a force of 50 pounds of pressure per square inch), minimizing any circulatory disturbances to the brain as contractions become more intense. Intact membranes also protect against excessive molding (to the point of deformity) of the baby's head during birth and subsequent drop in fetal heart tones. Finally, in cases where the umbilical cord is looped around the baby's neck (26 percent of the time), intact membranes equalize pressure on umbilical blood vessels so they do not become occluded during contractions. This means that your baby will be in a better oxygen-availability situation throughout labor, since all the baby's oxygen is supplied through the cord.

All of these demonstrated safeguards against compression of the skull and damage to the baby's brain are squandered when amniotomy is performed. As the careful work from Latin America conclusively shows, there is no benefit in rushing all women and their unborn babies through labor. Caldeyro-Barcia and others contend that there is probably a range of optimal duration of labor for each mother-infant pair during each labor, a period of time during which the baby receives appropriate stimulation in preparation for extrauterine life from contractions which pose no undue stress upon the healthy mother. Rupture of the amniotic sac produces unnecessary trauma for the baby and additional stress for the mother, since labor is suddenly so much more intense when the naked head is applied directly to the cervix, rather than the bulging membranes serving as the lead point in labor.

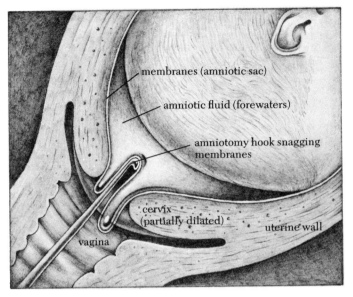

Performing an amniotomy.

Left, *Amniotomy hook (actual size).*

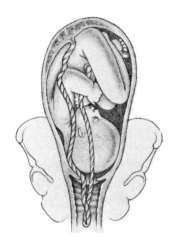

Prolapsed cord extending from vagina.

The procedure itself is rarely uncomfortable for mother or baby. The slender amniotomy hook (which resembles a long crochet hook) is inserted through the vagina and semidilated cervix until the hook catches a section of the membranes; the physician gives a tug and the membranes split painlessly, releasing a warm rush of amniotic fluid which escapes through the vagina. The procedure is so simple almost anyone could perform it; perhaps that explains its popularity.

Caldeyro-Barcia, however, states flatly that amniotomy should never be used as a method of inducing labor in a low-risk mother and infant. There is a danger of infection (discussed above) whenever the mother is hospitalized with ruptured membranes and being examined vaginally to determine progress. There is a danger in subjecting the still-rigid cervix to excessive strain by early amniotomy. There is a danger of having to perform a Cesarean if delivery is not accomplished within 24 hours of the amniotomy. There is a danger that the rush of amniotic fluid will bring the umbilical cord down into the vagina in front of the head. (This happens most often when the obstetrician has scheduled an induction based on the calendar and the baby is small or in breech position and, so, does not fill the pelvic basin enough to prevent the cord from prolapsing.) A prolapsed cord is one of the most serious emergencies in labor, because the cord will be compressed tightly between the pre-

senting part and the pelvis with each contraction and maybe also in between, so the baby is severely deprived of oxygen. Emergency Cesarean may be the only treatment for this condition.

Ask *early* about your doctor's practice concerning amniotomy. Be sure you have a written agreement of your labor preferences signed by the doctor and sent to the hospital as part of your prenatal chart. This will insure that, should your doctor or midwife not be present at all times during your labor (a very likely possibility), the nursing staff will have your individualized plan of management to consult instead of feeling obliged to stick with standard procedures. These provisos are especially important if you plan to use a teaching hospital where residents are learning on each patient and intervention is the norm.

Analgesia/Anesthesia

Pain medication is used in over 90 percent of births today in the United States, with fully two-thirds of all deliveries still being conducted under anesthesia and one-third with the mother unconscious. These practices persist despite the volumes that have been written about the harmful effects of these substances on the infant and the readily available proven alternative to pharmacologic pain relief, comprehensive education for childbirth that includes individualized nutrition counseling and progressive relaxation (not complicated breathing techniques) as key features. The accompanying chart outlines the effects of the

[*Continued on page 58*]

Intervention: Routine Care

Drugs and Their Sensory Effects in Childbirth

Drug	Mode of Administration	Sensory Effect

Barbiturates:
    amobarbital (Amytal)
    butabarbital (Butisol)
    pentobarbital (Nembutal)
    phenobarbital (Luminal)
    secobarbital (Seconal)
	Oral, IM (intramuscular injection), IV (intravenous)	Lowered blood pressure, slowed heart rate, disorientation, reduced anxiety
		In newborn: poor sucking ability

Tranquilizers:
    hydroxyzine (Atarax, Vistaril)
    diazepam (Valium)
    chlordiazepoxide (Librium)
    meprobamate (Equanil, Miltown)
    chlorpromazine (Thorazine)
    prochlorperazine (Compazine)
    promazine (Sparine)
    promethazine (Phenergan)
    propiomazine (Largon)
	Oral, IM, IV	Increased or decreased heart rate, increased or decreased blood pressure, drowsiness, dizziness, nausea, dry mouth, confusion, retention of urine
		In newborn: impaired ability to maintain temperature

Narcotics:
    morphine
    meperidine (Demerol)
    pentazocine (Talwin)
    alphaprodine (Nisentil)
	IM, IV
	Nisentil also given subcutaneously
		In newborn: disorientation, less interest in mother's voice, less consolable, less cuddly, lowered responsiveness, visual difficulties, bluish skin tone
		In mother: depression, nausea and vomiting, dizziness, itchiness
		In both: lowered breathing rate

Anesthetics:
    procaine (Novocain)
    tetracaine (Pontocaine)
    chloroprocaine (Nesacaine)
    piperocaine (Metycaine)
    propoxycaine (Blockain)
    prilocaine (Citanest)
    bupivacaine (Marcaine)
    mepivacaine (Carbocaine)
    lidocaine (Xylocaine, L-Caine, Seracaine)
    dibucaine (Nupercaine)
	Pudendal block
	Paracervical block
	Uterosacral block
	Caudal block
	Subarachnoid block
	Epidural block
	"Saddle" block
	"Spinal" block
	"Low" spinal
	"Local"
		Obliterated feeling, lowered heart rate, lowered blood pressure, drowsiness, restlessness, dizziness

Anticholinergics:
    atropine sulfate
    hyoscine or scopolamine
        (also termed an amnesiac;
[*Continued on next page*]
	IM, IV	Dry mouth, blurry vision, palpitations, dizziness, nausea, retention of urine, disorientation

Drug	Mode of Administration	Sensory Effect
not literally true. Also known as: "twilight sleep," "scope," "the bomb")		

Inhalation anesthetics:
    cyclopropane or
        trimethylene
    ether
    halothane (Fluothane)
    methoxyflurane
        (Penthrane)
    nitrous oxide
    trichloroethylene (TCE,
        Trilene, Trimar)
	Inhaled through mouth and nose	Lowered breathing rate, changes in heart rate, irregular heartbeat, increase or decrease in blood pressure, impaired kidney function, impaired digestive system function, impaired liver function, impaired uterine function, postpartum hemorrhage, nausea, vomiting, dizziness, disorientation, sleepiness, depression

Oxytocics:
    synthetic oxytocin (Oxytocin,
        Pitocin, Syntocinon)
    ergonovine maleate
        (Ergotrate)
    methylergonovine (Methergine)
    sparteine sulfate (Spartocin,
        Tocosamine)
	IM, IV, buccal tablets	Acute rise in blood pressure; drop in blood pressure; fast heart rate; anxiety; swelling; severe water intoxication; forceful, lengthy contractions; rupture of uterus; headache; nausea; postpartum hemorrhage
		In fetus and newborn: suffocation due to overly strong contractions, changes in heart rate

Anticonvulsants: magnesium sulfate	IM, IV	Parathyroid gland dysfunction, flushing, sweating, confusion, muscle weakness, sedation, low blood pressure, cardiac arrest, respiratory muscle paralysis

Antihypertensives:
    furosemide (Lasix)
    (label states: "Contraindicated in women of childbearing potential")
	IM, IV	Drastic reduction in blood volume, numbness, itching, blurry vision, lowered blood pressure, nausea, vomiting, diarrhea, elevated blood sugar, electrolyte imbalance, blood disorders, ringing in
		[Continued on next page]

Intervention: Routine Care

Drugs and Their Sensory Effects in Childbirth [*Continued*]

Drug	Mode of Administration	Sensory Effect
Antihypertensives: [*Continued*]		ears, swelling, headache, jaundice, acute pancreatic dysfunction, diminished kidney function

Diuretics:
    furosemide (Lasix). See
      above.
    ethycrinic acid (EDE)
	IM (Lasix), IV, oral	Lasix. See above.
		 Also, gout, abdominal pain

panoply of pharmaceutical preparations in current use on American obstetrics services.

Probably the most damaging aspect of drug use during labor and birth is that almost all of them, when taken in amounts large enough to be effective in the mother, constitute an overdose for the baby. Most of these preparations work by depressing the central nervous system of mother and baby, and they may combine in the body to produce metabolites of the original compound that are even more potent than the initial substance. This means that your baby may be limp, pallid, and unable to breathe on his/her own at birth.

In his moderately courageous monograph, "Effects of Maternal Analgesia on Neonatal Morbidity" (*Preventability of Perinatal Injury: Proceedings*, Karlis Adamsons and Howard A. Fox, eds., New York: Alan R. Liss, Inc., 1975), Howard A. Fox, M.D., who is director of the division of neonatal medicine and associate professor of pediatrics at the University of Kansas Medical Center, Kansas City, argues that perinatal mortality is no longer the sole measure of the skill of obstetrical and neonatal management. Fox calls for "refinement" of the system for evaluating effectiveness (risk versus benefit) of obstetrical medications.

"We can no longer use the absence of a limp, narcotized, apneic infant or indeed even the infant with a 'good Apgar' as the measure of success of maternal analgesic outcome," he notes. "Neonatal behavior long after delivery, neonatal thermoregulation, and the complexities of maternal attachment behavior are examples of more subtle kinds of outcome that must be considered as well." His paper ends with a forceful directive to his colleagues on the labor and delivery suite, "The analgesic drugs have no place in the *routine* management of the mother in labor. Increased atten-

tion should be given to nonpharmacologic means of achieving maternal comfort and when drugs are employed, the decision should be based upon a 'cost-benefit' analysis with the physician aware of the implications of their use and able to deal with the acute manifestations of their unwanted side effects."

So what should you do when you're deeply involved in your labor and a nurse walks in with a medication tray, announcing that it's time for "a little something to take the edge off"? We advise our childbirth students to reply politely with something like, "I'll let you know if I feel the need. I'm doing fine right now." Or, "I've discussed medication with my doctor and I'll talk it over with her/him again when s/he gets here. Thanks for thinking of me."

If the person persists or sends in heavy reinforcements, like the chief resident, who may recite all the reasons why you should take it now ("because later it will be too late"), it's important to have your partner take your side. Explain how well you're working together and refer them to your birth preferences sheet. If all else fails, just tell them straightforwardly that you know what their labor expectations are, but you also know you are within your rights to refuse any medication, procedure, or treatment you so desire. And just ask the nurse to chart that you "refused meds." This shows that she did what she was supposed to do in offering them to you. If all this results in an ugly situation (it does happen), tell everyone present you want them "off your case" and you'll sue anyone who touches you. A very confrontational technique, but it does get results!

Probably the best reason for not taking drugs during labor and birth is found in the package inserts which accompany the products. Most of these compounds carry warnings that they are contraindicated in children under six months of age—a category which certainly includes the unborn baby. A look at the warnings and side effects for Valium, widely used in obstetrics in combination with other drugs, suggests the sensory disruption that can follow its administration. It should not be used in occupations requiring complete mental alertness (isn't that what we're talking about?); should not be used simultaneously with other CNS depressants (often is in obstetrics—result: over-sedation and a mother and baby too groggy to care if the other is present); and can cause drowsiness, confusion, hypotension (lowered blood pressure, means less amount of blood flowing to baby over a given period of time), nausea, fatigue, depression, headache, slurred speech, tremor, blurred vision, acute hyperexcited states, anxiety, hallucinations, muscle spasticity, urinary retention, and rage.

One final comment: when mothers have been well trained in progressive relaxation and come to labor in optimal health, the presence of unendurable, agonizing pain is almost always a sign of a clinical abnormality. Being unmedicated up to this point of discovery of the problem is important, because if you had already accepted medication the true problem might never have been diagnosed. It is unrealistic to expect that giving birth will be like walking through a field of flowers—it's hard physical work of a kind you may never have done in your life—but it should not resemble torture, either.

Electronic Monitoring

Electronic monitoring (intrapartum assessment of fetal well-being) has been the single tool which has most assisted those trying to document the injurious effects of obstetrical intervention. From its introduction in the late 1950s as a research device, to today when virtually every out-of-the-way community hospital can point with pride to its fetal monitor, electronic labor surveillance has been widely touted as a way of insuring that all babies will be born in good condition. Would that it were so. The truth is that the definitive 1979 government report on their cost-effectiveness, *The Premature Delivery of Medical Technology: A Case Report*, by David Banta, M.D., of the United States Office of Technology Assessment (available free from: Publications and Information Branch, National Center for Health Sciences Research, 3700 East West Highway, Hyattsville, MD 20782), demonstrates that electronic fetal monitoring contributes nothing to the safety or well-being of

"low-risk" mothers and babies. Even more startling, since monitoring was first introduced as an aid to management of the mother and infant at "high-risk," is the report's conclusion that there is inadequate scientific evidence to support the claim that monitoring may have a beneficial effect on maternal and infant health as the risk of disease and disability increases. This means that the millions spent on monitors and monitor research in recent years, by hospitals and well-intentioned philanthropic organizations looking for ways to reduce infant mortality, has been money ill-spent. To add insult to injury, large numbers of the 600 studies reviewed by Banta show that electronic monitoring, in and of itself, *increases* the risk of pregnancy complications in the very subjects it is supposed to be safeguarding!

Remember, the premise that conditions the thought processes of nearly everyone involved in the monitoring controversy is that labor itself poses a problem for the baby's survival. Or, as Martin Stone, M.D., president of the American College of Obstetricians and Gynecologists expressed it in his 1979 inaugural address to the ACOG membership, "The trip through the birth canal is the most dangerous trip we ever take with the greatest chance of our dying of any one day in our lives. It has been said that as a result of this hazardous journey all of us are a little bit brain-damaged. . . ."

In the case of electronic monitoring we need to realize that the Banta report terms "purely speculative" the idea that monitoring can save many babies' lives and prevent brain damage due to oxygen deprivation. Robert C. Goodlin, M.D., professor in the department of OB/GYN at the University of Nebraska Medical School, goes even further. A veteran of years of experience in monitor research, Goodlin wrote in "When Is It Fetal Distress?" (*American Journal of Obstetrics and Gynecology*, May 1978) that "the fetus likely to suffer intrapartum fetal death is *ill prior to the onset of labor* [emphasis added]. . . . The healthy, term fetus tolerates labor and is *not* living through a particularly dangerous time period with regard to either death or permanent injury." Goodlin's position, while not popular with many of his colleagues, concurs with comments in the Summer 1974 edition of *Birth and the Family Journal*:

Of all perinatal deaths, anoxia (lack of oxygen) accounts for only 20 to 22 percent. Many of these are secondary to fetal anomaly, placental placement, and delayed delivery of the head

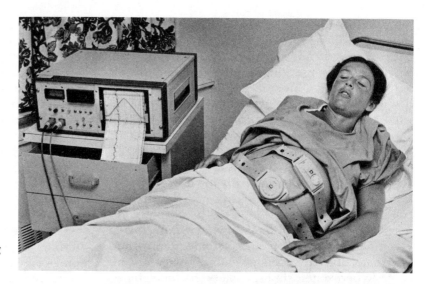

External electronic fetal monitoring abdominal straps.

in breech deliveries—problems which monitoring cannot solve. Sixty-five to 70 percent of perinatal deaths occur before labor begins at all. Infections, malformations, and other maternal diseases account for three-quarters. Probably the one single factor that would most reduce our perinatal mortality would be good maternal nutrition. In countries with the lowest perinatal mortality, such as the Netherlands and Sweden, more effort is spent insuring adequate nutrition and little on fetal monitoring. . . .

Another interesting twist to the monitoring debate came from Andre E. Hellegers, M.D., of Georgetown University, Washington, D.C., whose observations appeared in the August 17, 1978, issue of the *New England Journal of Medicine*. Noting that there has been no series of controlled studies of monitoring, yet monitoring has been almost universally accepted by obstetrical practitioners, Hellegers asserts, "Monitoring has become so common, and it has such strong advocates, that many engage in it without conviction about its value, but simply out of fear of being accused of not having done 'all that could be done.'" That is, in case of a poor outcome (which monitoring is supposed to prevent), your physician can cite the monitor tracing as evidence that his/her care was up to the standard of practice in your area.

There are three ways information about the baby's response to labor can be obtained:

external monitoring—An ultrasound transducer is attached to the mother's abdomen

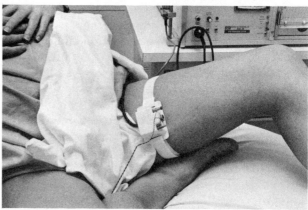

Internal electronic fetal monitoring wires and leg strap.

with a tight cinch strap; the transducer picks up the fetal heart rate which is then relayed by an electrical cord to the console and recorded on a strip of paper in the same manner as an electrocardiograph. A second strap around the mother's abdomen holds a pressure gauge in place; the gauge measures and records the occurrence of uterine contractions by sensing changes in the tautness of the mother's skin before, during, and after contractions take place. The well-trained attendant can read the monitor paper strip and get a good indication of how the baby is tolerating labor (provided the machine is working correctly; see below). internal monitoring—A catheter is inserted into the uterus to record the strength, not just the occurrence, of contractions. The catheter contains wires which protrude from the vagina en route to the console and are kept from becoming dislodged or entangled by means of a Velcro strap which holds them to the mother's leg. A spiral stainless steel screw-in electrode is pushed through the baby's scalp (hopefully, no further) to obtain direct information about the baby's heart rate; this electrode, too, is connected to the console via wires attached to the mother's leg. Obviously, the cervix must be somewhat dilated (a minimum of two centimeters) and the membranes ruptured in order to gain access to the interior of the uterus and the baby's head.

fetal blood sampling—As an adjunct to indirect (external) or direct (internal) monitoring, the proficient attendant will obtain a specimen of the baby's blood and have the blood gases analyzed in a laboratory before performing a Cesarean when a monitor tracing seems to be indicating "fetal distress" and conservative measures to improve the baby's performance have not worked. Fetal blood sampling is a sophisticated, but very risky, way of monitoring the monitor; when performed skillfully it can provide better data upon which to decide whether an operative delivery is warranted, thereby preventing hasty Cesareans carried out for no other reason than a few unusual tracings on the machine. The blood sample is obtained by inserting an endoscope (a tube with a light at the tip) through the cervix to illuminate the blood vessels of the presenting part (usually the baby's head, although the buttocks can also be used), then puncturing the skin and artery with a fine-bore needle to withdraw some blood. If the blood acidity is normal, labor progresses uninterrupted unless fetal heart tones remain abnormal; if the blood tests confirm acidosis, another sampling is done within 30 minutes with operative delivery scheduled immediately if this test shows a continuation of blood gas disturbance. Great care must be taken not to incise the scalp too deeply, since unborn babies have a markedly longer blood coagulation time than the rest of us, and, so, can hemorrhage to death from what might seem to be a very small cut. Numerous infant deaths due solely to fetal blood sampling have in fact been reported already in the medical literature by those experimenting with this technique for wider use.

Because women move in and out of their childbearing years in generational groups, there is always a fresh crop of expectant mothers who can be convinced by their doctors that the latest thing is the best thing. And it makes no difference whether the products work or not or are harmful or not. Electronic monitors are just the latest in a series of obstetrical gadgets convincingly presented to the medical profession and the public as a lifesaver for mothers and babies.

Apart from the fact that the use of monitors is based on an unscientific appraisal of the dangers inherent in human labor and birth, why else should you avoid them? Basically because they contribute enormously to the sensory distortions in labor that remove childbirth from the realm of physiology and place it into one of pathology. In order to be monitored, you have to accept these conditions:

- the tension of the belts strapped tightly around your abdomen at a time when you may not want to be touched at all because the uterus is so hard at work;
- the immobility caused by lying nearly flat on your back (the most painful position for labor and the least effective in moving the baby down) for fear of causing unusual tracings by your usual movements;
- the sound of the beeping amplifier and the flashing of the oscilloscope, not to mention the feed of paper from the machine (the monitor creates the atmosphere in the labor room);
- the good chance that nursing attendants will be paying more attention to the monitor than to you (many hospitals now have their machines hooked into a central display center so OB staff can follow all the monitors from one location—this has reduced the number of nurses needed for patient management under the guise of providing better care—some monitor manufacturers now term their machines "the electronic nurse"!);
- the 33 to 67 percent chance that the machine itself will not be recording the data it receives from you and the baby accurately (the machines have to be replaced every three to five years, because there are so few technicians to service them properly);
- the good chance that your doctor will not know how to interpret the monitor tracings accurately—one of the major reasons for the ten-fold increase in Cesareans since moni-

Intervention: Routine Care

toring became standard procedure at many institutions, and one of the variables over which you have the least control (there is a false positive rate of approximately 40 percent in detecting distress);

- the fact that there is no standardization of monitoring equipment, so tracings from one machine are not comparable to the tracings from a machine made by another manufacturer, and it is more difficult for personnel to recognize troublesome fetal heart rate patterns, more difficult to train people in interpreting the tracings, and more difficult to report on the scientific research using these machines;
- the repeated repositionings of the monitor belts required as the baby's position changes during labor require that your concentration and relaxation work with your partner will be interrupted;
- the difficulty of doing progressive relaxation when you are snared in a jumble of belts, wires, cords, and cuffs;
- if internal monitors are the rule, the 300 percent higher rate of infection for you, due to the open-channel uterine pressure catheter (makes a direct passageway for bacteria from vagina to uterus), and for your baby, due to the contamination of the amniotic fluid and wound in the baby's scalp where the electrode is attached (scalp abscesses occur once in every 200 to 300 babies monitored at Los Angeles County Hospital, for example);
- the good possibility that your blood pressure will fall as the result of the on-the-back position that produces the best tracings, thus *creating* fetal distress which the monitor will dutifully record—a distress which would not have occurred if you had not been forced to assume an unphysiologic position for labor;
- the good possibility that your labor will progress more slowly due to the unfavorable positioning and higher levels of anxiety, leading to the diagnosis of "failure to progress" and a potential Cesarean;
- the pain that probably accompanies application of the fishhook electrode to your baby's head at a time when the baby is already coping with enormous sensory input.

Probably the last word on monitoring comes from the widely publicized study of Albert D. Haverkamp, M.D., at the University of Colorado School of Medicine, Denver General Hospital, "The Evaluation of Continuous Fetal Heart Rate Monitoring in High-Risk Pregnancy" (*American Journal of Obstetrics and Gynecology*, 125: 310–20, 1976). Comparing the results of two groups of "high-risk" mothers who shared characteristics of age, parity, race, weeks of gestation, baby weight, and reason for monitoring, Haverkamp and colleagues concluded that the group whose labors were monitored by nurses using stethoscopes at 15-minute intervals (the classic method of labor evaluation in premonitoring days) did better on a number of measures than those in the electronically monitored group. "Cesarean sections were significantly more prevalent in the monitored group (16.5 percent) than in the auscultated group (6.6 percent). The Cesarean section rate for fetal distress in the monitored group (7.4 percent) was also significantly higher than that of the auscultated group (1.2 percent)." In measurements of infant outcome, no significant differences were found in mortality, Apgar scores, cord blood gases, and nursery illnesses, leading one to the conclusion that the only effect of electronic monitoring, even for the high-risk mother and infant in this study, is to increase the Cesarean rate with no improvement in infant outcome. This is the summary finding of the Banta report as well, three years and 599 studies later, so we find it very hard to accept claims to the contrary, regardless of the source from which they emanate. Just to reiterate, it is within your rights to refuse electronic monitoring and in light of the best available evidence it is in your best interest to do so.

Separation from Labor Support People

In many institutions, labor partner(s) are required to leave the laboring woman during admitting and prepping procedures (which often take up to an hour); whenever the mother is being examined internally (the partner may be asked to leave the room 15 minutes before the doctor arrives!); whenever medication is used—even though the mother remains awake; whenever the mother is confined to bed and must use the bedpan; upon the order of a physician; when the mother is taken to the delivery room; when the mother is actually giving birth; or when the mother is in the recovery area.

These policies effectively reduce the labor support to intermittent visits rather than a continuous presence, making the labor partner's job of promoting the mother's comfort and relaxation much more difficult. Many of these practices are based on the traditional way things are done in a given hospital and are not written, official hospital policy. On your hospital tour, ask for copies of the written regulations dealing with labor support—there probably aren't any. Even where there are vague restrictions, make sure your doctor has your preferences clearly in mind. (This takes a lot of effort on your part; the average OB/GYN practitioner sees 30 to 40 patients a day in the office and on hospital rounds, so making yourself stand out from the crowd takes a bit of persistence.) In almost all cases, where the doctor orders that a labor partner be admitted to the labor and delivery floor and you make it clear that you *want* your partner around no matter what else is happening, your wishes will be respected.

One of the greatest causes of anxiety and tension during labor is being left to labor alone. One of the most common fallacies first-time mothers have about labor is that someone will be with them all the time. (The usual fantasy involves the presence of the doctor who usually doesn't arrive until you are quite close to delivery unless s/he happens to be in the hospital for some other reason.) Unless you bring your own full-time labor helper, you are unlikely to find anyone at the hospital to fulfill this function.

In your home, of course, you are surrounded by people you have chosen to be present and whose presence means something special to you and your family. It is a completely different relationship (even extending to the physician) than that in the hospital where, just by showing up, you automatically forfeit what Chicago physician Mayer Eisenstein, M.D., calls your "home court advantage." Bringing at least one person of your choice with you as a companion throughout labor, birth, and the early postpartum hours helps to even the scorecard a bit. The presence of a loving partner, under the best of circumstances the baby's father, has been proven to reduce the mother's need for medication, thereby shortening labor.

For more detailed information about the psychological and medical advantages to continuous companionship during labor—and the benefits of the practice to hospitals, doctors, and nurses as well as to the family—read and share with your medical consultant:

Why Natural Childbirth? A Psychologist's Report on the Benefits to Mothers, *Fathers, and Babies,* by Deborah Tanzer, Ph.D., and Jean L. Block (New York: Schocken, 1976)

Husband-Coached Childbirth, by Robert A. Bradley, M.D. (revised ed., New York: Harper and Row, 1974)

Fathers in the Delivery Room: Recommendations to Hospital Administrators and Physicians on the Desirability and Safety of the Practice, by International Childbirth Education Association (revised ed., ICEA Bookcenter, P. O. Box 20048, Minneapolis, MN 55420, 1975)

Insistence on One Style of Labor Coping

Not only do you have to show up, you also have to play by their rules! In most cases, this means acting as though you're not really having a baby at all. Barbara Katz Rothman, a medical sociologist at Baruch College, analyzed this phenomenon in "The Social Construction of Birth" (*Journal of Nurse-Midwifery,* Vol. 22, No. 2, Summer 1977). Citing the work of Szasz and Hollender as reported in the 1956 American Medical Association's *Archives of Medicine,* Rothman discusses how women are socialized to accept hospital routines, even down to how they are supposed to respond to the stress of uterine contractions. Certain forms of labor coping, such as patterned breathing, are "acceptable" to hospital staff, while other expressions of labor response, such as groaning, are "unacceptable." Implying that the range of what is "acceptable" is determined on the basis of what is comfortable for the staff—and not the mother—Rothman brings us to the crux of the matter, the thinly veiled struggle of wills that is played out whenever hospitalized birth takes place.

It has been suggested that there are three basic modes of patient-practitioner relationships. Let us consider each with regard to childbirth. The first is the Active-Passive relationship, particularly applicable to the unconscious patient in an emergency situation. The doctor makes all decisions, and the patient is "worked on" in much the same way one does mechanical repairs. In the childbirth situation this relationship is typified by the doctor using forceps to pull the baby out of an unconscious mother. The doctor not only has complete control once the mother is unconscious, but it is the doctor who has the authority to define

Intervention: Routine Care

normal, variations from normal, and obstetrical emergencies, as well as the "state" of the patient. . . .

The second model of practitioner-patient relationship is Guidance-Cooperation. The practitioner guides and directs the patient who, if she is a good patient, takes guidance and direction easily. In childbirth, I believe that this is best typified by the in-hospital, "prepared" childbirth. The laboring woman is there to be coached. All of her preparation has taught her to work within the framework of the institutional rules. She learns, for example, techniques for breathing through an uncomfortable transfer from bed to table, and she does not learn to question the necessity of such a transfer. She learns where to place her hands so that they will not be strapped down on a delivery table. She learns what the rules are and how to avoid breaking them.

The third possible relationship is Mutual Participation, in which practitioner and patient work together toward a common goal. In childbirth, it is probably possible, though very difficult, to achieve this relationship in an institutional setting. It flows naturally, however, in a home birth where the attendant is clearly hired by and guest of the mother. The hospital patient is in no position to be an equal participant in her birthing. She is outnumbered and outpowered. She may be allowed to act as if she were an equal participant—even bring a patient advocate (husband, coach) with her, but should she stop playing by the rules and become disagreeable, difficult, or disruptive, as defined by the birth attendants and hospital staff, her true powerlessness is made clear. Her advocate is there only as long as the hospital attendants choose to allow him/her there.

It is perhaps for this reason that so much emphasis is put on control of both pain and the expression of pain in preparation for childbirth classes. According to the rules of the game, if the laboring woman chooses to deal with her pain by crying or calling out, she has forfeited her right to decision-making. Much is made in childbirth preparation circles of being in control in labor, while all that is meant by that is being in control of expressions of pain. A woman who maintains a fixed, if somewhat glazed, cheerful expression, and continues breathing patterns regularly, is said to be "in control" as she is carted from one room to another and literally strapped flat on her back with her legs in the air.

Episiotomy

The episiotomy is the quintessential surgeon's view of the perineum: we have to cut through muscles in order to preserve them! In her exceptionally thorough, clearly illustrated, and readable book, *Essential Exercises for the Childbearing Year* (Boston: Houghton Mifflin, 1976), Elizabeth Noble, R.P.T., past president of the Obstetrics Section, American Physical Therapy Association, details an episiotomy prevention program any woman can implement on her own. She comments:

Unlike the cervix, which over a period of many hours in the first stage of labor gradually and passively is thinned out (effaced) and dilated, the vaginal canal has considerably less preparation for the passage of the baby. . . . Of course, the hormonal changes that have occurred in pregnancy make the birth canal softer and more elastic, so it expands and becomes very thin under the pressure of distention. This stretching causes the perineum to become numb, although until that point the sensations that accompany the stretching are described as "burning," "prickling," "pressure creating a desire to move the bowels," or "a buildup of tension like that before orgasm."

The advantages claimed for the episiotomy include minimizing stretching, pre-

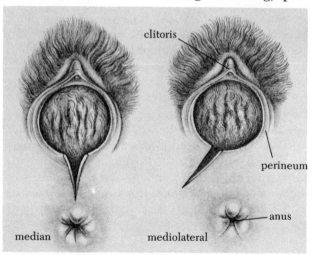

Two types of episiotomy incision.

venting perineal tears, and reducing compression of the baby's head. It may shorten the second stage of labor, when there is resistance from the pelvic floor. (The mother is tensing the muscles to counteract the pressure and stretching, withholding rather than releasing and *giving* birth.) Episiotomies are also given in instrumental deliveries and even when the mother has been given anesthesia, which results in total relaxation of the pelvic floor, but eliminates her voluntary assistance in bearing down. . . . Once the perineum is cut, however, the incision may be extended during the birth, anyway . . . and it has never been demonstrated that routine episiotomies reduce damage to the pelvic floor structure; in fact, incision and repair may lead to poor anatomical results. . . . Sexual response, we have seen, can actually be marred because the vagina becomes too lax or too tight subsequent to surgical repair.

In North American obstetrical practice, episiotomy is practiced over 90 percent of the time; in the Netherlands about 6 percent of births require it. The rate of pelvic floor surgery required later in life is the same in both countries, leading us to question the obstetrical dogma that surgically opening and reconstructing the vaginal outlet has anything to do with preventing gynecological problems.

How best to preserve your perineum during childbirth? Noble provides several recommendations:

- Eat well so you'll manufacture plenty of hormones and healthy, elastic tissue that will stretch well during birth.
- Make use of gravity during birth by positioning yourself in a 45-degree-or-better propped position (*never on your back!*), on your side if the birth is happening too fast and your pelvic floor hasn't had a chance to distend gradually, or on all fours if your baby is posterior to rotate the head into the most favorable position for birth.
- Keep your legs loose and relaxed in front of you, spread comfortably apart, throughout the pushing stage so your perineum isn't stretched tight as a drum (as is the case when you're strung up in stirrups, flat on your back) before the baby's head comes anywhere near it.

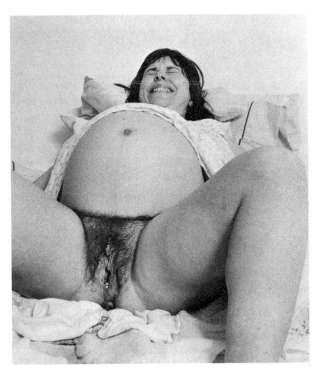

Making birth noises at peak of pushing contraction (legs unrestrained).

- *Do not pull up on your legs or push against any resistance with your feet—this tightens the pelvic floor muscles and impedes the gradual emergence of the baby's head you're aiming for.*
- Bear down only when the urge to do so is irresistible (at the peak of the contraction) and allow air to escape as you bear down. (You will probably make sounds like grunting or humming as you do this—it's the same sort of exhalation with effort you've noticed if you've watched weight lifters work out—and it reduces strain on your abdominal muscles and pelvic floor.)
- Keep in mind that the *uterus* is doing the work in pushing the baby out—good prenatal nutrition grows a strong uterus that won't play out during this strenuous phase of labor; the same principles of cooperation with the working uterus that you used in the first stage of labor also apply here—release uninvolved muscle groups elsewhere in your body and pay attention to those muscles that are in action.
- As you feel the stinging associated with maximum distention of the pelvic floor, reach down to feel the baby's head so you

Intervention: Routine Care

can gauge whether you need to keep pushing or release a bit. (Remember that your skin will be numbed by this time, so you won't get this impression without touching or looking to see what's happening.) Think of Sheila Kitzinger's description of the parting and opening of the vaginal lips as "the blossoming forth of a lovely flower"; a British childbirth educator, she writes most evocatively of birth as a psychosexual experience, one of many in a woman's cycle of sexuality; this perspective provides a major reason why tampering with the birth process can scar not only the body, but the spirit, so deeply. Remember that the more gradual the birth, the less likely the baby will have head deformities, bloodshot eyes, or breathing problems due to trapped mucus. As Caldeyro-Barcia reported in the Spring 1979 *Birth and the Family Journal* article, "The influence of Maternal Bearing-Down Efforts During Second Stage of Fetal Well-Being," when mothers are encouraged to bear down without holding breath only when they felt the need to do so, the bearing-down efforts lasted no more than five to six seconds each. When the mothers were instructed to bear down for ten seconds or more while holding their breath, the fetal heart rates dropped markedly, due to excessive pressure on the infants' heads during the prolonged bearing-down period.

Because of the presumed inevitable lack of oxygen flowing to the baby during these second-stage bearing-down efforts, doctors have traditionally favored hastening the second stage as much as possible. (See Forceps, below.) However, Caldeyro-Barcia's conclusion is just the opposite: *the second stage of labor may be somewhat longer when mothers bear down spontaneously and release breath, but mother and baby are better off.* This approach gives the perineum more time to stretch, reducing the need for episiotomy, as Noble and others have maintained. Judged on virtually all measures, spontaneous uterine pushing is better for mother and baby.

Forceps

Forceps are metal blades of many different designs, used to extract or rotate the baby's head in difficult deliveries; most forceps procedures today

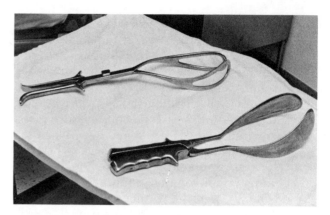

Two types of obstetrical forceps.

are done as a result of interventions imposed on the labor and birth as discussed previously. Many obstetricians have been trained to perform routine early episiotomy under anesthesia, then application of forceps to deliver the baby (since the anesthesia interferes with the mother's own uterine activity and bearing-down efforts) as the *preferred method* of delivery for all obstetrical cases. This approach makes delivering the baby the doctor's job—and reduces the mother to a passive spectator, or very sick patient, depending on the degree of anesthesia used and the skill of the surgeon. A standard handbook of obstetrics, *Human Labor and Birth,* by Harry Oxorn, M.D., of the University of Ottawa, and the late William R. Foote, M.D., of McGill University, lists these dangers from forceps operations, some of which are possible even with the most skillful operator:

> **dangers to you**—lacerations of pelvic floor tissue and muscle, extension of episiotomy, rupture of uterus, hemorrhage from lacerations, injury to bladder or rectum, infection of genital and/or urinary tract, fracture of coccyx (tailbone)
> **dangers to your baby**—cephalhematoma, hemorrhage and damage to the brain, late neurologic aftereffects, difficulty in breathing at birth, skull fracture, facial paralysis and brachial palsy (weakening of the arm) due to facial/neck/spinal nerve damage, bruising (forceps marks on cheeks and side of head), cord compression (when cord is inadvertently caught between forceps and head), death (when injuries from these hazards are massive)

In cases where the baby is lodged in an unfavorable position, or the mother is truly exhausted from an arduous labor, forceps can be a lifesaving instrument, but it seems rash to assume that the procedure is good for all mothers and babies—especially in light of the very serious, possibly lifelong complications that can result. Even in situations where there has been good progress in labor until the baby's head reaches the perineum and gets "stuck" between the pubic bone and coccyx, a common problem when the mother is flat on her back and the pelvic outlet reduced to its smallest diameter, the best solution is to stand the mother up and let her squat. This opens the outlet to its widest dimension and shortens the birth canal all at the same time, making much more room for the baby to pass through. Just moving the mother into an upright, propped position and getting her legs down from stirrups may be enough to do the trick in many cases, even when the baby is posterior.

Obviously, the sensations and actual vectors of force are radically changed when forceps are applied to extract the baby, rather than the baby emerging with a push from behind. The delicate spinal and neck vertebrae are easily pulled out of alignment by excessive and forceful extension of the infant's head. In a 1966 study of 1,250 infants, reported in the *Journal of the American Osteopathic Association* (Vol. 65: 1,059–75), researchers noted a direct relationship between excessive strain on the newborn's head and spine with newborn behavior many professionals have long held to be "normal"—that is, observed commonly in babies born the standard American way. Vomiting, tremors, irritability, and hypertonicity (holding muscle groups rigid) in these babies were identified as central nervous system responses to the excessive strain associated with instrument-assisted delivery. To summarize, everything possible should be done to avoid the need for forceps and, in the few cases where they are legitimately required, they should be used with as minimal amount of traction on the baby's head as possible. In this regard, the addition of a pressure gauge to the handles of forceps has been advocated so the limits of safety are not exceeded.

Lithotomy Position for Birth

Caldeyro-Barcia has commented that, "except for being hanged by the feet," there is no worse position for birth. It would be difficult to devise a birth position more incompatible with physiology. Requiring the mother to lie flat on her back with her legs strapped high and wide into stirrups, even when she is awake and unmedicated, is a common

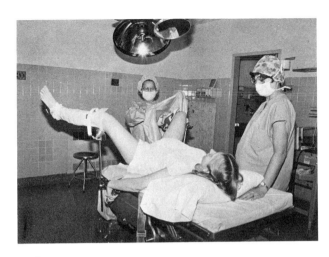

Lithotomy position.

cause of chronic back problems, exaggerated separation of the abdominal muscles (diastasis recti), and extensive cutting and repair of the skin and muscles which comprise the pelvic floor (episiotomy). He does not mention the feeling of fright that overcomes many people when they are tied and in pain—this psychological effect of the lithotomy position is undeniable. This archaic and damaging ritual has no justification other than obstetrical tradition. You do not have to accept this as a birth position, and it is wise to make plans in advance to bring your own backrest to the hospital if they are unable to provide you with an adaptable delivery bed or table. (Instructions for making your own backrest are available from: American Foundation for Maternal and Child Health, 30 Beekman Place, New York, NY 10022.) Other alternatives are to have your partner and a nurse support you from behind with their arms during contractions, or, least functional, to bring several pillows into the delivery room with you and use them to prop your back.

Cesarean Delivery

The skyrocketing Cesarean rate amounts to what, in another context, Sture Hedenstedt, M.D., of the Karolinska Institute of Stockholm, has termed "surgical vandalism." Nobody denies that there are large numbers of unnecessary Cesareans being performed or that mother and baby are subjected to higher rates of morbidity and mortality when Cesarean delivery is carried out. On the sensory level, an unnecessary Cesarean short-circuits the mother's concern for her baby and forces her to pay a great deal of attention to herself in order to begin to recuperate from the major abdominal surgery a

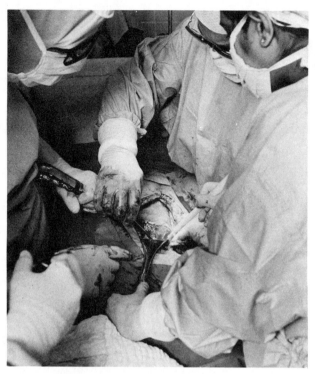

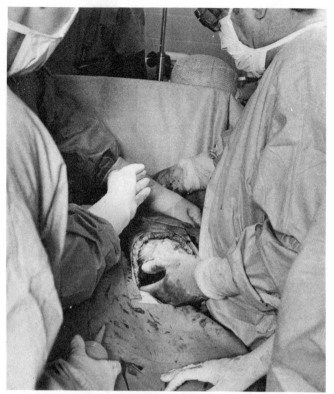

Above, *Opening the abdomen to expose uterus (retractors hold back abdominal wall).* Top right, *Reaching in to grasp baby's head.*

Cesarean entails. (See accompanying series of photographs.) It is the ultimate intervention in childbirth, often a culmination of a series of "lesser" interventions. For a comprehensive discussion of the Cesarean question, read Bonnie Donovan's *The Cesarean Birth Experience: A Practical, Comprehensive, and Reassuring Guide for Parents and Professionals* (Boston: Beacon Press, 1977), and contact C/SEC, a national Cesarean support and information group: 23 Cedar Street, Cambridge, MA 02140, or Cesarean Alliance, a group offering education for vaginal birth after Cesarean (V-bac): 10 Great Plains Terrace, Needham, MA 02192. C/SEC also sponsors an annual seminar in Boston dealing with issues in Cesarean birth, including why the rate has risen (a ten-fold increase in ten years in many areas) and what the individual mother can do to protect herself from an unnecessary Cesarean in the first place.

Other printed sources of information about Cesareans include:

Frankly Speaking (revised 1978). C/SEC's manual dealing with the subject.
Cesarean Reprint (BFJ, 110 El Camino

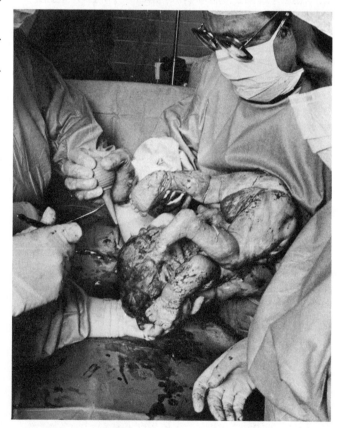

Delivery of body.

Right from the Start

Real, Berkeley, CA 94705, 1977). Contains articles from *Birth and the Family Journal*, "Having a Section Is Having a Baby"; "Teaching about Cesarean Birth in Traditional Childbirth Classes"; "Minimizing Emotional Sequellae of Cesarean Childbirth"; and two charts with references to the medical literature on complications of Cesarean to the mother and the baby. Order from BFJ.

Your local childbirth education group should include a full session on Cesareans as part of its standard series. International Childbirth Education Association (ICEA) guidelines propose that such a class discuss:

1. indications for a Cesarean (mother and baby) and the controversy surrounding some of these;
2. steps to take during pregnancy and labor to reduce the need for a Cesarean;
3. indications for and conduct of a trial of labor;
4. relationship between certain obstetrical practices and the need for Cesarean;
5. anesthesia: types, advantages/disadvantages of each;
6. what to expect during the procedure and afterward;
7. how to make an unavoidable Cesarean more family-centered;
8. vaginal delivery after previous Cesarean; who is a candidate and what is the protocol to be followed;
9. emotional reactions to Cesarean birth.

Victor Berman, M.D., and Salee Berman, R.N., in their chapter on risk assessment in *The Pregnancy-After-30 Workbook* (Emmaus, Pa.: Rodale Press, 1978), address all of these issues. We have found in our own work with pregnant women that the need for Cesarean in women who have taken our classes is 3 to 5 percent, a figure far below the national rate of 20 to 25 percent. The approach we use with our own classes is woven throughout this book: emphasis on *primary prevention* of situations that create Cesareans. Recovery after Cesarean and special handling of the baby born by Cesarean are presented in chapters 5, 6, and 8.

Overall, keep thinking of the importance of the birth process in preparing yourself and your baby for the next few months of your life together. Remember that the best services and individuals respect the need you and your baby have for one another and encourage your close association in the hours or days after birth when you are in their direct care. Deciding how you want your baby to be handled after birth and exercising your parental prerogatives in the matter involve dealing with a different set of people than during pregnancy. It also means learning about the enormous physical changes occurring in your child from the moment of birth until that first pediatric checkup at four weeks after birth. The decisions you have made during pregnancy and birth will have contributed much to your child's ability to cope with these changes and deepen his or her emotional attachment to you and your family.

Chapter 4

The First Breath
Transitional Care

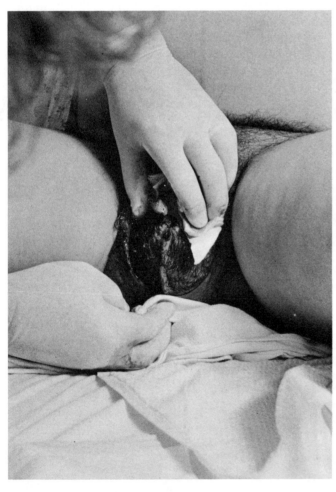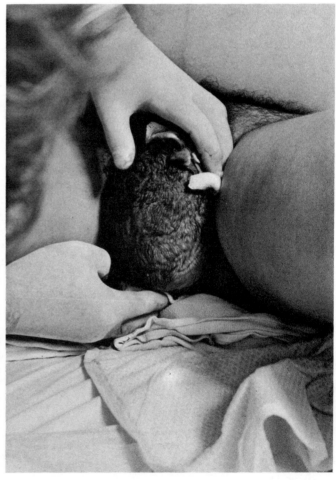

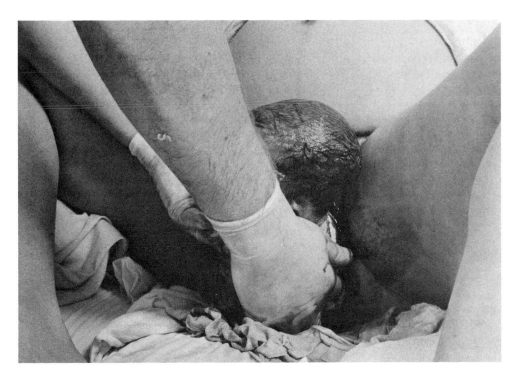

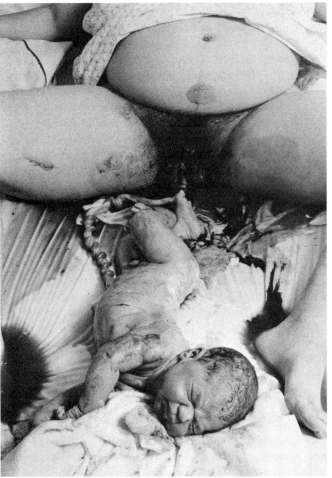

Healthy babies emerge from their mothers ready to be born. The critical test of this readiness is the newborn's first breath. Releasing that breath in a lusty cry confirms to all present the infant's safe transition to life outside the womb.

Hearing her child's cry and gazing upon her infant for the first time may rouse the mother to a state of near rapture. She may cry out herself as she reaches spontaneously for her baby. Once reunited, each is comforted by the physical presence of the other. The close contact they have enjoyed thus far in their shared lifetime is reestablished, and a major milestone in the development of mother and child is marked. Respectful attention to the needs of you and your baby during this profoundly sensitive period proves to be of paramount importance in your ever-growing attachment.

Referred to by one writer as a "physiologically displaced person," the just-born infant is spurred on toward that first breath by a host of stimuli. True, the newborn needs to eliminate carbon dioxide and take in oxygen, so the diaphragm contracts in response to that need. Commonly, however, there is a period of several minutes during which the baby continues to receive dwindling amounts of oxygen through the still-attached umbilical cord. So it's possible that other factors may be equally important in initiating the baby's first intake of air.

The First Breath: Transitional Care

Chief among these might be the multitude of major environmental changes to which the newborn is subjected in even the most gentle of birth circumstances. Where moments before there was powerful pressure on all the baby's body surfaces, there is suddenly no touch at all except from a solid surface. Wetness and warmth are replaced by air and chill. Darkness becomes light. Limbs accustomed to being tightly encased now encounter neither resistance nor support. Sound enters the ear with unprecedented acuity. Smells and tastes are brand-new. All of these stimuli occurring at the same time no doubt have a strong effect on the baby's central nervous system, perhaps enough to trigger respiration by themselves. In our view, these experiences do not necessarily constitute trauma for the baby as some writers, such as the French obstetrician Frederick Leboyer, believe. Rather, they should be viewed as positive steps along a continuum of development for which the healthy, full-term, well-nourished, undrugged newborn is amply prepared by the events of normal labor. However, Leboyer's other point—that standard handling of the newborn by the majority of medical personnel unduly stresses the baby—is certainly well taken.

Once the baby's chest is relieved of pressure from the vaginal walls, it is possible for the chest walls to expand a bit, lowering the internal pressure of the chest cavity. Since nature seeks always to equalize air pressures, air rushes into the baby's nasal passages and mouth en route to the still-collapsed lungs. The air moves from larger pathways to smaller ones aided in its free passage by surfactant, a substance manufactured by the mature lungs only in the last few weeks of pregnancy. Pressure from within the newly inflated airways is balanced by the flow of blood for the first time into the capillaries serving the lungs. This prevents rupture of the lung due to the considerable pressure exerted by the inrushing air.

Because the lungs contain no reserve air, the first inhalation is extraordinarily deep, pushing the diaphragm, intestines, and abdominal wall downward and outward. When the abdominal muscles respond by pulling themselves back into their customary position, the diaphragm is pushed back to a resting position, exerting upward pressure on the expanded lungs. Thus, air is forced from the lungs, passing by the vocal bands on the way out and resulting in the classic first cry.

Subsequent breaths are usually easier than the first, since thereafter the lungs stay partially in-flated even when at rest. Depending on the temperature of the room and the baby's activity level, the respirations may vary from 20 to 100 per minute, with an average of 45 per minute—considerably more than your usual adult rate of 16 per minute.

While your baby's first breath is getting underway, other imperceptible, but equally crucial, adjustments in the circulatory system are also taking place.

- The major opening between the chambers of the fetal heart (the *foramen ovale*) closes, sending large amounts of blood up through the bronchial tree for the first time—making plenty of blood available for this function is the major argument for allowing the umbilical cord to remain intact until it has stopped pulsating.
- Within minutes after the *foramen ovale* closes, a second heart opening, into the aorta, also closes permanently (the *ductus arteriosus*), thus insuring that all blood reaching the left side of the heart for pumping to other parts of the body has been circulated first through the lungs and is fully oxygenated.
- The blood vessel permitting blood from the umbilical cord to travel directly to the fetal heart without passing through the liver (the *ductus venosus*) closes as a result of contraction in a muscle sphincter at the site of the navel, thus halting the circulation of blood through the cord.

All these adjustments are required in order to meet the new demands placed on the heart, lung, brain, liver, and other vital organs. While the load on the heart, for instance, might seem to be reduced after birth, since it no longer has to pump blood through the placental blood vessels, it turns out that, due to lower temperatures outside the womb coupled with the general increases in muscular, digestive, respiratory, and endocrine functions, the heart is working much harder than ever! The baby's pulse typically runs 125 to 130 beats per minute, but can rise to 180 when the infant is crying vigorously.

The newborn's blood has some unique characteristics which seem designed to give the baby the best possible chance for a good start in its new environment. The white blood cell count, for instance, which normally measures 7,000 cells per cubic mm of blood, is elevated at birth to around 45,000. This high level of white blood cells provides the infant with a strong first line of defense against infection. Coming from a sterile world into our microbe-filled one makes this an especially important compensator mechanism for the newborn. Red blood cells are similarly increased in number, with hemoglobin concentration often in the range of 18 to 20 g per 100 cubic cm of blood. This falls to 12 to 14 g within the first week to ten days after birth.

The presence of all the extra cells in the same volume of blood means that the newborn's blood is considerably thicker than an adult's. To offset this increased viscosity and prevent undesirable coagulation, a clotting factor, prothrombin, is present in the baby's bloodstream at 20 to 40 percent lower levels than usual. This, too, may be an adaptive mechanism for survival, since many infants are born with small hemorrhages into their eyes, scalp, and skin (particularly when instruments have been used during delivery). If the blood were to clot at the normal rate during the birth process, it might result in irreparable damage to these structures.

Why is your baby born with proportionately more red blood cells than you have? The answer has to do with the way your baby obtains oxygen during pregnancy. As with all other substances essential to your unborn baby's growth, in order for the child to receive oxygen, you have to take it in. The oxygen concentration of the atmosphere is approximately 20 percent. When you inhale, the inner surface of your lungs is brought into direct contact with oxygen-laden air. Red blood cells circulating through the capillary network that services the lungs pick up oxygen much like a freight-train car taking on a load. As the red cells travel throughout the body they release their oxygen cargo into the bloodstream wherever it is needed. One of these sites, of course, is the maternal "lake of blood" that perfuses the placenta. (See chapter 1.) At this point, however, the percentage of oxygen contained in the mother's blood is much lower than the 20 percent found entering the lungs. To compensate for the proportionately lower amount of oxygen present in its source of oxygen (the lake of maternal blood) than will be present after birth through the lungs, the unborn baby's body simply manufactures more red blood cells to pick up and distribute all the oxygen the baby's organs and tissues require for growth and development. It is analogous to adding more cars to the freight train.

After your baby is breathing on his/her own and has access to the higher concentration of oxygen in the air through the lungs, the extra red blood cells that were so necessary to life *in utero* become superfluous. They are broken down and excreted by the liver. Should the liver be impaired in this process, for whatever reason, a by-product of the red cell breakdown, bilirubin, can rise above normal levels. Because of its orange pigmentation, an excess of bilirubin tints the skin, eyes, and excretions yellow. Medically, this condition is termed jaundice or *icterus*. When the yellow coloration is simply the result of breaking down the red cell overload following birth, it is called physiologic jaundice. Generally, this type of jaundice does not appear until the second or third day after birth, is transient, and requires little treatment except to provide the baby with plenty of fluids (ad lib breastfeeding) and to expose the baby to sunlight to aid in the breakdown of the bilirubin. (See chapter 6.)

If your baby is born jaundiced or develops jaundice in the first 24 hours after birth, however, other courses of action are usually necessary, since in these cases the jaundice is a symptom of an underlying disease process, not just the normal clearance of supplementary red blood cells. Babies born with severe jaundice due to an unanticipated Rh incompatibility or blood group incompatibility, for instance, might have to undergo a blood transfusion soon after birth. Most of the time, with quality prenatal care, such problems are diagnosed well in advance of the birth and appropriate therapy can be instituted, sometimes even while the baby is still in the womb. These procedures and the indications for them are discussed in chapter 6. We mention them there because an emergency of this sort, while exceedingly infrequent, significantly alters the course of events in the immediate postnatal period for mother and baby.

Apart from the jaundice issue, your baby's color at first glance, perhaps more than any other feature, may come as a surprise. Instead of the rosy-cheeked cherub with satiny skin we've been dreaming of for months, suddenly we're face-to-face with a gray blue, squirmy being who's likely to be dripping with any combination of amniotic fluid, mucus, vernix, and blood. You needn't worry about the colors. Your baby has looked this way *in utero* throughout pregnancy, courtesy once again of the unique way the unborn's blood and circulatory system handle carbon dioxide.

The same transport mechanism previously

The First Breath: Transitional Care

discussed, the red blood cells, are used to pick up carbon dioxide wherever it is formed and discharge it through the placenta into the mother's circulation. Then it is carried by her red blood cells to her lungs where it passes readily into the air, the carbon dioxide concentration of the atmosphere being only 0.4 percent.

The carbon dioxide attached to the hemoglobin in the red blood cell changes its color to blue. You can observe this in your own body by looking at the bright blue veins in your arm, all of which contain blood laden with carbon dioxide en route to your lungs for cleansing. In the case of your unborn baby, though, the carbon dioxide has to diffuse through the placenta rather than the lungs—and the concentration of carbon dioxide in your blood is much higher than in the atmosphere—so the carbon dioxide leaves the baby's body much more slowly than it will after birth.

The higher concentration of circulating carbon dioxide is an ongoing condition of intrauterine life, which changes dramatically the moment the baby's lungs begin to function. Then, the carbon dioxide leaves the body much more efficiently, and the baby's overall color shifts from gray blue to pink—usually within a minute or two. The baby need not be wailing in order for this to happen; regular, quiet respirations accomplish the carbon dioxide transfer equally well. The baby who is gently handled may give only a few loud cries following birth, then settle into a period of observant

alertness. There is no physiologic need for prolonged crying in the newborn. As Lee Salk, M.D., once commented, "If crying is good for the lungs, then bleeding must be good for the veins."

The Apgar Scoring System, a method for assessing your infant's condition at birth, evaluates five factors associated with potential difficulties in the period just following birth. (See chart.) The highest possible score on each item is two, for a total of ten. A score of seven or above is considered good, four to six fair, and three or below poor enough to require resuscitative measures. The Apgar score is *not* of value in predicting your baby's future intelligence or general state of health. It is strictly a shorthand method of indicating the baby's condition at one and five minutes after birth and whether assistance will be required in getting the baby started breathing on its own.

The Apgar rating will be entered on your baby's permanent birth record—its reliability, of course, depends on the objectivity of the person (usually the doctor) doing the scoring. Sometimes babies in only fair condition receive a seven or better on paper, since a low Apgar is commonly considered an unflattering reflection on the obstetrician in charge (labor too rushed, excess sedation and/or anesthesia used, delay in instituting resuscitative measures in the clearly depressed infant, etc.). In short, the Apgar simply expresses numerically what any interested observer (mother) can see for herself: is my baby breathing, crying,

The Apgar Scoring System

| Factor | Possible Score | | |
	0	1	2
Pulse	Absent	Less than 100	More than 100
Respiratory Effort	Absent	Weak cry, irregular	Good cry
Muscle Tone	Limp	Some movement of extremities	Active movement
Reflex Irritability (catheter is briefly introduced into baby's nose or a short slap is given to the baby's foot)	No response	Grimace	Cough or sneeze; vigorous cry and withdrawal of foot
Color	Blue or pale	Body pink Extremities blue	Pink all over

Right from the Start

moving, and "pinking up"? If so, most mothers respond, *"Let me have my baby!"*

The sensations of holding your own child in your arms for the first time defy description. Emotions you may never have experienced with such intensity well up from your innermost spaces. You may cry. You may laugh. You may laugh and cry. You may babble, repeating phrases of endearment to the baby over and over. You may be struck almost dumb. Whatever your reaction, it will be your personal response to the reality of your baby's presence—to that child's look, smell, and feel. It will be one of the most intimate moments of your life, a time you will recall with tenderness for years to come, an encounter your child will enjoy hearing you describe many times as s/he grows up.

Within the bounds imposed by concern for the baby's well-being, there is no *right* way to greet your baby. What counts is having the opportunity to fondle, inspect, and love your baby in your own way. Just as you and your lover find your own ways to give each other pleasure and a sense of security, so, too, will you find the appropriate ways to meet the special needs of this baby. All you need are privacy and time to find your way together.

Because your baby needs to be kept warm, and because your body is the best radiant heat source yet invented, skin-to-skin contact in the minutes after birth is far preferable to swaddling or placing the baby alone under an electric warmer. Numerous studies of neonatal heat loss in various delivery room situations (baby naked under warmer, baby swaddled under warmer, baby swaddled and handed to mother, baby handed to mother naked for skin-to-skin contact, baby and mother covered and under radiant heat panel installed in ceiling) show that body temperature falls immediately after birth in the conventional delivery room. Celeste Phillips, R.N., reviewing the reasons for this heat loss in an article, "Neonatal Heat Loss in Heated Cribs vs. Mothers' Arms" (*Journal of Obstetric, Gynecologic and Neonatal Nursing,* Vol. 3, No. 6, November/December 1974), notes that body heat is lost from the skin surface by (1) evaporation, (2) radiation, (3) convection, and (4) conduction.

In the newborn, she explains, evaporation occurs when a baby wet with amniotic fluid comes in contact with the dry, air-conditioned air of the delivery room. Radiant heat loss, which accounts for two-thirds of the total loss in hospital nurseries, happens when heat leaves the body surface by transferring to the cooler surfaces of surrounding

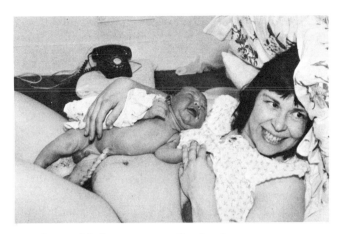

Mother and baby moments after birth.

objects, particularly the walls of the incubator/isolette. Citing the findings of Lutz and Perlstein (*Nursing Clinics of North America,* March 1971, pp. 16, 17, 22), Phillips states that the incubator does not guarantee protection from radiant heat loss, because "the relatively thin sheet of Plexiglas comprising the wall of an incubator is very sensitive to room temperature changes and, as measured, can vary in its various surface temperatures by as much as 10°C from the temperature reported on the incubator air thermometer." Heat loss by convection is due to air currents and is aggravated by air conditioning. Conduction results in heat loss when cooler objects come into direct contact with the baby's skin (cold diapers, blankets, scale, instruments, hands, bedding). If the room is chilly (less than 75°F) you can towel the baby off yourself with a soft, absorbent, prewarmed receiving blanket to prevent excess heat loss as fluids evaporate from the baby's wet skin. Then, you snuggle together under a sheet or blanket. Your body heat will be contained in a mini-climate that's just what baby needs to relax and enjoy your embrace.

Reporting in the journal *Pediatrics* (Vol. 46, p. 187, 1970), investigators Marshall Klaus, M.D., John Kennell, M.D., and Peter deChateau, M.D., described behavior of mothers on first contact with their babies which they believe to be species-specific. They found that undrugged mothers in the hospital who receive their naked, unwashed babies soon after birth usually begin by touching the baby's limbs with their fingertips, then proceed to massaging the trunk with their full palms while beginning to establish eye-to-eye contact. Making eye contact appears to stimulate the mother's ability to relate to her infant as a person and is described by mothers as very rewarding.

The First Breath: Transitional Care

Jean Liedloff, the British journalist and ecologist, reflects on the meaning of these early moments together in her penetrating book, *The Continuum Concept* (New York: Warner Books, 1979):

> Imprinting, geared into the sequence of hormonally triggered events at birth, must take place right away or it would be too late; a prehistoric mother could not have afforded to remain indifferent to a newborn baby even for a few minutes.
>
> If the imprinting is prevented from taking place, if the baby is taken away when the mother is keyed to caress it, to bring it to her breast, into her arms and into her heart, or if the mother is too drugged to experience the bonding fully, what happens? It appears that the stimulus to imprint, if not responded to by the expected meeting with the baby, gives way to a state of grief.
>
> When, then, a modern hospital suddenly produces a baby hours, or even minutes, after the mother has gone into a physiological state of mourning, the result is often that she feels guilty about not being able "to turn on mothering" or "to love the baby very much," as well as suffering the classic civilized tragedy called normal postpartum depression . . . just when nature had her exquisitely primed for one of the deepest and most influential events of her life.

As you carefully take in each of your baby's features you may notice many ways a newborn differs from babies who are even just a few weeks older. Not every baby displays all these normal variations, but your baby is likely to have several of them. The accompanying series of captioned photographs should help you identify the various conditions you discover in your own baby and give you an idea of their natural course or form of treatment, if any. Should you observe anything else worrisome about your baby's physical or emotional condition, do not hesitate to bring it to the attention of your doctor, midwife, or attending nurse. Nobody is more attuned to your baby's needs than you are, so your perceptions can be very valuable in pinning down whatever the problem might be.

Because of the considerable evidence that the period after birth is an especially sensitive time for parents and other members of the newborn's family who may be present, a call for reappraisal of

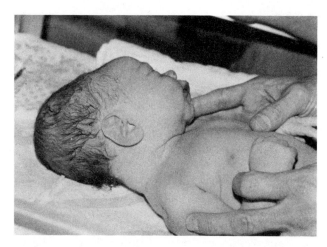

Molding of head (enables baby's head to pass through vagina).

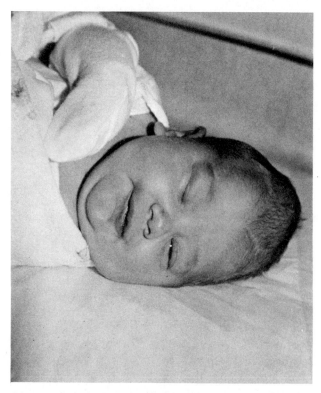

Caput succedaneum *(swelling due to pressure during labor).*

standard operating procedure in hospitals has arisen within and without the medical community. Diony Young, a consultant in maternal and child health, summarized recent research in a 1978 pamphlet of the International Childbirth Education Association (ICEA), *Bonding: How Parents Become Attached to Their Baby.* (Available at ICEA Bookcenter, Box 20048, Minneapolis, MN 55420.)

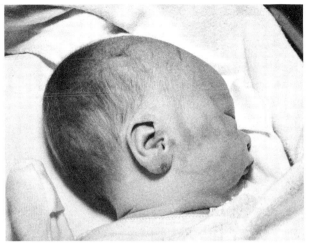

Forceps marks (bruises caused by pressure of instruments against skin).

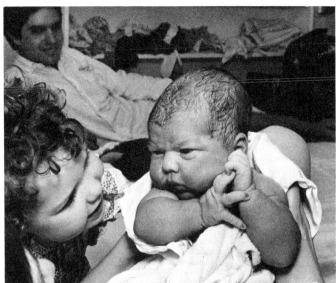

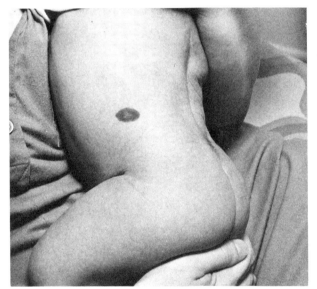

Birth mark

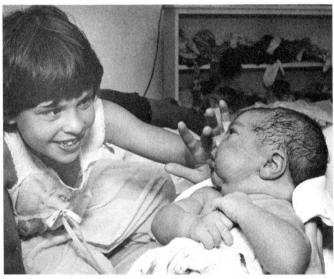

Top right and above, *Newborn facial structure (flat nose, receding chin, fat cheeks).*

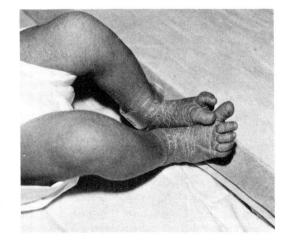

Peeling skin at creases.

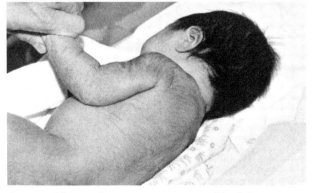

Lanugo (downy hair covering parts of body).

The First Breath: Transitional Care

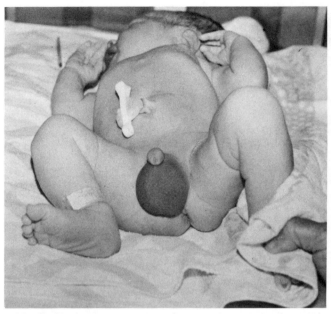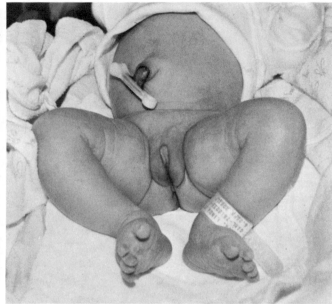

Enlarged genitals (due to maternal hormones)—male and female.

Sucking reflex (baby may have been sucking thumb in utero).

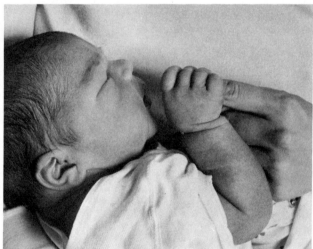

Grasp reflex.

During this period, the baby is alert and ready to respond to his/her environment. At the same time the mother and father are physically and emotionally attracted to their baby, and reciprocal reactions of great richness and complexity occur between the parents and the baby. . . . Many recent studies have examined the interaction and responses of mothers and babies when they are together. Maternal bonding behavior includes cuddling, kissing, fondling, touching, smiling, nurturing, rock-

Right from the Start

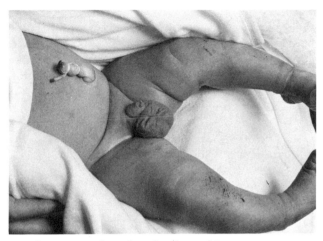

Cord stump tied—infant has bowed legs.

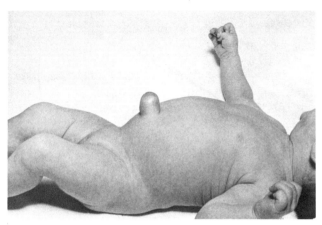

Umbilical hernia.

ing, prolonged gazing, soothing, and talking in a high-pitched voice. (Babies seem to respond particularly to high frequencies in human speech.) Fathers exhibit the same attachment behavior as mothers when they have early and extended contact with their newborns.

New techniques for measuring newborn behavior have been developed which show that babies are much more discriminating and responsive than was formerly realized. At birth the alert newborn is attracted by a variety of visual, sound, and other sensory stimuli, particularly by the eyes and other features of the human face. When the newborn baby is in a state of quiet alertness and thus receptive to stimulation (rather than asleep or crying), s/he reciprocates with behavior such as gazing, imitating, crying, listening, startling at a loud noise, following with his eyes, clinging, and body movement. . . . It is now known that babies can see at birth and that the alert, un-medicated baby will focus on a moving object at a distance of 10 to 15 inches. A mother seems to be particularly attracted to her baby's eyes, and she will position her head so that her eyes can meet her baby's eyes (*en face* position).

Because of these significant findings, some neonatologists (physicians who specialize in caring for newborn babies) recommend that during the first hour after birth the parents be encouraged to spend a period with their babies in complete privacy. . . . Many physicians now recognize the importance of parents having early and extended interaction with their newborn baby during the sensitive period to enhance the natural bonding process. During a prenatal visit, parents should tell their physician or midwife about their desire for early contact with their newborn baby, and thus they and the physician or midwife can discuss and plan the necessary arrangements together. . . . In hospitals with a family-oriented philosophy and practice, the staff derive a profound satisfaction in caring for the

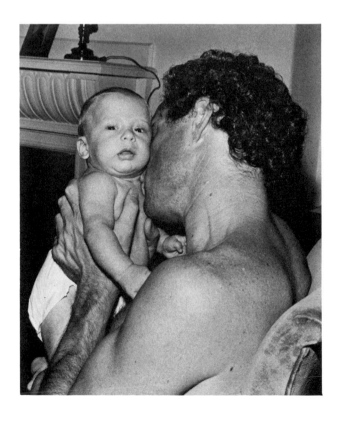

The First Breath: Transitional Care

new family and knowing that they have contributed toward the establishment of bonding.

Gene Cranston Anderson, Ph.D., associate professor of maternal-child nursing at the University of Illinois Medical Center, Chicago, wrote about mothers and newborns as mutual care givers in the September/October 1977 issue of the *Journal of Obstetric, Gynecologic and Neonatal Nursing.* Focusing on breastfeeding as an integral part of the mammalian maternal-young interaction pattern during the period immediately following birth, she comments:

> This is the practice in most human primitive cultures and is thus assumed to have been the general rule as our species evolved. It would therefore seem reasonable to propose that such interaction might have survival value. . . [and] that the mother and her newborn need to be free to interact with each other in self-regulatory fashion from the moment of birth.

When you put your baby to the breast as soon after birth as the baby seems calm, Anderson notes, the ongoing interaction is replete with sensory stimuli ideally suited to furthering bonding. In several instances, these stimuli are familiar to the baby, having been an important part of life before birth. (See chapter 1.)

- The baby is closely held, now in mother's arms, rather than in the womb.
- The gentle rise and fall of her chest with the rhythm of her breathing is reminiscent of the rocking provided by her movements during pregnancy.
- The warmth of her skin reproduces the internal warmth of her body.
- Suckling her breast stimulates all the extremely sensitive nerve endings on tongue, lips, cheeks, and palate just as the infant was previously accustomed to doing by sucking its own thumb *in utero.*

To illustrate her point that the baby's need for this interaction is urgent, immediate, and continual even if it goes unfulfilled, Anderson discusses a videotape she produced with the cooperation of the medical director of the University of Illinois Hospital Nurseries: *Hand-Mouth Activity in the Transitional Newborn: Intention to Suck?* (Hawthorne, N.Y.: Ardine Publishing Co., 1976). It records the routine care received by a typical newborn between 20 and 80 minutes after birth with special focus on hand-mouth activity. Anderson challenges the idea that this activity is random, proposing instead that it is intentional for the purpose of sucking.

During 47 minutes in the supine position, this newborn's hand went past his mouth 115 times, his hand touched his face 113 times and his mouth 133 times. His mouth opened unrelated to crying 142 times and his fingers entered his mouth for two to three seconds 72 times. He engaged in active sucking, with attendant total quiescence, for an average of 41 seconds five times. Once crying began it occurred the majority of the time, and this newborn's behavior rapidly disorganized. Hard crying with associated Valsalva maneuvers [breath-holding with buildup of abdominal pressure and strain on the blood vessels—EDITOR] became interspersed with increasingly intense hand-mouth activity. However, no further sucking occurred. Placement in the prone position, at least after this baby's earlier experiences, did not relieve crying or facilitate sucking. When a pacifier was offered, deep sucking commenced immediately, as did the total cessation of gross motor activity, startles, and crying. This behavior continued for the next 70 minutes. The film concludes with this question: Assuming the quiescent state reflects comfort, wouldn't it have been better for this baby to be so quieted by his mother "on cue," rather than by a man-made object on demand?

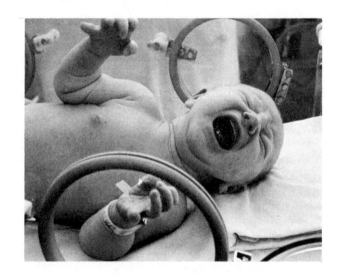

Enforced separation of mother and baby soon after birth is still too often the rule and not the exception in hospitals where "rest" for mother and baby is often identified as the birthing pair's most important postpartum need. Judging from the preceding passage, the baby sentenced to isolation in a typical newborn nursery gets little "rest," but seems bent on reestablishing physical contact with someone, anyone (anything) in a frantic attempt to maintain some sense of belonging in the world.

Mothers also fare poorly when their just-born babies are removed from their presence. Denied the stimulus of suckling at the breast which causes rhythmic contractions of the uterus, most women giving birth in hospitals receive instead a hormone injection to trigger separation of the placenta. Continued separation from her baby (often for 4 to 12 hours) increases her risks for postpartum hemorrhage since she lacks adequate breast stimulation for the release of oxytocin, the naturally occurring hormone which causes the uterus to stay tightly clamped down until the placental site heals. In addition, thousands of mothers have told us how being kept from their babies led to anxiety, inability to sleep (even though they were tired after a long labor in many cases), and feelings of depression or "not knowing what to do with myself." Yet the common solution to these negative feelings and serious physical health hazards engendered by mother-baby separation is to offer the mother medication to make her uterus contract and sleeping pills plus pain relievers to induce sleep.

A final consideration that argues strongly for breastfeeding shortly after birth is the substance the baby ingests in early feedings, colostrum. We'd be wealthy women if we had a penny for every time a mother has been told her breasts are empty until three or four days after birth, that colostrum is just an inferior form of milk, or even more astounding, that it's actually "bad for the baby." To the contrary, colostrum is the perfect food for your newborn baby because it contains:

- a great deal of lactose (milk sugar) which makes it sweet (the baby's favorite taste—yes, s/he can discriminate very well between sweet, sour, salty, and bitter), thereby rewarding the baby's sucking efforts and encouraging more of them at frequent intervals (the newborn's sucking reflex, according to Russian research, is at its peak 20 to 30 minutes after birth);
- higher concentrations of amino acids, the

protein building blocks so essential to growth and repair of healthy tissues;
- a form of protein that is nearly 100 percent digested and assimilated by the baby, thus reducing the strain on baby's eliminative systems;
- laxative properties that assist the baby in clearing its bowel of meconium, the tarry, sticky, semifluid which consists mainly of mucus mixed with swallowed amniotic fluid, cast-off cells from the baby's skin *in utero*, and biliverdin, which gives it its greenish black color;
- living cells, lymphocytes and macrophages, which have the ability to attack and digest foreign organisms and certain harmful bacteria that may enter the baby's gastro-intestinal tract at or soon after birth;
- specific antibodies effective against viral infections such as polio, Coxsackie, staph (very prevalent in hospitals), and *E. coli*, the bacteria commonly involved in neonatal diarrhea.

An excellent film detailing these points is "Breastfeeding for the Joy of It"—rental from: Cinema Medica, 664 North Michigan Avenue, Chicago, IL 60611.

The value of colostrum is so widely recognized by veterinarians and animal breeders that donated colostrum is made available to newborn animals whose mothers are unable or unwilling to suckle them. Lambs, calves, foals, piglets, kids, kittens, and puppies all do poorly when denied their mothers' colostrum. According to Jackie and C. E. Spaulding, D.V.M., in their book, *The Complete Care of Orphaned or Abandoned Baby Animals* (Emmaus, Pa.: Rodale Press, 1979), 80 percent of calves who don't receive the necessary colostrum for the first three days of life die, presumably because the colostrum contains antibodies and vitamin A that protect the calf against bovine diseases for the first few weeks of its life.

Cans of artificial puppy formula display this warning on their labels, "CAUTION: Feeding newborn mammals a milk-formula always entails some risk. Your veterinarian should be consulted for advice concerning sound management practices and the feeding of Borden ESBILAC."

In light of what is now known about the importance of human colostrum for human babies, perhaps similar advisories should become mandatory on packages of artificial formula intended for

The First Breath: Transitional Care

their consumption. Or, at the very least, human babies should receive a serving of donated colostrum as their first food if their mothers are unable or unwilling to breastfeed. It would far surpass in nutritional and immunological benefits the standard hospital offering of distilled or 5 percent glucose water. It might also go far toward reducing the occurrence of neonatal hypoglycemia. (See chapter 6.)

Getting your baby to "latch on" the first few times is a learning experience for both of you. Like so many other aspects of baby care, it's a matter of learning what feels comfortable for the two of you and what works best in different situations. Some fundamentals:

- Don't offer the breast *immediately* after birth—wait until the baby seems calm or indicates by sucking on his/her fingers that the breast would be welcome.
- Make sure you're in a position that's comfortable for you and that allows you to hold the baby securely. (Side-lying or propped up is preferable to lying almost flat on your back.)
- Support the baby's neck and head in the bend of your elbow with that hand tucked under the baby's legs. This frees your other hand for guiding the breast to the baby's mouth.
- Using the thumb and forefingers of your

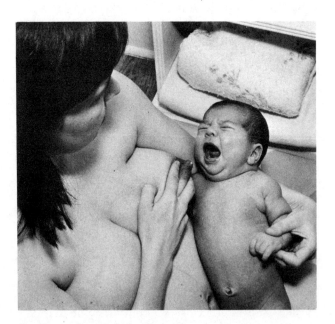

Compress breast behind areola.

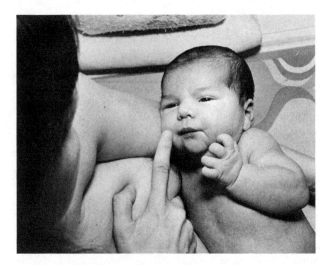

Stroking cheek stimulates baby's rooting reflex.

free hand, gently compress the breast tissue just behind the areola so you are introducing a soft, flattened rectangle into the baby's mouth rather than trying to push a mass of soft, rounded tissue into a basically rectangular opening.

- If the baby is paying attention to something else, keep holding the breast as before, but just lift a finger to stroke the baby's cheek that's closer to the offered breast—don't tickle, don't poke, just keep moving the finger up and down next to the corner of the baby's mouth, and soon that stimulus will trigger the baby's rooting reflex, so s/he will turn toward the finger and inadvertently discover the breast.
- Be prepared for a mighty tug and some chomping at first as baby gets the feel of drawing fluid from the breast.
- Check to be sure the baby is taking in almost all the areola during suckling, otherwise baby will be obtaining little nourishment, and your nipples will soon become raw and cracked from being vigorously nibbled.
- Keep nursing until your placenta separates by itself (in most cases ten minutes or so). This is the best way to prevent retained placental fragments which are so common after manual removal of the placenta or a "trapped" placenta that can happen when the placenta shears off all at once due to a too-strong uterine contraction (caused by the after-birth hormone injection).

Right from the Start

82

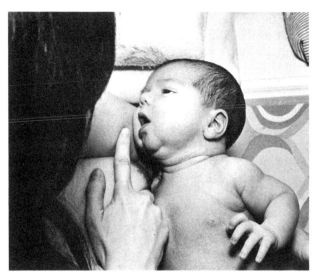

Baby turns toward stimulus.

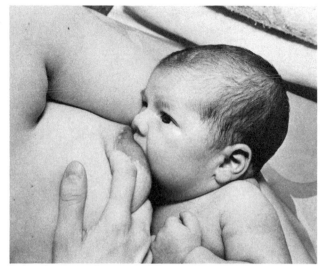

Baby discovers breast and begins suckling.

- If your baby urinates, don't be upset: you'll soon be showering off, anyway, and it's a sign that all is well with the baby's urinary tract—incidentally, urine itself is a sterile fluid and that of babies getting enough to drink is very dilute.
- Apgar ratings and almost all other necessary procedures can be carried out while you are holding your baby. Should you need to have an episiotomy repair, baby can be transferred to father's arms for continued cuddling.
- Silver nitrate can be withheld until the family hour is over. As a result of all the recent discoveries about the undrugged newborn's ability to see at birth and the importance of direct eye contact between mother and child, a great controversy now rages over the treating of babies' eyes with silver nitrate or similar preparations, such as premixed Argyrol (preferred in some hospitals since it can't be mixed in too strong a concentration inadvertently). These preparations, used to combat gonococcal conjunctivitis (which can cause blindness), are presumed to blur the baby's vision.

Since it is virtually impossible to prove that you *don't* have gonorrhea, and since the consequences for your baby's vision are so important, we feel *delaying* the silver nitrate or Argyrol rather than *eliminating* it to be the wiser choice. Our rationale:

1. Gonorrhea produces no early symptoms in 80 percent of women who have actually contracted the disease.
2. Pregnancy does not protect you from contracting gonorrhea from an infected individual—in fact, due to the increased alkalinity of the vagina during pregnancy, you may be more susceptible than at any other time except when on birth control pills.
3. The cervix is the most common site of infection—and, of course, it is through the cervix that the baby must pass in order to be born.
4. The gram stain method of testing women for gonorrhea is practically worthless, since other organisms in the vagina can easily mask the gonococcal bacteria.
5. The culture test, while more accurate, requires 16 to 48 hours under controlled laboratory conditions for the bacteria to multiply, making it of no value if you've thought about asking to be checked for gonorrhea upon admission to the hospital in labor—by the time the test comes back you may already have left the hospital with your new baby.
6. If you have your baby at home and decide to forgo eye drops, take special care in checking the baby's eyes for the first three to five days, and take the baby to a clinic or doctor's office imme-

The First Breath: Transitional Care

diately at the first sign of any unusual discharge. (See chapter 8.)

7. If the baby does contract gonorrhea, s/he will have to stay in the hospital or be returned to the hospital nursery for close supervision until the disease is cured, not a happy situation for the family that values close contact between mother and baby throughout the early weeks.

This is one instance where an ounce of prevention is truly better than a pound of cure.

Taking care of you and your baby in the manner we've been describing obviously constitutes a major departure from delivery room practices that have become entrenched in most hospitals over the past 50 years. For your quick reference, a Newborn Care Preferences sheet covering the immediate postpartum period and the time you spend in the hospital or birth center is included in chapter 5. It should assist you in discussing your care plan with medical care providers in advance of the birth and, if signed by your obstetrician and pediatrician and attached as part of your official prenatal care chart, can help insure cooperation on the part of other hospital personnel.

If you can't find a hospital in your area that makes these provisions for family bonding and subsequent care of mother and baby as an ongoing unit, you should write your requests and mail them to the hospital administrators with a copy to your local childbirth education organization (which is able to provide in-service workshops for hospital workers). Enclose with your letter the recently approved "Joint Position Statement of the Development of Family-Centered Maternity/Newborn Care in Hospitals." (Copies available from: ACOG, One East Wacker Drive, Suite 2700, Chicago, IL 60601.) Formulated by an Interprofessional Task Force on Health Care of Women and Children, the report has been endorsed by the American College of Obstetricians and Gynecologists (ACOG), the American Academy of Pediatrics, the American College of Nurse-Midwives, the American Nurses' Association, the Nurses' Association of ACOG, and the American Hospital Association. It "urges all interested hospitals to form committees, composed of physicians, nurses, and other health professionals and members of the community to develop and implement family-centered care programs," while also offering a description of recommended program

components as "general guidelines to be adapted to local needs and desires" by individual institutions. Volunteer to serve on your hospital's committee as a community member.

The recommendations include:

- participation by father or another person of the mother's choosing during labor and birth, and postpartum;
- flexible rooming-in to encourage "maximum desired mother/infant contact, especially during the first 24 hours";
- sibling visitation in a special family room if the mother elects to remain in the hospital;
- encouraging mothers to breastfeed;
- offering an optional early discharge plan.

The statement also notes, realistically we feel, that the major change in hospital practices needed to make these programs work is an "attitudinal" one. Before being swept away with enthusiasm for this enlightened statement, however, let's remember that activists in the childbirth reform movement have been pressing for these changes for 20 years. Without being cynical, it's also important to recognize that this new flurry of concern for "family-centered maternity care" has arisen in direct proportion to the growing number of home births and out-of-hospital birthing facilities being established across the country. In your own area, you will have to be the judge of how strong and sincere your local hospitals' commitment to these precepts truly is. The important thing is not what appears on a position paper, but what services actually become available to the childbearing public.

Without advance preparations or formal agreements, unfortunately, you and your baby are likely to be placed on the delivery room assembly line. According to that time-worn routine, you can expect to be processed like this:

- As soon as your baby's head is born, a bulb syringe is inserted into the baby's mouth and nasal passages "to clear out mucus"— this may be necessary for babies who are heavily sedated due to medications given their mothers during labor, but the unmedicated baby whose mother is in a semi-upright position has its mucus drained by a combination of pressure from the vaginal walls and assistance from gravity. Another point: too vigorous suctioning can cause hemorrhage of delicate mucous membranes or stimulate the vagus nerve leading to a reduced heart rate or cause the baby to suck in, thus forcing a plug of mucus far down into the lungs—exactly what suctioning is supposed to prevent!

- The umbilical cord is cut within 30 seconds after birth, so baby does not obtain all the blood from the placenta that is rightfully a part of the baby's blood supply and is critically needed to perfuse the newly functioning bronchial tree—this may create breathing problems in the neonatal period.
- The delivery room is kept at approximately 65°F, theoretically to inhibit the growth of staphylococcus bacteria, but far too cold for your comfort and a tremendous shock to the baby's system which has been accustomed to your 98.6°F. This also contributes to excess heat loss in the newborn, the major factor in rushing the baby to the newborn nursery as soon as possible for temperature stabilization in an isolette.
- The full complement of operating room lights will be turned on, blinding both you and the baby. An alternative: focus needed extra light on the attendant's work space, but keep the rest of the room dim or at everyday illumination levels.
- Your first look at your baby may be as s/he is being hung by the feet ("to drain mucus") which suddenly snaps the child's spine straight (it has been curled for months) with the full weight of the heavy head exerting undue traction on the baby's delicate neck—is it any wonder the infant howls in protest?
- If the baby is slow to breathe, the attendant may slap the buttocks, back, or feet. If that doesn't do it, a tube will be introduced through the mouth, down the windpipe, and into the lungs, and resuscitation begins. (Laws require the presence of resuscitation equipment as standard equipment in delivery rooms everywhere; David C. Abramson, M.D., director of nurseries at Georgetown University Hospital, Washington, D.C., estimates that approximately 15 percent of all newborns are "noticeably distressed" in the delivery room.)
- In some institutions, the baby's stomach contents are routinely suctioned out via a tube inserted through the nose, down the back of the throat, and into the stomach—the rationale: since mothers have been sedated, the baby's reflexes are likely to be depressed, so, if the baby vomits, gastric secretions may be aspirated into the lungs.
- The baby will be given a quick wipe-off (in some places with a paper towel) to "get rid of the unattractive vernix and blood," held up briefly for the mother to see, then placed naked on an open tray with radiant heat source above.
- The nurse then inserts silver nitrate drops in the baby's eyes, gives a quick visual inspection for major defects, inks the baby's feet and your thumb for identification on charts, and attaches ID bracelets to baby's wrist and ankle to match yours.

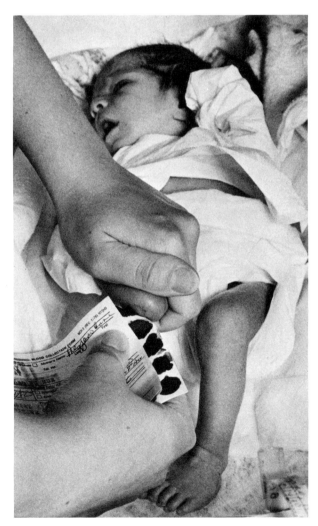

Taking footprints.

The First Breath: Transitional Care

- The baby is then wrapped, placed in a wheeled cart, and whisked away to the nursery where s/he will remain for anywhere from 4 to 12 hours before being brought to you for a reunion.

Clearly, this form of handling, while providing plenty of sensory stimulation, violates the baby's basic need and inborn expectation for *pleasurable* stimulation. It seems especially unwise in light of the critical physiologic adaptations happening at this time.

Mother and baby deserve to be cared for as a continuing biological and social unit just after birth, in the early hours after birth, and for weeks and months thereafter. After the birth has been accomplished, knowledgeable family members and friends can usually provide this care in the comfort and security of the parents' own home, far better than institutional routines set up, for the most part, for the convenience of the hospital staff. For this reason, when mother and baby are healthy, more parents today decide to leave the hospital hours after birth, rather than days later.

Right from the Start

Chapter 5

The Early Hours
Coordinated Care

Scene: A Newborn Nursery in a typical community hospital. Plastic cradles on wheeled metal stands are lined up in neat rows. A shelf beneath each cradle holds disposable diapers, disposable plastic-backed sheets, blankets, shirts, washcloths, liquid soap, baby lotion, formula and water bottles, and a thermometer. Everything looks neat, clean, and efficient. Then the scene starts to roll.

Breakfast is over, and the babies have just returned from being fed by their mothers. A nurse and an aide are busy diapering their charges and noting what the babies have produced. Some of the babies are sleeping contentedly, but it appears many of them feel that their breakfast was inadequate. The crying would disturb most outsiders, but the nurses continue to work with no apparent strain. They give the irritable babies sugar water or a pacifier.

As the pandemonium subsides, enter Delivery Room Nurse, pushing a glass box on wheels. In the box is Baby Boy Brown, newly delivered from his mother, Mrs. Darlene Brown. Baby's occasional cries are muffled by the cover on the box. Air enters through vents in the sides. Traces of dried blood and vernix cover his face, and two purplish bruises extend from his temples to his jaw. He is swaddled in towels marked Delivery Room. Nursery Nurse enters, lifts the cover of the box, and unwraps the towels.

Nursery Nurse: You're really busy back there today.

Delivery Room Nurse: Our third boy this shift. The new students will have enough circs [circumcisions; see chapter 7] to keep all of them happy.

Nursery Nurse (gathering papers): Is he okay?

Delivery Room Nurse: Sleepy and a little blue, but breathing. You know how much energy it takes them to get born.

Nursery Nurse: Well, he'll get plenty of rest here. Two aides called in sick. Luckily he won't need much after I get him admitted. Okay, let's check him in. Mother's name?

Delivery Room Nurse: Darlene Brown.

Nursery Nurse: Check. Mother's admission number?

Delivery Room Nurse: 7704228163.

Nursery Nurse: Check. Sex?

Delivery Room Nurse: Male.

Nursery Nurse: Check. Obstetrician?

Delivery Room Nurse: Dr. Mehdi.

Nursery Nurse: Check. Pediatrician?

Delivery Room Nurse: Dr. Varga.

Nursery Nurse: Check. Hour of birth?

Delivery Room Nurse: 0945.

Nursery Nurse: Check. Footprints?

Delivery Room Nurse: Here.

Nursery Nurse: Thanks. Apgar?

Delivery Room Nurse: Six at one minute, nine at five.

Nursery Nurse: Check. Silver nitrate?

Delivery Room Nurse: Done.

Nursery Nurse: Check. Void?

Admitted to Nursery 7/6   Time 10:05 AM

Bracelets, sex, and weight checked with   Owens   By Harris

Date	Time	Nurses Notes
7/6	10:30 A	Baby boy Brown admitted to newborn nursery at 10:05 A
		after NSVD at 9:45A. Length 19½" weight 7'8" head 13"
		chest 13½" rectal temp. 96.8°. apical P 128 Resp 40
		Vit K given IM. Forceps marks noted bilateral.
		Birthmark noted - size of quarter on left side below waist.
		Umbilical cord moist, no oozing. Clamp tight.
		Color mottled. No abnormal molding. Mucusy, suctioned
		10cc, clear. Meconium passed in nursery - due to void.
		Placed in infant warmer in no apparent distress.
		Dr. Vargas office notified.
	10:45 A	Admission bath given. Tolerated well. Color, cry,
		respiration, activity good. Condition of cord good.
		Placed in open cradle.
		D. Harris RN

DATE   Discharge Physical Done By   PKU Done   Date

Condition

Bracelets checked and removed by   Discharged to

Date   Time   By

Nurse's nursery admission chart.

Delivery Room Nurse: No.

Nursery Nurse: Check. Meconium?

Delivery Room Nurse: No.

Nursery Nurse (She quickly looks Baby over; he sneezes and shivers.): Heavy mucus there. Forceps marks noted.

Delivery Room Nurse: Right. The junior resident tried first.

Nursery Nurse: Of course. Feeding method?

Delivery Room Nurse: All of Dr. Varga's babies are put on the bottle. I don't think she's the breast-feeding type, anyway.

Nursery Nurse (pointing to stretcher being wheeled down the hall with snoring figure on it): Is that the mother?

Delivery Room Nurse: Yes. She'll get plenty of rest. Dr. Mehdi always gives them enough to sleep through the first day.

Nursery Nurse: Well, thanks. Hope we don't see too much of you this shift. (Delivery Room Nurse leaves.)

Nursery Nurse (to Baby): Okay, let's get your vital statistics. (Lifts Baby out of cradle by ankles and holds against tape measure. Baby hangs, unresistant.) Stretch out there, Baby, will you? Got to be accurate. Nineteen and a half. (She lays the baby down on a table and places the tape measure around his chest and then around his head.) Chest 13½, head 13. Okay, let's get your weight. (As she puts Baby on scale he starts to move, making it difficult for her to read the numbers.) Seven pounds, eight ounces. Biggest this week! (She puts him back in the cradle. He starts to tremble and shriek. She goes to her work table and prepares an injection of vitamin K.) That's a good baby, exercise your lungs. (She wipes his thigh with alcohol and injects the medication.) There! Now we can circ you without you bleeding all over the place. (She places a stethoscope on his chest and listens intently, counting his breaths and looking at her watch at the same time.) Apical pulse 128, respirations 40. Okay, now what's your temp? (She places a thermometer in Baby's rectum, removing it several minutes later. It is followed by a stream of thick, tarry, greenish black stool.) Couldn't you wait until I got your diaper on at least? (She cleans the thermometer and reads it.) Only 96.8. Better get you warmed up a bit. (She wipes off the meconium and puts him, naked, into a warming cradle. She places him on his side and props him up with a rolled blanket. She fiddles with the dials. She looks Baby over very quickly, checking that his cord clamp is secure and noting a small, dark birth-

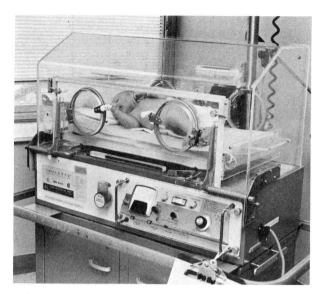

Baby in temperature-controlled isolette.

mark on his left side. Leaving the infant care area, she sits down at her desk and begins to write her admission note. She calls the pediatrician and then goes in to help the two aides who are struggling to feed all the babies who are not allowed out on the floor to be fed by their mothers. This includes three babies born by Cesarean, two babies in phototherapy treatment [see chapter 6], and four babies whose mothers have elevated temperatures. She passes the infant warmer containing Baby. He is sleeping, and has gone from a mottled blue color to a warm-looking red. He trembles and sneezes as if on cue.) Mucus bothering you? (She gets a bulb syringe, opens the warmer, and proceeds to suction Baby's nose and mouth. The warmer is still turned on.) Gee, it's noisy in there! It's a wonder you can get any sleep. (The phone rings. She closes the warmer and goes to answer it.) Newborn Nursery, Charge Nurse speaking. (It is Dr. Varga's secretary. Dr. Varga will be at the nursery at 11:00 A.M. to examine Baby. He will be meeting three of the third-year medical students there to teach them newborn assessment.)

Well, Baby, you're getting your first visitors. Better get you cleaned up for them. (She prepares an open cradle for Baby. It is made up with a cotton sheet covered by a disposable plastic-backed sheet. She spreads a blanket in the cradle, lays out a shirt and disposable diaper, and gathers up liquid soap, baby lotion, alcohol wipes, washcloth, and towels. She wraps Baby in a towel and carries him, as she was trained to, in the classic football carry,

The Early Hours: Coordinated Care

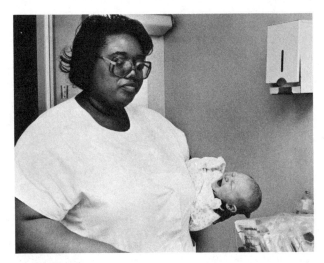

Football carry.

his head in her palm and his body balanced on her hip. She starts the water and tests the temperature. As she washes him she checks his body for abnormalities.) Okay, Baby, eyes, ears, nose, face all normal. Those forceps marks will fade soon. (She holds his scalp under the water as she scrubs out the dried blood and vernix.) Lots of hair, lots of vernix. (She washes this protective coating, *vernix caseosa,* from Baby's neck and chest.) Ten fingers, ten toes, you've got everything you need. (She starts to wash his genitals, retracts his foreskin, and he voids.) Well, you won't have to worry about that being done too many more times. (She finishes his bath, wipes his cord area with alcohol, dresses him, and puts him in the waiting cradle. She returns to her desk to chart the bath. Enter Dr. Varga with his entourage of medical students.)

Dr. Varga: Nurse!

Nursery Nurse: This way, Doctor. (She brings him to the examining area where several babies are waiting. Dr. Varga proceeds to teach the students the basics of newborn assessment. (Dr. Varga and students leave to make pediatric rounds. Nurse rediapers Baby, who is crying and has passed more meconium during the newborn exam. She wraps him in blanket and places him back in his cradle. Baby falls asleep after crying for 15 more minutes. Nurse is busy reviewing hand-washing procedures with a group of student nurses assigned to the nursery today for the first time. Three more babies are admitted to the unit during the next two hours while Baby sleeps fitfully.) *Nursery Nurse* (to students): Time to get everybody ready to visit Mama! Diaper your babies and wrap them firmly.

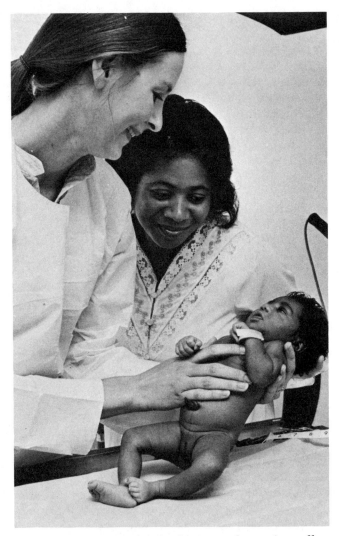

Mother and midwife checking newborn (overall appearance).

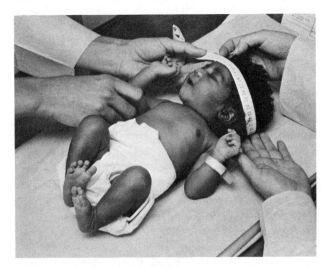

Measuring head circumference.

Right from the Start

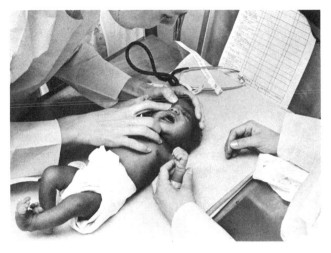

Checking eyes for evidence of jaundice.

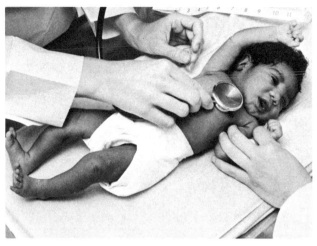

Listening to lungs and heartbeat.

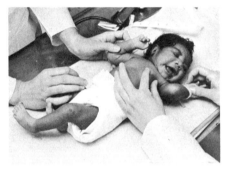

Feeling degree of breast engorgement (due to maternal hormones—swelling gradually recedes).

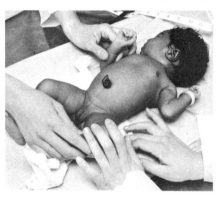

Checking cord for possible bleeding.

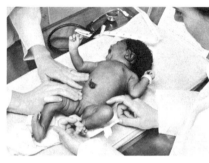

Palpating abdomen to locate internal organs.

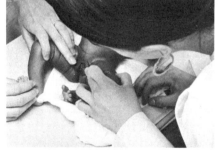

Determining sex organs.

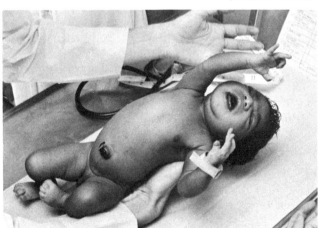

Above and bottom right, *Moro (startle) reflex (when suddenly without support, baby flings arms apart, then together).*

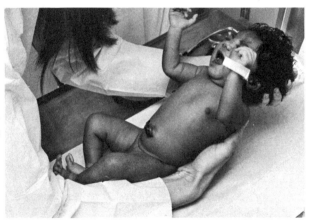

The Early Hours: Coordinated Care

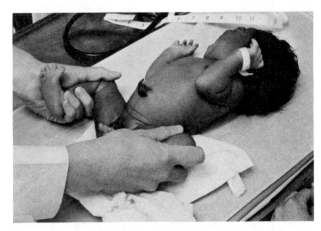

Checking for hip dislocation.

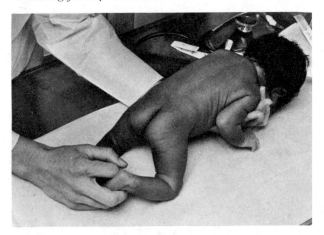

Checking spinal alignment.

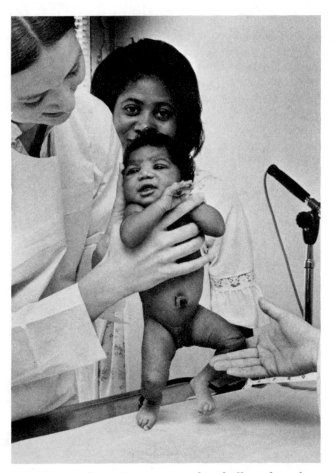

Stepping reflex (when supported and allowed to place soles of feet on a surface, baby lifts and drops knees).

Place a bottle of the appropriate formula in the lower left-hand corner of the cradle and a burp towel across the baby's chest.

First Student Nurse: My baby's cradle card says "Breast"; what am I supposed to do?

Nursery Nurse: Send a bottle of glucose 5 percent out with the baby. You can give the formula when the baby comes back—check Dr. Varga's orders in the order book. Place two alcohol wipes in the cradle and have the mother wipe each nipple with one after she washes her hands. This is her third feeding, so tell her she's allowed to nurse four minutes on each side this time. Check your watch to make sure she doesn't go over. Don't want her to overdo it. You'll find that the breastfeeders always take more of your time.

Second Student Nurse: What about these in the corner?

Nursery Nurse: Their mothers have temperatures above 100.6°F. You can feed them when you get back. Don't take too long chatting. (Student Nurses

wheel babies out and down the halls. Nurse picks up Baby Boy Brown, who is making loud smacking noises and squirming in his blanket.)

Nursery Nurse (inserting nipple of glucose bottle into Baby's mouth): Here, I know what you need. (Baby licks nipple, grimaces, and Nurse reinserts it.) Come on now, don't be a fusspot. This is the only flavor we have today. (Baby takes a few half-hearted sucks.) Guess you're really not hungry yet. We'll try again in a few hours. (She checks diaper, rewraps Baby, and places him back in the cradle.) (Student Nurses return, eager to feed the remaining babies.)

Nursery Nurse: Make sure to wash your hands. Don't spend a lot of extra time playing with the babies. We have to get them all ready for showing during visiting hours. (Student Nurses diaper babies, then stand around feeding them. There's only one rocking chair in the nursery and the Head Nurse is sitting in it writing charts.)

Nursery Nurse: Remember to burp them after

Right from the Start

every ounce! (Student Nurses check diapers and change the soiled ones.)

Nursery Nurse: Now, place babies on their sides and cover them with a pink or blue blanket. Tuck it in firmly all around so it looks neat. Put the ones who just came in up front. Nobody's seen them yet. (Student Nurses arrange the cradles in rows, and Nursery Nurse murmurs approval while raising the shades covering the plate glass window. Five anxious relatives are already assembled waiting to get a peek. Mr. Brown arrives a few minutes later after trying unsuccessfully to rouse his wife who is still groggy from the anesthesia used at birth. He motions through the window to one of the Student Nurses, asking her to hold the baby up so he can get a better look, but she gestures back that it's against the rules. He looks at the baby a few more minutes, then turns resignedly to spend some more time with his wife.)

These scenes are played out roughly ten thousand times a day in hospitals across the United States. They vary so little from place to place that anyone trained in newborn nursing could easily report for work in a different unit every day for years and be able to fit right in, competently processing the little charges as they are deposited at the door. A factory efficiency expert's dream, the repetitiveness, uniformity, and orderliness make it simple to keep track of the work accomplished (and charting details is a big part of the work load). This system also facilitates unlimited interchangeability of caretakers with little effect on the quality of service provided. Interactions with the babies are routinized as well, making it possible for one nurse to see to the elementary physical needs of a dozen or so infants.

All these facets contribute to making the newborn nursery one of the most cost-effective operations in the modern hospital. But is cost-effectiveness an appropriate measure of its desirability? What are the short- and long-term consequences of denying our infants personal care in the days after birth?

Dr. Betty Lozoff and co-workers state in the *Journal of Pediatrics* (91: 1–12, 1977), "There is no medical reason why healthy mothers and babies should not be together from the time of birth to the time of discharge from the hospital." Yet, in the United States today, there comes a time when almost every one of us is compelled by hospital policy to surrender our baby to the care of strangers. No matter how well we have been prepared for labor, birth, and the immediate postpartum period, nothing can adequately ready us for the moment when someone in charge officially declares that we are no longer personally necessary to our babies—that, in fact, we and they are two distinct entities best cared for by two sets of workers in segregated facilities. Two decades of research documenting the deleterious impact of separation on mother and infant suggest that re-evaluation of this nearly universal practice is long overdue.

The central newborn nursery came into being as "scientific" childbirth supplanted social childbirth in the teens and twenties of this century. Richard and Dorothy Wertz discuss in detail the medical and cultural reasons for the shift from home to hospital confinement in their book, *Lying In: A History of Childbirth in America* (New York: Free Press–Macmillan, 1977). A comparison of characteristics of the two modes of birth presents a pretty strong case in favor of central nurseries as childbirth for a variety of reasons became organized on a disease care model.

Ironically, the more "scientific" childbirth became in the name of preventing life-threatening complications, the more sickening and debilitating it turned out to be for mother and baby. Most often, as the result of needless "standard procedures," neither mother nor baby was up to any socializing for two or three days after the birth. Instead of a period of "lying-in" at home to rest, regain strength, initiate nursing, and become acquainted with her new child while family and friends took over the responsibility of running her household, women delivered "scientifically" faced the prospect of two or three weeks of hospitalization in a slow, agonizing "recovery" from their "illness" which their doctor had "cured" by means of surgery. Under these conditions, the baby is an enormous drain on the mother's strength and may even be identified as the cause of her suffering.

On the other side of the coin, the mothers were commonly viewed with suspicion by the nursery staff as potential carriers of infection to their "sterile" babies. Though the hospital stay has been considerably shortened (probably due more to economic considerations than to the wishes of doctors or hospital administrators seeking to keep their occupancy rates high), the attitudes of this bygone era linger, conditioning the care available to us and our infants in the days after birth.

Today's central nursery may actually be a series of holding rooms through which the newborn is promoted as certain developmental landmarks are reached. In a large institution, there may be one room for the babies less than one day old, one for premature babies or others whose weights require that they be fed more often than the standard every 4 hours, a "suspect" nursery for "unsterile" babies born outside the hospital walls and for babies whose mothers' membranes were ruptured more than 24 hours prior to delivery, a special unit for babies born addicted to their mothers' drug habits, intensive care units for babies with serious medical problems, an observation area for babies born by Cesarean, and some space for the leftovers—the healthy babies who require "minimal" nursing care. And that's exactly what they get.

As any woman who has ever had a new baby to take care of will tell you, she spends at least a half-hour every 1½ to 2 hours breastfeeding, changing, and playing with her child. In the central nursery, however, the baby is lucky to get a half-hour of attention out of each 8-hour shift. The reason: the 1-to-12 ratio of nurses or aides to newborns makes it impossible to give anything but a modicum of care to each. To individualize care under these circumstances would throw the nursery into chaos. The solution: accustom each baby to the 4-hour feeding schedule and refuse to make exceptions even when babies cry out for more contact. Then justify the wailing with the rationalization that babies *need* to cry in order to keep their lungs in good working order.

Out of the 15 minutes allotted to each baby for feeding, time must also be taken to weigh, cleanse, diaper, and burp the baby, then change wet bedding. An additional requirement is a minute or two set aside to chart everything the baby did during the contact period: number of ounces taken; number of wet diapers; color, consistency, and amount of stool; condition of rash; and quality of cry. On the late-night shift when few babies (even those who are perfectly well) are taken to their mothers for feeding and staffing is reduced below that of the day and evening shifts, it's no wonder many harried nurses resort to propping bottles for slow eaters, even though this practice is generally frowned upon by nursing administration.

Like so many other first-time mothers, we went along with the routines, all the while trying to ignore the nagging worries we had about our babies' safety and our simple curiosity about what they were doing in the nursery at any given moment. When we reported to the nurses that the baby had been fussing the whole time we were trying to breastfeed, we believed them when they purred, "That's odd—s/he's so good in the nur-

sery." We knew there must be something wrong with *us*, with the way *we* did things, that made our babies so unhappy. Only after having other babies did we finally realize that our real mistake was in letting other people take care of them.

It was hard to challenge the doctrine that anonymous, hired experts were better for our babies in the early days after birth than we were, but talking over our experiences with other mothers and analyzing what made us and our babies feel better eventually forced us to that conclusion—all without benefit of scholarly research into the question. As with so many other topics we later investigated for this book, the research merely served to confirm what mothers everywhere already had observed and responded to in their own infants.

If the skin is the most important sensory organ for picking up stimuli from the environment and transmitting them to the brain for appropriate response, one cannot help but be moved to pity for the newborn confined in an isolette. If an adult were subjected to similar treatment, cries would be heard from all quarters against this "cruel and unusual punishment." Myron A. Hofer, M.D., of the Department of Psychiatry, Albert Einstein Hospital, New York, writing in *Biological Psychiatry* (10: 149–53, 1975), concludes that the damaging effects of early separation of the baby from its mother are the effects of sudden loss of a primary source of information about the outside world. Experiments with sensory deprivation in humans show that people can keep functioning when they experience loss of sight, smell, or hearing; however, a loss of skin stimulation results in rapid degeneration of their physical as well as emotional health. In the newborn such important functions as respiration, heart rate, temperature regulation, and neuromuscular coordination are directly affected by the amount and appropriateness of tactile stimulation.

The philosopher Bertrand Russell remarked over 50 years ago that it is our sense of touch that gives us our sense of reality. Babies separated from their mothers, then, presumably experience a primitive, all-engulfing terror—a feeling of being permanently cut off from all familiar sensations with no way of comprehending that the situation is temporary. Dr. Selma Fraiberg, the University of Michigan child psychotherapist, states in *Every Child's Birthright: In Defense of Mothering* (New York: Basic Books, 1977) that this separation anxiety returns in waves in later life whenever the child is removed from human companionship. The common problem of getting infants and older children off to sleep at night is an example of how this early anxiety experience may complicate daily life long after the newborn period.

Fraiberg also worries about the effects of indifferent caretaking on the child's ability to form enduring attachments. Though writing primarily about older children who are being "stored" in day-care facilities, which she finds inadequate in the extreme, her concerns seem relevant to the care of infants in central nurseries. "All love, even in later life, begins with a feeling of exclusiveness," she writes, and "a human infant has within him all the human capabilities for profound and enduring attachments and the full gamut of emotions which we read as signs of love and loss." The formation of a primary human bond, she observes, "including love for a partner, normally takes place, without psychiatric consultation, in ordinary homes and with ordinary babies, during the first year of life."

Fraiberg's answer to the problem echoes that of other researchers in human development: "The diseases of nonattachment can be eradicated at the source by ensuring stable human partnerships for every baby. If we take the evidence seriously we must look upon a baby deprived of human partners as a baby in deadly peril. This is a baby who is being robbed of his humanity. . . . Strong bonds are formed only when there are human partners to provide satisfaction of the baby's biological and social needs through feeding, play, comfort, sensory, and motor experience." It seems only logical to initiate this program at birth.

In the early days after birth, the infant tries to integrate functional responses to the bewildering array of incoming stimuli. Intermittent handling unrelated to the infant's signals of needing attention (primarily crying) subverts these fledgling efforts. The result: behavior that is disorganized and unpredictable. Hofer of Albert Einstein Hospital notes in another article, "Physiological and Behavioral Processes in Early Maternal Deprivation" (in *Physiology, Emotion and Psychosomatic Illness*, D. Hill, ed., London: Elsevier, 1972), "It would seem that the separation experience in an unfamiliar environment initially leads to a state of increased excitability which normal mothering tends to regulate."

Babies tended in the conventional hospital manner display disruption of sleep-wake cycles; resistance to calming by rocking, stroking, or carry-

ing; increased digestive problems (vomiting, malabsorption, colic, diarrhea/constipation); and delayed developmental skills (holding head up, visual tracking, hand-mouth coordination). Sound like what we've heard described as "normal" newborn behavior? While this behavior may be typical, it is decidedly *not* normal. It merely reflects the impersonal, insensitive, automatic handling most infants receive in hospital nurseries.

The old idea that the central nursery is a protective sanctuary where the infant is kept safe from infection, chilling, mucus problems, and overexhaustion is being challenged by professionals who work there. These four considerations, plus those of jaundice and feeding, are the major reasons given for keeping babies out of their mothers' care during the first few days after birth. Unfortunately, as Betty Cahill's article, "The Neonatal Nurse Specialist—New Techniques for the Asymptomatic Newborn" (*Journal of Obstetric, Gynecologic and Neonatal Nursing*, January/February 1974) points out, the system of care in the conventional central nursery often engenders these problems instead of preventing them!

In the early hours after birth, for instance, routine care encourages heat loss by:

- wrapping the infant in blankets during transfer from delivery room to nursery in unheated isolette;
- giving sponge bath in open air before the infant has stabilized his or her own body temperature;
- failing to observe the infant at frequent intervals to identify persistent subnormal body temperature;
- wrapping the infant in blankets so that visual signs of chilling (periods of no breathing, skin turning blue, sluggish activity) are obscured;
- failing to assess the gestational age of each baby, so that some babies who appear to be of normal weight but are actually immature and in need of more frequent feeding and closer monitoring of temperature, go on to develop hypoglycemia and excess weight loss as they use up their energy stores trying to maintain their body temperatures.

Avoiding these mistakes with the baby born at home or taken home hours after birth is a prime function of the birth attendant.

Two other conditions in babies that contribute

The Early Hours: Coordinated Care

to practices some parents find objectionable are hemorrhagic disease of the newborn and jaundice. Hemorrhagic disease of the newborn results when the lowered prothrombin levels in the baby's bloodstream (see chapter 3) cause bleeding. An injection of vitamin K is given to newborns as a routine preventive measure. Researchers around the world report widely varying incidence of the condition, ranging from 1 in 100 infants to 1 in 400 to 500. Interestingly, early papers in the field from the 1930s and 1940s remark about the higher rate of the disease among premature and underweight-at-term babies. Later investigators, however, commonly fail to make this important distinction, writing about the problem and describing it statistically as though all babies are subject to the same risk of developing it. Parents have even been told that all babies *invariably* suffer hemorrhagic disease unless the vitamin K injection is given soon after birth to restore the clotting time of the baby's blood to normal!

Many parents wonder if the injection is really necessary, if there are forms of the vitamin that could be administered in some other way (such as by mouth), and if there are possible side effects of the vitamin K itself. Given what we've already learned about what babies have to endure in standard hospital nurseries, an injection of vitamin K seems to make little difference one way or the other for most babies. However, these questions are interesting because they prompt us once again to examine the idea that "all babies are alike at birth" and, so, are best handled uniformly.

Human beings obtain vitamin K two ways: from a limited number of foods which contain it and from our own intestines where it is synthesized in response to the presence of foodstuffs. There are two naturally occurring forms of vitamin K, both of which are fat-soluble. K_1 was first isolated from alfalfa in 1939 by Henrik Dam, a Danish biochemist. K_2, only 60 percent as potent as K_1, is the form manufactured in the intestine. Vitamin K_3 (menadione) is a water-soluble, synthetic product available for giving by injection in liquid form or orally in tablet form.

The amount of vitamin K required in human nutrition is unknown, but since large amounts are excreted in feces it seems reasonable to conclude that adults synthesize far more than they need. Small amounts of vitamin K are stored in the liver where it serves as a catalyst in the manufacture of prothrombin and other clotting factors. Vitamin K crosses the placenta, so the well-nourished mother's diet should provide adequate stores in the liver of the unborn baby. In order to be absorbed into the bloodstream, K_1 and K_2 require the presence of bile salts in the intestine.

At birth, your baby has plenty of bile salts to assist in vitamin K metabolism. These substances are responsible for the green color of the contents of the newborn's bowel (meconium). However, since the baby's intestinal tract is sterile until food has been taken, independent synthesis of vitamin K is nil. On the other hand, the liver of the full-term, full-size, healthy neonate should contain stored vitamin K sufficient to meet the baby's needs until the intestinal flora can begin to function.

One reads throughout the literature on this subject that breastfed infants are more prone to developing hemorrhagic disease than those fed cow's milk formulas. (Cow's milk contains a much higher concentration of vitamin K than human milk.) One would expect this to be so; since calves weigh so much more at birth than human offspring their needs for the vitamin would be proportionately greater. Rather than insist that all babies receive a first feeding of cow's milk formula in the nursery (a standard practice for years regardless of whether the mother planned to breastfeed), or require that all babies receive vitamin K by injection, why not make sure that every pregnant woman has adequate sources of vitamin K in her diet so that the first secretion in her breasts (colostrum) will be rich in it?

We are increasingly impatient with studies purportedly telling us what's in "breast milk," as though it were a standard formulation manufactured by the breasts independent of the individual mother's nutritional intake. It is well established that when a mother eats foods high in certain nutrients, the level of these nutrients rises in her milk. By the same token, when her diet fails to provide adequate amounts, they are in scanty supply in her milk.

Human milk is not a miracle food or a miracle drug that appears after birth in just the right proportions for individual babies. It is a highly variable, complex substance which varies widely in its chemical composition from woman to woman. It is, therefore, unscientific and misleading to discuss its "nutritional value" apart from recognition of the nutritional status of the mother producing it. Consequently, we don't buy the idea that all human milk is low in vitamin K. What seems more likely is that many women simply do not eat adequate amounts of foods containing vitamin K, so their milk reflects this deficiency.

What to do about your own diet to obtain adequate vitamin K for yourself and the needs of your baby? Eat generously of the best food sources: alfalfa (use sprouts in salads and as a garnish on sandwiches or mixed in with tuna or egg salad), cabbage, spinach, kale, and cauliflower. Lesser amounts are available in tomatoes, cheese, egg yolk, and liver. Carrots, yeast, and wheat germ also contain small amounts. A daily salad containing a selection of these foods raw, plus one serving as a cooked vegetable, would go far toward meeting your goal, since the vitamin K_1 contained in foods is so much more active than the K_2 we synthesize.

Some writers have suggested a vitamin K supplement for pregnant women to be taken during the last month of pregnancy, but it seems to us eating food is much more enjoyable. Attempts have been made to administer vitamin K by injection to women in labor, but without remarkable success. It probably takes longer than a few hours for necessary amounts of the vitamin to cross the placenta and be stored in the baby's liver—and during labor that organ may be under exceptional stress if it must work to detoxify the baby's system of any drugs given to the mother during labor and birth.

Another factor contributing to the onset of hemorrhagic disease is the routine fasting of newborns for the first 4 to 12 hours after birth and, for the next two feedings, giving nothing but water or glucose water from a bottle. Surely, if there is serious concern for the baby's protection from spontaneous hemorrhage, all babies would be given colostrum within the first hour after birth. In this way the infant would receive not only whatever vitamin K it contains, but also benefit from the intestine-stimulating properties of its proteins and fats. When this is done, and mother and baby have been well nourished throughout pregnancy with respect to vitamin K and all other essential nutrients, the liver stores of vitamin K ought to more than suffice even when the baby does not receive vitamin K by injection.

It should go without saying that the baby should be put to the breast at least every couple hours thereafter to insure that these interdependent systems stay well regulated. This is exactly what happens when mother and baby enjoy a nursing period shortly after birth and subsequently are cared for as a unit in the mother's room for the rest of their hospital stay. In the days when vitamin K was not routinely injected and breastfeeding was restricted to a four-hour schedule, it's easy to see why breastfeeding became targeted as a predisposing factor in hemorrhagic disease of the newborn, when, in fact, nursery routines were contributing far more to its occurrence.

For those who are planning to give birth at home and choose not to administer vitamin K, Dr. David G. Vulliamy, an English pediatrician, describes what to look for as possible signs of hemorrhagic disease of the newborn in his text, *The Newborn Child* (2d ed., Baltimore: Williams and Wilkins, 1967):

- black stool (after the cessation of meconium excretion)—also possible due to maternal blood the baby ingested during birth; a test of the stool will show whether it's from baby or mother, because the baby's blood will have a much higher hemoglobin concentration than an adult's;
- vomiting bright red blood—blood ingested from a sore nipple during breastfeeding may be vomited as streaks of brownish red material;
- bloody discharge from umbilical stump;
- bleeding from circumcision wound;
- bloody urine;
- nosebleed.

These signs typically appear on the second or third day after birth. Though it is highly unlikely that hemorrhagic disease of the newborn will occur in a baby born to a well-nourished mother who initiates breastfeeding soon after birth and continues ad lib, it is one excellent reason for making sure you have good communication with a pediatrician or pediatric nurse practitioner. Contact them immediately if you have any indications that your baby may be in trouble. They will probably ask that you meet them at the emergency room of the local hospital to evaluate the baby and decide whether treatment is necessary.

Treatment depends on the severity of the disease, but usually involves readmission to the hospital for vitamin K injections (usually two injections 12 hours apart) and close observation until the bleeding tendency is brought under control. In severe cases, infusion of frozen plasma and/or a partial transfusion may be necessary to replace blood lost and correct the resulting anemia. Vulliamy notes that normal breastfeeding may be resumed as soon as the baby's condition is stable.

The Early Hours: Coordinated Care

Another consideration in the vitamin K controversy: there is evidence that menadione (vitamin K_3, the synthetic, water-soluble form) can cause neonatal jaundice, the other bete noire of the newborn nursery. As Louis S. Goodman, M.D., and Alfred Gilman, M.D., relate in their reference book, *The Pharmacological Basis of Therapeutics* (5th ed., New York: Macmillan, 1975), "Menadione is excreted in part as a glucuronide and *competes with bilirubin* for a detoxication mechanism of limited capacity in the newborn." In other words, vitamin K_3 causes less bilirubin to be excreted during the period the K_3 is being metabolized, and in some babies this may cause noticeable yellowing. As one might expect, Goodman and Gilman mention that this problem is seen significantly more often in premature and underweight babies whose livers are less functionally mature. In conjunction with other factors, vitamin K injections may be playing a significant role in the upsurge of neonatal jaundice reported here and abroad. Whether this type of jaundice is dangerous and what treatment, if any, should be instituted for it is another area of dispute. (See chapter 6.)

One final consideration looms large in the decision to administer vitamin K. This is routine neonatal circumcision, a procedure which is commonly performed in the hospital anywhere from a few minutes to a few days after birth, well before a baby could make enough vitamin K to deal with the bleeding this surgery causes. (See chapter 7.)

If you should find yourself in a situation where, for valid medical indications, you and your baby must remain in the hospital, you'll need to learn to cope with the hospital as a place to live. As maternity textbooks and written nursing objectives remind us, in the postpartum period the nurses' actions and attitudes are more crucial in determining the daily atmosphere and environment than are those of the doctors. These attitudes are transmitted to us directly and indirectly as long as we remain under medical supervision. Sociological studies such as Nancy Shaw's *Forced Labor: Maternity Care in the United States* (Elmsford, N.Y.: Pergamon Press, 1974) demonstrate that fact.

Rather than fostering feelings of independence, creativity, competence, and confidence, patienthood instead reinforces and rewards dependency, passivity, conformity, and inability to form judgments. Your daily routine, your diet, your medications, your access to friends/baby/family, your physical therapy, even your bathroom/bathing privileges are determined by others. It's easy,

under these circumstances, to start believing that nobody as powerless as yourself could possibly be of any value to a newborn baby.

These feelings are aggravated when professionals indicate that you're just not measuring up to their standard of motherhood. It's awfully hard, remember, to feel effective in caring for a newborn when you've been told the baby can't see you, doesn't need your milk (isn't hungry yet), can't hear a thing you say, has no feelings (poorly developed nervous system), only cries when you're holding him/her, and may be in peril of losing his or her life should you be harboring an infection or fail to notice the baby choking on some mucus.

How to cope when it seems you'll never have a moment to yourself and life "on the outside" seems a vague memory? Herewith a primer of hospital survival strategies. (See chart.)

Hopefully, neither you nor your baby will require prolonged hospitalization (more than a day or two). Instead, the vast majority of postpartum mothers who follow the guidelines for pregnancy and birth provided in this book and the others we've recommended along the way should be prime candidates for an early discharge plan. An example of such a plan was detailed in an article, "Maternity Day Care Program Offers Economical, Family-Oriented Care," in *Hospitals, Journal of the American Hospital Association* (December 1, 1977). Louise Hickey, R.N., and collaborators at the Melrose-Wakefield Hospital (Massachusetts) found that ". . . many of the hospital's obstetrical patients were without appropriate insurance coverage; and another group of parents was searching for a maternity program that would permit a safe, economical, home-centered postpartum course without the constraints of the hospital setting."

Features of the program, all of which are covered by Massachusetts Blue Cross, include:

- hospital charges for labor and delivery;
- 24-hour charge for mother's and baby's rooms and nursing care (baby rooms-in with mother after 4 hours in the central nursery for observation);
- three home visits (usually on the second, third, and sixth postpartum days) by an experienced obstetrical or pediatric nurse;
- one office visit to a pediatrician or family practitioner for well-baby care;
- an optional homemaker to perform routine household chores (*not* baby care!) five hours a day for five days, at the parents' request.

[*Continued on page 103*]

Right from the Start

How to Survive Hospitalization

1. Keep in the forefront of your thoughts: I am essential to my baby's welfare. My baby is essential to my welfare. We will grow stronger, quicker together.

2. Remember that your baby belongs to you, not to the hospital. Resist feeling that the baby is just "on loan" to you at appointed intervals.

3. Get enough good food to eat. Order double everything if you are in a hospital that allows menu choices; otherwise, have your friends and family bring nutritious food in to you every day. Keep an emergency food bag within reach in case you get hungry between meals (no food is served between 5:00 P.M. and 7:00 A.M. from the kitchen). Fill it with nonperishables: fresh fruits, dried fruits, nuts, crackers, whole grain cereals or granola, powdered milk (you can always get cold water), a day's supply of good cheese, carrots and a peeler, cocoa mix (find out where the nurses keep the hot water boiling for coffee and ask to use it), peanut butter. A pitcher of ice water will be kept on your bedside table—squeeze fresh lemons into it, add sweetener, and you've got refreshing lemonade.

4. Make it difficult for people to interrupt you so you get the rest you need; always keep your door shut if you have a private room and make boldface signs for each side of it saying "**Asleep—Do Not Disturb Unless to Bring Baby**" and "**Please Close the Door As You Leave**" (people always leave it open a crack); leave word at the visitors' registration desk that you will only see family members (or have your doctor leave the message); take your telephone off the hook while you nap or request of the switchboard that they not put through any calls until you wake up; do not sign up for a television—it just keeps your eyes open when you'd be better off really relaxing; do bring a transistor radio and tune it to one of the bland, "easy listening" music stations to drown out hospital noises; pretend to be getting up to go to the bathroom whenever anyone you don't wish to see comes by—tell them you'll let them know when it's more convenient for you to see them; if you have a noisy roommate, ask for a room change (get a private room whenever possible) or tell her you feel absolutely rotten (even if you don't) and you must get extra sleep (which is always true). Then draw your curtain.

5. Whenever possible, have a relative or friend care for the baby in your room if you can't get up (such as after a Cesarean) without a big struggle. Just having someone lift the baby out of the cradle and place him/her in your arms can save a great deal of unnecessary strain and effort.

6. Surround yourself with personal items that keep your identity intact such as your own sleepwear and slippers, toilet articles, soap, comb and brush, brand of toothpaste, perfume, powder, pictures of loved ones, *your own bed pillows*, a cozy quilt or comforter, a favorite poster or print to hang near your bed, a notebook for keeping track of questions you have for the staff, a camera for photographing the baby; avoid taking on that "hospital issue" look.

7. If confined to bed, ask to see a physical therapist for special exercises that can be done in bed to prevent blood clots from forming in your legs and loss of tone in your muscles; if no therapist is available, follow the program in Elizabeth Noble's *Essential Exercises for the Childbearing Year* (Boston: Houghton Mifflin, 1976); Noble, past president of the obstetrics section of the American Physical Therapy Association, presents clear instructions with diagrams and rationales for all stages of postpartum activity (including a most helpful series of movements for post-Cesarean mothers).

8. If up and about, walk around for a change of scene a few times a day—the traditional stroll is down to the nursery to look through the window and see how your baby is doing if the baby can't be with you, but there may be a solarium or reading room on your floor, too. Ask. This helps get rid of the sense of disorientation most people experience in large buildings, an essential feature of control in hospitals. You will hardly ever find a map in your hospital room saying "You are here" and marking the spot as one is accustomed to seeing in parks, public buildings, museums, or campuses.

9. Remember that you do not have to submit to examinations or interviews with anyone except those medical care providers you have hired. Your body still belongs to you even though it is temporarily housed within the walls of the hospital. The fewer examinations, the less your chance of contracting some sort of infection. *Insist that people wash their hands in your presence or put on sterile gloves before they examine you.* In most hospitals, you will be

[Continued on next page]

The Early Hours: Coordinated Care

denied all contact with your baby (no breast-feeding, no rocking, no cuddling) if you are running a temperature, so it's worth it to take every precaution in direct-contact situations. The best way to reduce the number of times you're exposed in direct-contact situations is to assume responsibility for as much of your personal care as possible. Instead of waiting for someone to come to do your perineal care, for instance, bring along your own hand-held mirror to note how well your stitches are healing, and ask the nurse or aide to check your skill in doing the tasks she would usually perform (such as cleansing, changing pads, and episiotomy care). The basics:

- Though tantamount to a medical heresy, the application of an ice pack to your perineum as soon as possible after birth (ideally in the delivery room or recovery room, but in any case as soon as you get to your own room) helps dramatically to reduce swelling of a fresh episiotomy wound—pack your own throat ice bag just in case nobody can get you something else (they can always get ice to fill it)—keep the bag in place as long as it feels comfortable—the next day, application of heat (via a lamp usually) may be useful in promoting healing, but doing your Kegel exercises will also stimulate circulation.
- The goal in promoting healing of the wound is to keep it clean and dry—this means wiping from front to back after urinating or moving your bowels, squirting with the solution in your peri-bottle (usually an antiseptic such as Betadine) whenever you use the toilet (if you squirt while you're releasing urine, the urine will be greatly diluted and less irritating to the incision)—another tip: try to lean forward while urinating so the flow doesn't even hit the episiotomy—change pads every two hours or even more frequently if needed—when in bed, leave the front flap of your sanitary napkin unhooked and just rest the back of your perineum on the pad so air can circulate to the episiotomy site (if you worry about soiling the sheet, ask for some large disposable underpads).
- Because your perineum is very vascular, healing should progress rapidly if the stitches have been done correctly and you're in good nutritional shape—by the day after you give birth, the scar should be just a thin red line with some dissolvable sutures crossing it.
- If your episiotomy looks swollen, inflamed, purplish, oozing with pus or blood, or if its edges are starting to separate (dehisce) make sure your doctor or midwife checks it right away—you may have a bleeding vessel in a deep layer of tissue that needs to be tied off (hematoma) or your stitches may have been put in too tightly.
- Later on, as the suture material is dissolved inside your tissues by enzymes, the sections on the surface come loose and you may find them (little, black, elastic threads) on your toilet tissue after you wipe or on your sanitary pad.
- If your tissues are sensitive, ask for some spray anesthetic, such as Perineze, or witch hazel you can dab on yourself as you feel the need. (You'll probably have to have a written doctor's order since these are viewed as medications.)
- If you feel you have to urinate or move your bowels, but fear of the pain prevents you, get some warm water and pour it over your perineum as you consciously release—the sensation of the water should stimulate your own normal eliminative functions.
- Realize that since you may have missed three meals on the day of birth, and probably had a thorough enema sometime during labor, you may not feel the need to move your bowels for a day or two—don't strain on a bedpan trying to fulfill someone else's schedule for this, just make sure you select plenty of fresh fruits, bran, and fluids, and get some exercise to stimulate bowel activity.

10. If you are recovering from a Cesarean, you have extra needs which you may have to express in a straightforward manner, since many people don't realize that a Cesarean is major abdominal surgery. Nancy Wainer Cohen, a co-founder of C/SEC and pioneer in vaginal birth after Cesarean (V-bac), lists these components of family-centered postpartum Cesarean care in her article, "Minimizing the Emotional Sequellae

of Cesarean Childbirth" (*Birth and Family Journal,* Vol. 4, No. 3, Fall 1977):

- locating Cesarean mothers in rooms with electrically operated beds, located as close as possible to lavatories and nursery;
- having other Cesarean mothers for roommates;
- encouraging sibling visitation;
- reducing traditional seven-day hospital stay whenever medically possible;
- help with the care of the infant at the mother's bedside (modified rooming-in);
- help with breastfeeding by qualified consultant (breastfeeding should start in recovery room whenever condition of mother and baby permit);
- keeping father informed if he is not present;
- baby not automatically sent to intensive care (judged on own merits);
- referral to local Cesarean support groups mother can call as needed to discuss her feelings or, in the case of an unexpected Cesarean, perhaps arrange help for family members at home (home care services).

Other aspects of your care will differ from those provided for women who have not had Cesareans:

- If you've had a spinal anesthetic, you will be advised to remain lying flat for up to 12 hours after the surgery to prevent the onset of a "spinal headache."
- If you've had general anesthesia, you may be groggy and alert for a few minutes by turns over several hours until the effect of the anesthesia has worn off.
- The intravenous apparatus will remain in place throughout your period of time in the recovery room (2 to 6 hours) and perhaps for as long as 48 hours—try to see if yours can contain some nourishment (vitamins/minerals/proteins) instead of just glucose solution.
- The catheter draining your bladder usually remains for 24 hours.
- You will graduate from clear fluids as your first food by mouth to a soft diet, then to a regular diet, based on how well your body adjusts to processing food once again.
- You will probably experience sharp gas pains and pain in your incision. See Eliza-

beth Noble's Cesarean recovery program for specifics of movements you can do in bed to minimize both of these, in *Essential Exercises for the Childbearing Year.* (Boston: Houghton Mifflin, 1976).

- You should request to see the physical therapist for special consultation whenever you feel the need.
- Expect to be urged to get up and walk within the first day after your operation—your incision will not be harmed by this and you will be assisted for as long as you feel the need—this is a most beneficial thing to do, since one of the most potentially hazardous consequences of staying in bed for days is the development of blood clots in your legs.
- Try to have your baby cared for at your bedside as much as possible by your mate, your mother, or other family member or friend until you are feeling like taking over more of the baby's care—this gives you a chance to get to know your baby much better than is possible at infrequent feedings.
- Lay pillows across your abdomen when nursing your baby to reduce strain on your incision and your back.
- Your stitches will be removed after four to eight days.

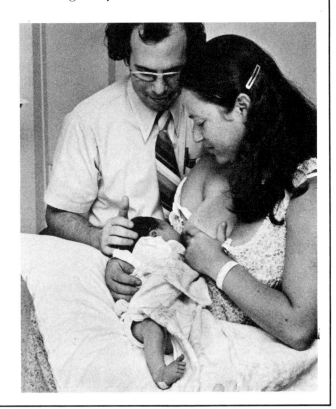

[*Continued on next page*]

The Early Hours: Coordinated Care

11. Open your window, if possible, to get some fresh air. Hospital air circulates throughout the building and can be rather stale. Air-conditioning and heating systems are notorious for removing most of the moisture from the air, which may dry your mucous membranes and make your nose and throat feel sore. Drink plenty of water to offset the dry environment, and if you have a private shower or hot water faucet turn it on a few times a day until things get steamy to make the air easier to breathe.

12. Refuse unnecessary pain medication, sleeping pills, uterine-contracting agents, tranquilizers, stool softeners, and *all* hormone injections (these last are very ineffective in suppressing lactation, anyway, and carry the potential for causing cancer). *Find out what every pill, liquid, or injection is and what it's being given for before you take it.* Orders can be mixed up easily, and even if it's a "standing order" for all your doctor's patients postpartum, that doesn't mean it's what you need. The best aid to sleep we've ever tried in the hospital and while traveling is a cup of hot milk (try it—the taste is quite mellow, veering toward a malted) followed by a session of nursing your baby. The tryptophan (one of the essential amino acids) in the milk is a natural soporific and the nursing stimulates a rush of natural hormones that relax you in a matter of minutes.

13. Should you waken in the night and find you can't get back to sleep, don't worry; it happens all the time when you're sleeping in a strange bed in a strange place among strangers. Try the hot milk again if you can rouse anybody from the nurses' station to warm it for you (keep the extra container from dinner for this purpose—usually there's a refrigerator on the floor where it will be kept for you if you ask). Try reading a very unexciting book or magazine, then lie back and go through the relaxation pattern you learned in your childbirth class, gradually releasing tension from head to toe until you feel loose and calm. Even if you can't actually sleep, at least your body will be benefiting from the deep relaxation.

14. Arrange joint conferences *in your room* between your obstetrician and your baby's pediatrician—otherwise, they may never see each other and plans for discharge can get delayed a day or two due to lack of coordination. Also, it's important that you be kept up to date on anything affecting your baby's condition, but nurses are generally instructed to be very tight-lipped about passing along information to patients. Getting word directly from the physician in charge makes misunderstandings less likely than if you hear something through a third party. However, if you feel nobody's giving you straight answers to questions, try to hang out within earshot of the nurses' station in the half-hour before the shift changes so you hear what is said about you and your baby in report. Call your doctors at their offices if you haven't had a chance to talk with them in a couple days—insist on holding until the doctor is available if the receptionist seems unwilling to call the doctor to the telephone and says she'll have him/her return your call later.

15. Never reveal any aspect of your personal life that you wouldn't want to become a permanent part of your medical record to any hospital staffer. Long, chatty conversations which you construe as friendly diversion can be taken out of context and given undue significance in nurses' notes. Aides and technicians may report anything they think is interesting to the head nurse. Seldom will you have a chance to review these notes for accuracy before they are filed and summarized, sometimes for release to financial institutions, insurance agencies, future employers, and government bureaus.

16. Keep in touch with "life outside" by making brief calls to neighbors, co-workers, and, of course, to little ones you may have at home (even if they visit you every day). Try to keep in mind that this will be a brief period of time in your life even if the days seem to creep along right now. You and your baby *will* be able to go home soon. Plan ahead for that day whenever you feel left out or discouraged. Remember how much you and your baby mean to each other and to your family. Spare yourself depressing speculations about the outcome of this hospitalization: as Mark Twain said, "I've had a lot of troubles in my life, and most of them never happened." The better you take care of yourself, the sooner you will be resuming your regular life in the best of health.

Only healthy mothers and babies qualify for early discharge. In addition, parents must demonstrate "the ability to care for the physical needs of the infant, including feeding, dressing, bathing, positioning the baby to aid in the drainage of mucus, and understanding the behavior patterns of the newborn. The mother must be able to care for herself—that is, she must recognize normal vaginal flow, the signs that would indicate impending hemorrhage, and the actions required in case of hemorrhage." These subjects are reviewed by maternity staff prior to discharge.

Forty percent of clients using the early discharge plan are in the self-pay category, as opposed to only 6 percent in the usual three-to-five-day-stay group. Families report considerable savings as a result of the fewer days' hospital charges for room, board, and nursery. For more information about similar programs in effect at hospitals and birth centers across the country, write to the National Association of Parents and Professionals for Safe Alternatives in Childbirth (NAPSAC) for their comprehensive listings of alternative birth services. (See Directory.) If your area lacks a program of this nature, contact your hospital and inquire when such a program is going to be implemented, as per the recommendations of the joint task force on family-centered maternity care. (See chapter 3.) Then volunteer to work on a committee to make your preference a reality.

Once we expand our perspectives about the importance of ongoing mother-baby interaction in the hours and days after birth, we see that we mothers and fathers can, by our own actions, eliminate or greatly reduce physical and psychic stresses on our infants just by requesting a few basic changes in routine postpartum management in the hospital and by carrying through on them at home. Progressive doctors, midwives, nurses, and hospital administrators can assist us in making the needed changes when they recognize that there is much more involved in baby care than giving just the barest physical attention, and that lifelong patterns of interacting with the child may be established in the early days after birth. What is so interesting about the new-old approach stressing coordinated care for mother and baby is that it's much more pleasurable for both. And, once they get used to it, less work for hospital personnel.

By way of review, we include a checklist of newborn care preferences for you to use as a basis of discussion with your medical care providers. Some points may be very important to you, others unimportant; so adapt the list to your own needs.

Newborn Care Preferences

(Copies available from: Cooperative Childbirth Network, 14 Truesdale Drive, Croton-on-Hudson, NY 10520. Send 25 cents and self-addressed, stamped envelope. Bulk order information on request.)

Preference	Rationale
1. Allow placental blood to transfuse through cord before cutting.	1. Placental blood is part of the infant's circulation, not the mother's. The blood is needed to perfuse the baby's bronchial tree. The smaller placenta makes the third stage faster.
2. Give infant directly to mother after birth, skin to skin. Cover both with receiving blanket to maintain warmth.	2. This is a highly sensitive time for both mother and infant. They need to comfort each other. Mother is best source of heat. Parents need to observe baby straight from birth.
3. Refrain from routinely suctioning the newborn.	3. Suctioning is a traumatic intervention. Babies born spontaneously to unmedicated mothers in the physiologic position have most mucus expelled by the time of birth. Baby's chest is compressed by the vaginal walls during the second stage, so drainage is accomplished automatically. The baby continues to receive oxygen through the cord until it is severed.

[Continued on next page]

The Early Hours: Coordinated Care

Preference	Rationale
4. Encourage the mother to breastfeed as soon as baby is calm.	4. Mother and baby need to comfort each other as soon after birth as possible. The breast stimulation triggers the release of oxytocin, causing rhythmic uterine contractions which gently separate the placenta. Colostrum is vital for the newborn because of its anti-infective properties.
5. Continue nursing until the placenta separates spontaneously from the uterine wall.	5. Patience is the key, not tugging on the cord or abdominal pressure. The natural process is safest and least traumatic.
6. If episiotomy has been done, repair with local anesthetic.	6. A local does not impede mothering.
7. Serve mother juice and other nourishment as desired.	7. Restore blood sugar to normal. Mother does not require an IV.
8. Delay administration of silver nitrate or other eye prophylaxis.	8. Mother and baby need to establish and maintain eye contact without intervention.
9. Mother and baby should continue uninterrupted nursing through the early postpartum hours.	9. Nursing releases hormones that trigger involution of the uterus. Incidence of postpartum hemorrhage is reduced.
10. Have facilities for parents to bathe baby, if desired.	10. Allows father or other support person to participate in baby's care and promotes bonding.
11. Perform newborn medical exam in parents' presence.	11. Gives parents time to ask questions about baby's physical development.
12. Do not hold baby upside down to obtain accurate measure of length.	12. Trauma can lead to dislocation of hips. Startles and frightens baby.
13. Do not weigh baby on cold, hard surface of scale. If necessary, weigh with several soft blankets, then subtract weight of blankets.	13. Baby's temperature regulation system is immature. Baby needs to be enfolded as in uterus or mother's arms.
14. No routine circumcision.	14. See chapter 7.
15. No routine medication to baby or mother (e.g., vitamin K, analgesics, oxytocics).	15. No medication has ever been proven safe for infants. Drugs are transmitted to baby in mother's milk. May promote jaundice.
16. Minimize number of persons other than family members coming in contact with baby.	16. Decrease incidence of neonatal infection. Reduce invasion of privacy of family.
17. If baby must be in nursery for special care, mother should be notified when baby needs nursing, so that she can go to nursery to be with baby.	17. Baby's need for special care nursery does not reduce baby's need for mother. Continuity of mothering is essential for all babies. If baby has a medical problem, mother's milk may be lifesaving.
18. Water and formula should not be given to breastfed infant.	18. Bottles interfere with mother-infant relationship. There is no safe, adequate substitute for mother's milk.
19. Mother and baby should be discharged as soon as they desire if there is no medical contraindication. Six to 24 hours is the typical stay for a normal birth.	19. This minimizes conflicts caused by leaving other children at home and reduces the chance of staph and other nosocomial infections. The infant is not subjected to hospital routines and feeding schedules. Mother can rest better at home when other household work is done by a helper.

Preference	Rationale
20. If mother stays longer in the hospital, she should have access to her baby whenever she desires. Baby should be brought to mother if in distress.	20. Baby needs to be fed when hungry. An experienced breastfeeding counselor should be available to assist mother with breastfeeding if needed, especially after Cesarean or difficult birth.
21. Visits by other family members should be facilitated at regular intervals. Healthy siblings should be encouraged to visit.	21. Frequent visits strengthen the family unit and allow the new mother to concentrate on the new baby without undue worry about other family members.
22. If baby has been born by Cesarean, mother needs additional help from staff to maintain rooming-in.	22. Cesarean mother should not be kept from caring for her baby but may need extra physical assistance to facilitate it.
23. Mother should be encouraged to have a relative or friend stay with her to assist with baby's care. This is especially important after a Cesarean.	23. Emotional support of friends and relatives is more easily accepted by new mother.
24. If baby has been born out of hospital and subsequently brought in because of an emergency, mother and baby should be in isolation together.	24. There is no advantage to isolating mother and baby away from each other as they share the same microorganisms. Mother's milk has protective factors that may be lifesaving for ill baby.
25. The mother has the right to be informed before the administration of any drug or procedure, whether that drug is medically indicated or for research, convenience, or teaching.	25. Mother has the right and obligation to give her informed consent at the time of any procedure or medication.
26. Parents should be allowed to review mother's and baby's charts while in the hospital. If chart is to be microfilmed and destroyed, it should be offered to the parents.	26. Parents need to be fully informed about the medical circumstances of their baby's birth. It should be retained for seven years past the child's majority.

The Early Hours: Coordinated Care

Chapter 6

In Distress

Intensive Care

What happens to your care plans if your baby is in distress and requires special medical supervision? Hundreds of thousands of parents each year face days, weeks, and in some cases, even months of anxious vigils in intensive care nurseries where access to high-technology care may mean the difference between life and death for their babies. The newborn with serious health problems (prematurity, low birth weight, congenital malformations, infection, nonphysiologic jaundice, and respiratory distress account for most admissions) needs the total life support system provided by the intensive care nursery. At the same time, this baby also needs all the comforting human contact we have seen is necessary for normal human development. In many cases, the procedures required to keep a baby breathing or to track a baby's progress, for instance, involve sensory experiences which are far from pleasing. For this reason, it's probable that these infants have an even higher index of need for pleasurable interaction with their mothers. Progressive administrators employ intensive care workers who recognize this need and make every effort to involve mothers and fathers in the day-to-day care of their child.

Services for critically ill newborns are located in just a few hospitals, due to the extremely high cost of maintaining a regional Neonatal Intensive Care Unit (NICU). The NICU is usually attached to a medical school, so babies in the unit are seen by many individuals: some provide direct care and others study the baby's illness as part of their training or research. Most NICUs also are training centers for registered nurses seeking advanced certification as a neonatal nurse-clinician, a sort of "supernurse" who can assume some responsibilities formerly assumed only by physicians.

Since everyone in the NICU is specially trained, and since the ratio of babies to nurses is far less than in the standard central nursery (3 to 1 instead of 12 to 1), a single day's care, without including the myriad laboratory and other tests or physicians' fees, costs $300 to $500. In addition to staffing, a major cost is the purchase and upkeep of sophisticated diagnostic and monitoring equipment, such as cardiac monitors, temperature sensors, inhalation devices, x-ray machines, incubators, and intravenous apparatus. In many parts of the country, seriously sick babies are airlifted by helicopters complete with emergency medical crews from community hospitals to the regional NICU, maybe 200 miles or more away. These newborn rescue flights, as you might imagine, are also very expensive. Many people feel that this money would be better spent in programs to improve the quality of prenatal care, particularly nutrition intervention, to *prevent* these problems. Many of these intensive care services are federally funded under new programs aimed at improving our country's poor showing in infant mortality statistics

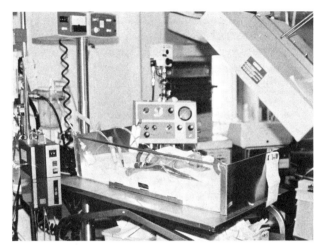
Premature baby receiving intensive care.

relative to other countries. Others are partially supported by grants from private foundations, such as the March of Dimes, which share this concern.

Were it not for the presence of the tiny babies, your first visit to an NICU might make you think of something out of "Star Trek": little lights flashing, buzzers going off, beeps and clicks emanating from complicated-looking machines replete with dials, gauges, and a tangle of electronic circuitry, and busy, determined people going about their work—everyone poised for the next crisis.

By far the leading cause for admission to neonatal intensive care units is **prematurity/low birth weight,** which, as we have seen, is preventable in over 90 percent of cases by insuring the mother's adequate nutrition every day throughout pregnancy. (See chapter 1.)

However, poor nutrition isn't the only cause for prematurity/low birth weight, and babies do get into trouble for reasons that have nothing whatever to do with what their mothers ate during pregnancy. Other reasons why your baby might have to be admitted to an NICU, even though your diet has been superb for a single baby, include:

undetected multiple pregnancy—Only half of the twins are diagnosed, so these pregnant women are on diets inadequate for carrying two or more babies to term—result: underweight babies born four to six weeks ahead of time.

undetected viral infection of the placenta early in pregnancy—Placental structure is damaged so even if plenty of nutrients are provided from mother's diet, they are poorly transferred across the placenta—result: underweight baby, possibly premature labor.

incompetent cervix—Inability of the cervix to remain closed until the usual time for labor to begin—some causes: congenital weakness in the cervix itself, damage done to cervix during a prior labor or previous abortion, surgery on the cervix such as a conization in which too much cervical tissue was removed—signs: very early (fifth or sixth month) and painless dilatation of the cervix, often with bulging membranes, then delivery of a very tiny (one- or two-pound) baby—with NICU some of these babies are now being saved.

genetic abnormalities and/or malformations—Sometimes require immediate and sustained treatment for survival.

preterm induction—Necessary for mothers with poorly controlled diabetes, heart conditions, or other medical conditions requiring treatment which could compromise the baby *in utero* (see chapter 3).

Cesarean birth—Many hospitals require that all babies born by Cesarean spend at least 24 hours in an observation nursery, regardless of the individual baby's condition—discuss this in advance with your baby's pediatrician so you can try to have your baby evaluated on his/her own merits should Cesarean birth become necessary.

severe jaundice—Due to blood group incompatibility, Rh incompatibility, or physiologic jaundice reaching higher-than-normal levels of bilirubin; aftereffects of obstetrical medication given to mother during labor and birth—baby may be seriously depressed for a day or two if large amounts of medication are used.

allergic reaction to certain medications—Alarming negative response may require constant and expert monitoring.

nosocomial infection—Hospital-acquired infection which may be highly resistant to conventional therapies.

bicornuate or other uterine anomalies—Structural deviations in the uterus interfere with uterine accommodation to developing baby and placenta, resulting in premature labor and a small baby.

Neonatal jaundice is another major contributor of babies to intensive care nurseries. We seem to be living through the "Jaundice Age," as the

In Distress: Intensive Care

threshold of treatment drops lower and the treatments become more readily employed. Since so many parents today have heard about jaundice, we feel an extensive look at the problem is warranted.

Jaundice, the yellowing of skin, mucous membranes, eyes, and excretions due to excessive circulating bilirubin, is not a disease. It is a *symptom* of diseases of the gallbladder, liver, and blood, such as obstruction of the bile duct, hepatitis, cirrhosis, cancer, poisoning, obstruction of the liver's collecting system, or hemolytic anemia. Bilirubin, an orange-pigmented by-product of the ongoing breakdown (hemolysis) of red blood cells, is introduced into the bloodstream on a constant basis. Under ordinary circumstances, the liver absorbs and excretes this bilirubin as part of its routine functioning. But when the liver and the flow of bile are compromised, or extraordinary numbers of red blood cells are being destroyed, bilirubin accumulates in the blood—eventually resulting in jaundice. In newborns, 12 to 15 mg of bilirubin per 100 ml of blood sampled is the cutoff point for treatment used by most physicians. The reason for concern: excess bilirubin can enter brain cells and cause serious brain damage, a condition called kernicterus.

Jaundice commonly progresses from the infant's head to feet, making it possible to estimate the level of serum bilirubin from the extent of the body involved. A more accurate assessment can be made using an icterometer, a device containing a color strip to be matched against the baby's skin color while the examiner applies pressure to the surface of the skin. If the baby's hips, arms, or thighs are discolored in natural light, most physicians will order a blood test (the sample is usually taken from the baby's heel) to get a precise measurement of bilirubin. The danger level for the onset of kernicterus is considered to be 20 mg of bilirubin per 100 ml of blood; however, babies who are underweight or premature, or who have low blood sugar (hypoglycemia) or infection, or who suffered asphyxia at birth, may develop kernicterus at lower levels of serum bilirubin concentration.

The ability of the body to clear bilirubin is based on a complex of factors:

- the amount of plasma proteins (manufactured in the baby's liver from the nutrients it receives from breast milk) circulating in the bloodstream and available to pick up and bind the bilirubin en route to the liver for conjugation and excretion—babies born to poorly nourished mothers typically have very low total serum proteins in samples of cord blood tested at birth, so they are at high risk for developing severe jaundice;

- maturity of the liver enzyme system which must conjugate bilirubin with glucuronic acid in order for the bilirubin to be excreted—again, the adequacy of the mother's diet during pregnancy is important in getting the baby's liver ready to function optimally after birth;

- whether the mother received certain medications during labor and/or birth (Valium, oxytocin, and epidural anesthesia have been implicated in numerous studies) which *compete* with bilirubin for binding sites on the plasma proteins or for conjugation by the liver enzymes—these drugs are toxic substances which must be eliminated from the baby's body after birth, so the task of bilirubin clearance falls behind;

- whether the baby has acquired an infection—bacteriological substances resulting from the infection circulate in the bloodstream and may also compete with bilirubin for detoxication by the liver;

- whether the baby has been fed water in addition to breast milk—both colostrum and milk from well-fed mothers are high in the specific proteins needed by the newborn for good liver function, but these proteins are not found in glucose water which so many breastfeeding mothers are encouraged to offer their babies at each feeding time in addition to the breast (the old idea that forcing water somehow helps the baby eliminate bilirubin fails to take into account whether the baby has adequate plasma proteins to do the job)—providing water when protein is needed simply doesn't work;

- whether the mother received 5 percent dextrose intravenous fluids during labor and birth—Singh and Singh report in the May 1979 issue of the *Archives of Diseases of Children* (Vol. 54[5], 400–403) that, since mother's and baby's body fluids are in continual transplacental communication, the electrolytes in the baby's blood become progressively diluted the longer the mother's IV infusion continues, resulting in red blood cells taking on extra water, swelling and becoming more fragile, and eventually bursting—this releases the cells' hemoglobin which boosts the bilirubin count even higher after birth;

- whether the baby received an injection of synthetic vitamin K (menadione) to prevent hemorrhagic disease of the newborn;
- whether the baby has bruises (such as forceps marks) or a hematoma (a pressure bump filled with blood) which result in extra numbers of red cells being destroyed.

Treatments for jaundice vary depending on the severity of an individual case. As Vulliamy notes in *The Newborn Child* (2d ed., Baltimore: Williams and Wilkins, 1967), "the condition must always be carefully observed because there is a point, not easily defined, at which 'physiological' jaundice becomes pathological." In a mild case in a full-term, full-size infant (up to 12 mg of bilirubin per 100 ml of blood), the baby will be alert and eating well and requires ad lib breastfeeding (to increase plasma protein synthesis by the liver and provide plenty of fluids) and full body exposure to sunlight (through window glass is okay) five minutes at a time five or six times a day. The light reacts in the skin with the bilirubin, changing it to a less bioactive substance with less danger of lodging in the baby's brain cells. Often the discoloration is relieved for a short time in babies with this degree of jaundice after they urinate or have a bowel movement. In both instances, bilirubin is excreted, accounting for the noticeable color change. This level of jaundice normally would not require hospitalization of a baby who had already been discharged, but you might want to keep in communication with your child's doctor or nurse-practitioner about it.

The jaundice typically peaks five to six days after birth and gradually subsides over the next week or so. Of course, in a smaller baby (the American Academy of Pediatrics [AAP] now classifies all babies born at term weighing under 6½ pounds as "small for gestational age," and therefore requiring closer supervision in the early neonatal period), there may be cause for concern at levels lower than 12 mg/100 ml, and you may be asked to bring the baby back to the hospital for continuous observation.

When the jaundice rises to the moderate range (13 to 18 mg/100 ml in the full-size baby), phototherapy in the central nursery is the most common,

though poorly understood, strategy for dealing with it. Ten thousand to 35,000 babies are estimated to receive phototherapy annually (up to 1 percent of all births). Like strong sunlight, blue fluorescent lighting has been found to convert bilirubin in the skin and superficial blood vessels to a harmless metabolite which is readily excreted. According to *Perinatal Press* (Vol. 1, No. 2) and a 1974 report on phototherapy by the Division of Medical Sciences, National Research Council (NRC), side effects of phototherapy are just beginning to be defined. Complete copies of the committee report and papers from an NRC workshop, "Phototherapy in the Newborn: An Overview," are available from: NRC, 2101 Constitution Avenue NW, Washington, DC 20418.

Phototherapy is more effective in checking a rise in serum bilirubin than in causing a significant fall after it has risen, consequently, any preterm or underweight baby with a reading higher than 10 mg/100 ml may be put under the lights as a preventive measure. Treatment may last two to three days with your baby's bilirubin count being taken every 12 hours. You may find that your baby is drowsy and/or disinterested in feeding when jaundice reaches this level.

Exchange transfusion (see later in this chapter for details) is the only rapidly effective means of removing bilirubin from the bloodstream and tissues when it reaches threatening levels. Vulliamy writes that the age of the baby as well as the baby's maturity is taken into account in trying to forecast whether an individual baby will soon have a natural drop in serum bilirubin or whether a transfusion has to be done. He uses the example of adopting a look-and-see attitude for another 12 hours about a 20 mg/100 ml count on a baby's fifth day, whereas a reading that high on the third day would be a clear indication for an exchange.

Transfusions are not without their own set of risks; however, even full-term, full-size babies are in danger of severe mental defects, cerebral palsy, or deafness subsequent to kernicterus at this bilirubin concentration. Obviously, babies whose jaundice is this severe need intensive care in the hospital. Since the jaundice generally persists in reduced severity after the exchange, the baby will still have to be monitored closely with serial estimation of serum bilirubin and probably other tests to determine exactly what is causing the jaundice (this is way out of the "physiologic" range). It may even become necessary to repeat the transfusion, depending on the baby's progress.

In Distress: Intensive Care

There are major differences between an exchange transfusion in an adult and in an infant that you should know about, in the unlikely event that your child will require one.

- The whole exchange lasts 1½ to 2 hours, because the infant's blood vessels are very small (each 10 ml, roughly a tablespoon, should take at least a full minute to inject)—object if the exchange is being done hurriedly, not if it seems to take forever.
- In addition to the individual conducting the exchange itself, a competent assistant should be present *throughout* to record the transfusion and report on the general condition of the infant by charting pulse rate, color, temperature, and respiration.
- To avoid undue cooling of the baby, many physicians prefer to carry out the procedure with the baby in an incubator. (This is especially true if the baby is underweight and/or premature.)
- The donor blood should pass from the storage bottle through a coil of tubing in a thermostatically controlled water bath at approximately body temperature—the baby has limited ability to warm itself without having to cope with the chilling from underheated blood.
- Human serum albumin, so necessary for providing binding sites for the excess bilirubin, may be substituted for some of the blood to increase the value of the transfusion in lowering the bilirubin count.
- The donor blood must be fresh (not stored more than four days).
- Most often, the transfusion is done through the umbilical vein.

(Summarized from *The Newborn Child*, by Dr. David G. Vulliamy, 2d ed., Baltimore: Williams and Wilkins, 1967.)

In rare cases, jaundice may be due to some difficulty apart from normal breakdown of the extra blood cells inherent in the newborn. One or more of the following, all of which require your cooperation with your baby's doctor, may be responsible when bilirubin rises to dangerous levels:

- Rh incompatibility (approximately 1 percent of all pregnancies), in which the Rh-negative mother who has previously been sensitized to Rh-positive red blood cells is now carrying an Rh-positive baby—the antibodies she has built up to the Rh-positive blood cells can cross the placenta and attack this baby's red blood cells, resulting in severe anemia and jaundice of the newborn—commonly this form of jaundice appears at birth or within the first 24 hours, as distinguished from "physiologic" jaundice, which usually does not show up until the third day;
- ABO incompatibility (approximately 1 in 200 babies are affected), in which mothers with type O blood are carrying a baby with either type A or type B blood—25 percent of type O mothers' blood also contains anti-A and/or anti-B antibodies which can cross the placenta and destroy the red blood cells of the A or B blood-type baby—many of these cases are mild and require no treatment, but the clinical sign is the onset of jaundice within 24 hours after birth and a rapidly rising bilirubin count;
- G-6-PD deficiency, most common in Middle Eastern and Oriental babies—a lack of an enzyme which makes red blood cells easier to break down and help dispose of bile pigment in the liver;
- congenital *spherocytosis*, the presence of unusually fragile red blood cells—usually diagnosed by laboratory analysis and a history of the condition in either parent;
- sepsis—jaundice due to infection—may involve reluctance to feed, drowsiness, and/or vomiting—a common site is the urinary tract;
- malformation of the bile ducts—usually causes fluctuating jaundice with dark, bile-stained urine and pale stools;
- congenital *toxoplasmosis*—arises from a maternal infection during pregnancy;
- congenital syphilis—since testing for maternal syphilis is almost universal in standard prenatal care, this cause can be ruled out in almost every case—however, if you have not had a blood test for syphilis during pregnancy, be sure to inform your baby's doctor of this should the jaundice not seem to be caused by anything else—syphilis responds to penicillin therapy.

While the diagnosis and treatment of pathological jaundice is complicated and can involve many extra days spent in the hospital for you and your baby, we need to keep these complications in proper perspective. A small minority of newborns experience these serious problems, and with thorough prenatal care, proper maternal nutrition every day of pregnancy, minimal interference with birth, and no separation of mother and baby after birth, the incidence could probably be lower.

Trying to maintain some continuity of infant care in even the direst of emergencies provides benefits to parents and babies. Since most NICUs lack personnel to orient parents to the unit, you may find the accompanying charts of NICU procedures and tests helpful should your child require intensive care.

Neonatal Intensive Care Unit Procedures

Procedure	Why Is It Done?	How Is It Done?	What Can Mother Do?
Isolation	To minimize the chance of infection (Sepsis). Tiny babies are not able to local-ize on infection an it spreads rapidly through body.	Strict hand-washing procedures. Must remove watches and rings before touching baby. Cover clothing with gown. Baby is in isolette or incubator with air filter. *Whenever possible, touch babies in isolation to provide some plea-surable stimulation.*	Follow rules. If baby can-not be removed from isolette, place hands and arms through porthole and cradle baby. Request, if medically permissible, time to take baby out for holding, feeding. Talk and sing gently to soothe baby.
Tempera-ture Con-trol	To assist the baby in maintaining the proper body tem-perature.	In isolette, where feasible. Under radiant warmer when isolette would be too confin-ing for doctor or nurse to work in or when bulky equipment is needed. Sensors attached painlessly to baby's skin regu-late warmth.	Cradle baby in your arms, sing and talk gently. Nurse baby if possible.
Exchange Trans-fusion	To sharply lower the degree of jaundice in a seriously affected baby.	Under surgical asepsis, the physician inserts an umbilical catheter through which he withdraws small amounts of the baby's blood, replacing it with donor blood.	Donate blood to the blood bank to replace what has been used. This reduces your bill and keeps blood available for other emergencies.

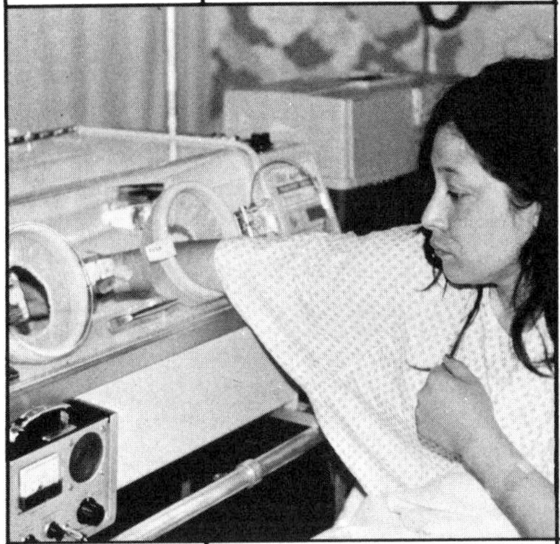

[Continued on next page]

In Distress: Intensive Care

Procedure	Why Is It Done?	How Is It Done?	What Can Mother Do?
Monitoring	To provide a continuous account of baby's vital signs: heart rate, respirations, temperature. They buzz to alert the nurse of possible problems.	Sensors are attached painlessly to the infant. They are extremely sensitive and give off many sounds—clicks, buzzes, rings—which may be misinterpreted.	Ask nurse to explain the equipment to you so that you do not become unduly alarmed.
	Continuous temperature and vital signs monitoring equipment.		
Intravenous Fluids	To provide fluids and nutrients for babies who are unable to get enough by sucking. To provide a route for giving medications.	A scalp vein is most frequently used because it is the easiest spot. Some of baby's hair may have to be shaved off. Arm and leg veins are also used.	Handle baby carefully so as not to dislodge IV catheter.
	Intravenous apparatus.		

Right from the Start

Procedure	Why Is It Done?	How Is It Done?	What Can Mother Do?
Oxygen	To provide enough oxygen so that the proper level is maintained in the blood circulation.	A hood is placed over the baby's head and a mixture of oxygen and air is circulated for the baby to breathe. There are also devices for babies with serious lung problems that assist the inhalation. *Oxygen hood.*	Massage baby's body to lessen the isolation.
Postural Drainage and Suctioning	To loosen mucus in the lungs and remove it so that baby's breathing will not become obstructed.	Nurse taps baby's chest to loosen mucus, then places a tube in the windpipe. Then, using her mouth or a machine, she suctions the loose secretions. *Nurse suctioning baby's airway to remove trapped mucus.*	Communicate your concerns to the nurse. Don't be shy: if you want to learn a skill, ask the nurse to teach you.
Umbilical Catheter	To obtain blood samples without having to puncture baby's skin repeatedly.	Physician places catheter in baby's umbilical blood vessel.	See Temperature Control and Intravenous Fluids.

[*Continued on next page*]

In Distress: Intensive Care

Procedure	Why Is It Done?	How Is It Done?	What Can Mother Do?
Gavage Tube	To provide nourishment for a baby who is too weak to suck.	The tube is inserted into the nose and the end placed in the stomach.	Express breast milk according to the policy of the institution. Discuss your desire to nurse baby as soon as possible.
Gastrostomy	To provide nourishment for an infant who has no gag reflex.	Surgeon makes an incision in the abdomen to allow a feeding tube to be placed directly into the stomach.	Express breast milk and donate to baby according to the policies of the institution. (See how-to hints, following.)
Bilirubin Lights (phototherapy)	To reduce the degree of jaundice in the baby.	Baby's eyes are covered with pads or bandages. Baby is undressed and placed under the lights for the prescribed amount of time.	If medically possible, baby can be removed from phototherapy for breast-feeding.

Gavage feeding.

Phototherapy for jaundice.

Procedure	Why Is It Done?	How Is It Done?	What Can Mother Do?
Medica-tions	1. Antibiotics: to treat or attempt to prevent an infection. 2. Diuretics: to reduce the blood volume, lessening strain on heart. 3. Calcium gluconate and sodium bicarbonate: to correct electrolyte imbalance. 4. Others: ask doctor or nurse.	Medications are usually given IV (intravenous) directly into the vein through a tube or IM (intramuscular) in a muscle, usually the top of the thigh.	Inform nursery staff of known family allergy to any medications.
Diagnosis of Infec-tions by Culture	To find specific organism that is causing the infection, and which medication will be most effective.	Samples are taken of baby's spinal fluid, blood, urine, umbilical cord stump, mouth, throat, and any obvious lesions. These are placed on culture dishes to grow until organism can be identified. Antibiotic-inoculated paper is placed on culture to determine its effectiveness.	See Medications.
X-rays	To find out if baby has a lung infection. Also used for other diag-nostic purposes.	X-ray machine is washed with antiseptic and brought to baby. Baby is held still for the length of time it takes to get the x-ray taken.	After done, hold baby and comfort.

Many NICUs prefer to feed preemies breast milk whenever possible. To keep your milk flowing even when your baby can't suck at the breast:

1. Start expressing by hand or with a physiologic electric pump (the Egnell is by far the best) as soon after the birth as possible.
2. Express every two to three hours during waking hours. Try to express at least once during the night.
3. Eat and drink something nutritious every time you express. Dietary fats such as butter, oil, or margarine help keep nipples soft and supple.
4. Use the sterile containers provided by the hospital or sterilize your own by placing them in a large pot, covering with water, and boiling for 20 minutes. Drain the water carefully. Do not touch the insides of the bottles.
5. Your nipples produce their own antiseptic lubricant that's better than any cream or lotion you can buy. If your nipples feel dry, itchy, or sore, plain hydrous lanolin (an animal fat—don't use it if you are allergic to wool) is available in tubes at the drugstore. Anything else—alcohol wipes, tincture of benzoin, pHisohex, Zephiran, perfumed creams—should be marked with a skull and crossbones. Poison to healthy nipples!

In Distress: Intensive Care

Test	Why Is It Done?	How Is It Done?
Blood Sugar (glucose)	To measure amount of glucose in the blood, an aid in diagnosis.	A drop of blood is obtained by sticking baby's heel. Blood is placed on Dextrostix or similar indicator.
Blood Count, Other Blood Tests	To aid in diagnosis, determine condition of baby, determine effectiveness of therapy.	Blood is withdrawn from scalp vein under aseptic conditions and sent to laboratory for appropriate tests.
Urine Tests	To aid in diagnosis, determine condition of baby, determine effectiveness of therapy.	Urine collection bag is affixed to baby's genital area. When voiding has occurred, bag is removed and urine sent to laboratory for tests.

Urine collection bag.

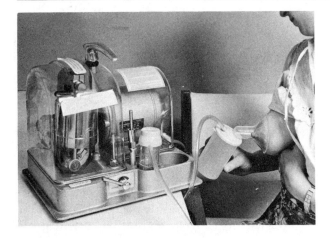

Using the Egnell breast pump.

6. Before you start to express, massage the breasts gently.
7. Some women like to use warm compresses, especially if there is any fullness or engorge-ment. Use a heating pad or washcloths wrung out in warm water. Apply for 10 to 20 minutes before expressing.
8. If you're renting a pump make sure you get complete instructions or a demonstration.
9. To hand express, follow the accompanying photos.
10. How long to express? When you start pumping, the milk comes in a stream. When the stream slows down to just a few drops, stop and try the other side. Excessive or too vigorous pumping can damage the delicate tissues.

Studies by Klaus and Kennel among others show that, when preemies and other ill newborns receive appropriate pleasurable stimulation as an adjunct to their medical treatment, both mother and baby do better. A study by psychologists at Grady Memorial Hospital, Atlanta, Georgia, "Care of the Critically Ill Newborn: Stimulation—a

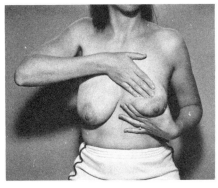

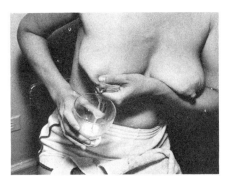

Massage breast to stimulate flow of milk.

At first, a few drops will flow as milk ducts behind areola are compressed.

A steady stream flows with continuing squeezing and drawing out of the areola.

Corollary to Physical Care," reported in the April 1976 issue of the *American Journal of Nursing* confirms their findings. Infants and their parents were involved in a special program in which parents were encouraged to express their feelings about their sometimes unattractive babies and gradually to assume some responsibility for their care. Initially, the staff was skeptical about the program, but ultimately they were convinced that the special-care regime benefited everyone.

Parents were taught methods of stimulation including:

- presentation of visual objects to the baby before each feeding;
- shaking rattles to encourage babies to orient to sound;
- talking or singing to the baby while facing baby squarely (baby's preferred object is the human face);
- holding baby in various positions and rocking in a rocking chair drawn close enough to the incubator so that the baby could be removed without being unhooked from essential apparatus;
- making sure baby had the same caretaker each day;
- covering eyes at night to establish day-night cycle;
- giving gavage-fed babies a pacifier during feeding so they would associate the feeling of a full stomach with sucking;
- placing their faces nine inches or so away from babies' faces whenever their eyes were open.

D. Gary Benfield, M.D., and collaborators from the Children's Hospital at Akron, Ohio, sug-

gest ways of helping families cope when their critically ill newborn is transferred to a regional NICU far from home in their article in the *New England Journal of Medicine* (Vol. 294, No. 18, pp. 975–78, April 29, 1976):

- Maintain an open visiting policy so parents can come to see and care for their baby when it's most convenient for them.
- Install a toll-free parent-nursery telephone line so parents can have their questions answered whenever the need arises.
- Initiate counseling early in the hospital course so parents know what to expect.

Morris Green, M.D., of the Department of Pediatrics, Indiana University School of Medicine, also had the parents' needs in mind when he commented in "Parent Care in the ICU" (*American Journal of Diseases of Children*, Vol. 133, No. 11, November 1979):

For the parents, time seems both to slip away, yet remain frozen in place. Geographically displaced, their work and lives disrupted, their biological rhythms in disarray, bewildered, anxious, and terribly tired, the parents in the delirium of crisis are simply unable to comprehend what is happening. . . . The highly sophisticated biomedical care of sick infants and children in ICUs often contrasts starkly with the undeveloped care of their parents. Parent care in many centers seems a sporadic improvisation by the most inexperienced staff.

One mother, a clinical psychologist, shared

In Distress: Intensive Care

her family's NICU experience with us since she has found that the stress may affect parents and family life for prolonged periods of time, even well after the crisis itself is over.

Though I was disappointed at having to stay in the hospital, it was five days after my Cesarean and everything was going fine—until the chief pediatrician walked into my room and very abruptly told me he had just transferred my previously healthy baby boy to the intensive care unit. He was very vague—couldn't tell me what was wrong with my baby, just that he had a rash and a sudden high temperature. I was terribly scared but was somewhat relieved to hear that I could go up to the unit and see my son. Though it was still quite painful for me to walk about, I managed to make it to the elevators and took one alone to the ninth floor. There was nobody from the postpartum floor or the nursery to escort me.

I just kept saying to myself there must be some terrible mistake: my baby is big and strong—he doesn't belong here. They must have meant some other baby, not mine. I was shocked when I reached the evaluation room to see my baby naked, undergoing all sorts of testing procedures with three or four workers hovering over him, writing things down on charts and taking samples of blood.

I was not allowed to hold my son at this point and someone indicated to me that it was time for me to go—there were lots of things they had to do and there was nothing I could do for my baby now. I was still kind of numb from all that had happened in the space of a half-hour, so I went back to my room to call my husband and my mother who had been planning to take the baby and me home the next day. The thing that began to haunt me was the lack of specificity about what would be done to my baby and for how long. I felt brushed-off and helpless, terribly confused, and completely unprepared for the reality that was to confront me when I returned to the unit a few hours later.

I'll never forget my first sight of my son in the incubator. It was all the worst fears a mother could have come true. He was hooked up to three machines with electric wires, three tubes were inserted into his body (arm, nose, and umbilicus), an intravenous bag was dripping via a tube into his scalp and there were bruises on his arms and legs. Again, nobody was with me to explain any of this. I just stood there, weeping, not knowing what to do for several minutes until someone noticed me.

Throughout the nine days of my baby's hospitalization in the ICU I felt that while the baby was being screened for every possibility (they never did find out what was the matter) the assistance to parents was nil. I started talking to other mothers once it seemed likely that my son would pull through. I had made a huge effort to get the hospital to provide me with an Egnell electric breast pump so I could maintain my milk supply. But almost everyone else had resigned herself to losing her milk and foregoing the entire breastfeeding experience. I really had to twist arms to get my electric pump, since all the hospital usually provides is the manual squeeze-bulb contraption that inevitably takes forever and causes very sore nipples. Since babies in the ICU need easily digestible food, it seems to me that electric pumps or a breast milk bank ought to be a standard part of the ICU.

One other thing people should know in advance in case their baby has to go to the ICU is that the routines there are physically and emotionally exhausting for parents and for the baby. It seemed to me that my son was never given a chance to rest and regain his strength. Every time he dozed off someone would step over, shake his leg forcefully to get blood down, then cut his heel with a razor blade to take a blood sample.

My mother came to the hospital every day, but since she wasn't allowed into the ICU to relieve me, the most I got was some desperately needed moral support. We have talked about the experience a lot since, and we agree that we both aged years in those nine days. Much as we appreciated the medical sophistication of the ICU workers and much as we desperately needed them, we found that it's the families' aching hearts that aren't understood. We were lucky—our ordeal only lasted nine days and I was able to stay in the hospital the whole time (my husband stayed at home with our other three children). At the end of our stay, my sympathy was going out to those families whose whole lives were being disrupted for weeks or months, for whom all of daily life was uncertain because of the baby's illness.

Green of the Indiana University School of Medicine made some specific recommendations for dealing with this all-too-common situation.

- Every ICU should make some provision for the parents' comfort—especially a place to sleep.
- The infant's diagnosis and treatment should be carefully repeated *many times* so parents can grasp the meaning—many times parents are unreceptive when first told of their child's condition and/or prognosis; they naturally are always hoping for the best even under the most unfavorable circumstances.
- Though many people may be involved in the care of the baby, one person from the staff should be the chief source of information.
- This person should schedule daily contact with the parents for a full report on the baby's progress.
- The family pediatrician should be used as a liaison with the family and be welcomed as a visitor to the infant.
- The family should be advised when a visit or conversation with the family pediatrician has taken place.
- If parents are dissatisfied with the care their

baby is receiving, a conference with the physician, charge nurse, social worker, and parent service representative should be scheduled immediately.
- *Prior* to the administration of any life support technology, such as a respirator, parents should be fully informed of the criteria for its discontinuance.
- Since the intensive care unit implies some chance for therapeutic success, babies with chronic conditions should be cared for in a long-term facility, not the ICU.

Because of the rising rates of admission to NICUs many childbirth education groups across the country now sponsor special groups for parents of prematures and other infants with serious problems. Some hospital have done likewise, in response to parents' requests and the increasing awareness of the physical and emotional wear and tear a baby's hospitalization can mean for the entire family. One group which is organizing national chapters and has a staff of professional advisors is Parent-to-Parent, a group begun under the auspices of the NICU follow-up clinic at San Francisco Children's Hospital. For more information, contact: Parent-to-Parent, NICU Follow-up Clinic, San Francisco Children's Hospital, 3700 California Street, San Francisco, CA 94118, (415) 387-0583.

Chapter 7

Circumcision

Ritual Care

To circumcise or not to circumcise? That is the question. Half of new parents are relieved at the birth of their child to find they needn't make that final decision—they've been blessed with a girl. For the other half, a reappraisal of infant circumcision underway in medical circles may furnish a welcome answer to their dilemma.

Circumcision as ritual surgery, to distinguish "the men from the boys" or "our kind from their kind," is one of the oldest operations on record. Though many people attribute the institution of the practice to the Jewish patriarch, Abraham, as recorded in Genesis 17:11: "and ye shall circumcise the flesh of your foreskin; and it shall be a token of the covenant betwixt me [God] and you," circumcision and ritual scarification of the genitals had been carried out in Egypt and elsewhere in the world for thousands of years before Abraham.

Today, circumcision may be considered for medical, social, or religious reasons. Cultural norms seem to play a large part in any individual decision: 95 percent of European men remain intact for life, while in the United States approximately two-thirds of all baby boys undergo the procedure. In some American medical centers, the figure approaches 90 percent. Serious reservations about routine neonatal circumcision, now being vigorously expressed both by physicians and parents' groups, may result in American statistics resembling those of Europe in just a matter of years.

David Grimes, M.D., of the University of North Carolina School of Medicine, said at the 1977 annual meeting of the American Society for Psychosomatic Obstetrics and Gynecology, "No other procedure is performed so often for such questionable reasons on such unwilling patients . . . in addition, the vast majority of newborn circumcisions are performed without the parents' informed consent." *Ob. Gyn. News* (Vol. 13, No. 7), reporting Dr. Grimes' presentation, noted that parental consent is routinely given before the operation is done. In one study, though, information about the benefits and risks of the surgery was not provided to three-fourths of the parents. Two-thirds of another group reported that their physicians *never said anything* to them about the operation. Under these circumstances the consent given could not properly be termed "informed."

To make a responsible decision, most of us probably need to know more about two things: the penis itself and the distinction between medical and religious circumcision. There is an enormous difference.

Take a few minutes to review the penis, and, if you have no male children, try to identify the major landmarks on a friend's baby or on your mate. There is the obvious difference in size between an adult male's penis and that of a newborn, but the structures are the same. If your model has been circumcised, all that should be missing is the foreskin (prepuce). If the foreskin is missing, you will not be able to feel that it is exactly the same in texture as the rest of the skin covering the penile shaft and (if your model is an adult) that it is fully retractable. This is true, incidentally, for 99 percent of males over the age of 17.

It is *not* true for 99 percent of newborn babies, according to Lowell R. King, M.D., professor of urology and surgery at Northwestern University Medical School. He explains in a review article, "The Pros and Cons of Neonatal Circumcision" (*Surgical Rounds,* December 1979), that at this age the foreskin is still joined at its deepest layers to the glans because it is still in the process of differentiation (glans, penis, and foreskin all develop from the same block of less differentiated embryonic tissue).

We have seen that many of our babies' organs and systems are not yet fully developed at birth, so it should come as no surprise that this is also the case here. Therefore, the traditional test of whether your baby needs to be circumcised (is his foreskin retractable?) turns out to be absolutely invalid as an indicator.

A thin mucous membrane which you won't be able to see or feel lines the underside of the foreskin, next to the glans. It secretes protective fluids which prevent the tip of the glans, the meatus (opening through which urine passes), from becoming inflamed, ulcerated, and scarred by ammonia burns (caused when the urea in urine is changed to ammonia in the baby's diaper). This protection is important, because if the meatus becomes scarred, its opening is constricted and the urinary stream can be narrowed, occasionally to the point of total blockage. In cases of constriction or occlusion of the meatus a second surgical procedure, a meatotomy, is required to restore the opening to its normal size and functional capacity. The foreskin itself, of course, protects the rest of the sensitive glans from this and similar insults.

If the foreskin is normally nonretractable at birth and serves a protective function in the newborn, why dispose of it? Most long-held medical reasons for performing neonatal circumcision are now termed unproven by the bulk of contemporary researchers, primarily urologists and pediatricians. And, as more attention has been focused on the circumcision debate in recent years, significant risks from the procedure have been spelled out more clearly. The most commonly cited reasons for neonatal circumcision have been:

cleanliness—Removing the foreskin means the boy won't have to clean under it when he gets older, and, perhaps most significantly in the minds of many mothers, they won't have to teach the boy how to clean himself at all in this area. (We still have a great amount of lingering prudery about handling our own genitals in this society, despite the barrage of public nudity and sexual imagery used to sell everything from designer jeans to toothpaste.)

protection against penile cancer—There are more deaths every year in the United States from circumcision than from cancer of the penis, and general lack of hygiene is now viewed as the probable factor in the onset of cancer, not the mere presence of a foreskin. (In Sweden, where circumcision is extremely rare, there are 15 deaths per year from carcinoma of the penis out of a male population of 3.7 million, so clearly some factor other than the foreskin is to blame.)

protection of a future wife from cervical cancer—Low socioeconomic status, poor nutrition, early initiation of sexual intercourse, multiple sexual partners, venereal disease, and poor personal hygiene are now known to be far more important in the onset of cancer of the cervix than whether one's husband is circumcised. (In both Israel, where most sexual partners are circumcised, and in Scandinavia, where most are not, the rate of cervical cancer is far below that of the United States, so we must conclude that other factors are responsible.)

protection from psychological stresses—Do the old "like father, like son" and "being one of the boys" arguments really mean anything? Does a little boy really equate the look of his organ with that of his father's when there are such obvious differences in size and hairiness? If most people stop circumcising their sons, won't the circumcised then have to bear the psychological/social stigma? Does a second unnecessary operation justify the first? Is explaining a different-looking penis so much harder than explaining baldness; facial, underarm, chest, and pubic hair; calloused feet; wrinkles; graying hair; or scars from operations to a child?

improvement of one's self-image—The idea that the circumcised penis is more attractive than the uncircumcised is a highly acculturated point of view and one which many people share with primitive tribes around the world who have used circumcision and body scarification as beautification procedures since the dawn of time.

prevention or treatment of *phimosis* (narrowing of the end of the foreskin so it cannot be pulled back over the glans) and *balanitis* (inflammation of the glans)—Removal of the foreskin is much more likely to *cause balanitis* than to prevent it in the newborn, since the glans is then exposed to constant friction and irritation from wet diapers (in an adult who is bound for combat duty in the tropics or the desert, circumcision may be warranted to prevent parasitical infection, as was discovered during wartime), but *phimosis* cannot even be fully diagnosed until a boy is between ages five and ten, since it's not until this time that 90 percent of boys' foreskins are fully retractable, anyway. (Many babies have a seemingly small opening in the foreskin which enlarges as the baby grows and in a few years poses no problem to full retraction for the purposes of cleaning the penis.) Of course, if your son has repeated infections of the penis in infancy, that would be a legitimate medical indication for a circumcision due to *phimosis* and/or *balanitis*.

correction of an overly long foreskin—This occurs often enough to mention, but it still does not warrant cutting away *all* the foreskin, just the droopy excess! Some people also feel that the penis may grow to fit the foreskin, so in such cases a decision about circumcision should wait until the boy is older.

Careful study over a three-year period of all these possible reasons for circumcision of infants led the Ad Hoc Task Force on Circumcision of the American Academy of Pediatrics to conclude in 1975 that *"there is no absolute medical indication for routine circumcision of the newborn"* [italics ours] and that health benefits previously attributed to it could be accomplished with considerably less risk to the boy by teaching him a program of good penile hygiene. (For a copy of the complete report, write: American Academy of Pediatrics, 1801 Hinman Avenue, Evanston, IL 60201.)

The risks of medical circumcision detailed in the task force report become more evident the more we learn about the surgery itself.

There are four ways to perform circumcision: the dorsal slit method, the clamp method (Gomco or Yellen), the Plastibell method, and the "freehand" method (used in older males and in religious circumcision, discussed later). In medical circumcision of infants, no anesthesia is used, and the baby is completely restrained on a circum-

cision board to reduce the possibility of movement during the procedure. There should be a suction unit on hand to clear the baby's nose and mouth should he vomit during the operation. The safest policy is to have laboratory results of the baby's bleeding and clotting times available before the surgery; however, in institutions where neonatal circumcision is permitted in the delivery room or nursery just after birth this preventive measure against hemorrhage is not taken.

It's important to realize that it's not just babies with hemophilia who bleed, often uncontrollably. A deficiency of any of the many clotting factors in the blood can produce the same unhappy result. Consequently, a family history free of hemophilia does not mean the baby is safe from potential bleeding disorders. For this reason, the American Academy of Pediatrics recommends that, when circumcision is desired by the parents, it not be carried out for at least 12 to 24 hours after birth and then only by an experienced individual specially trained in this operation.

All too often, the Ad Hoc Committee on Circumcision found, there is a tendency to regard circumcision as such a minor surgical procedure that inexperienced, unsupervised people are assigned to do it. If you choose circumcision for your son, you should be present, if for no other reason than to verify who actually performs the operation. Your comfort and solace will also be important to your baby after the surgery is concluded.

The March 15, 1978, issue of *Patient Care* featured an article, "Circumcision: Rite, Rationale, or Both?," prepared in consultation with professors of urology, obstetrics/gynecology, and pediatrics, which reviews the techniques of medical circumcision procedures and aftercare. The series of illustrations based on that article that follows, details each method, along with the special problems associated with each. Interestingly, nowhere in the article is the subject of the baby's pain and continuing postoperative discomfort discussed as a problem connected with the surgery. Yet, as mothers will tell you, babies who were pleasant and content prior to the operation often become difficult to comfort, startle easily, cry excessively, sleep fitfully, and demonstrate other behavior indicative of suffering for days afterward. Given what is now known about the acuity of the baby's sensory abilities immediately after birth and from then on, it hardly seems possible that "the baby doesn't feel it at all," as so many of the medical and nursing textbooks tell us.

Complications of Medical Circumcision

Complication	Cause	Treatment
Hemorrhage	Undetected bleeding disorder (can be fatal).	Vitamin K, transfusion.
	Severing of deep penile blood vessels.	Insert stitches.
Fistula (abnormal opening between urethra and skin)	Too much foreskin drawn through clamp (urethra crushed).	Surgical repair—often requires two separate operations because of location (base of glans).
	Bleeding requiring sutures (stitches accidentally sever urethra).	
Denuded Penile Shaft (penis shortened)	Too much foreskin removed.	Bury penis in scrotum until penile skin regenerates, then surgically release.
Scarring and Constriction of Circumcision Edge (*phimosis*)	Too little foreskin removed.	Recircumcision (usually at time of mother's postpartum checkup).
Divided Glans (split urinary stream)	Improper application of clamp (one edge into meatus).	Surgical repair.
Wound Infections (from pus sores to gangrene, blood poisoning, bone infections, lung abscesses—can be fatal)	Improper surgical technique (insufficient attention to asepsis). Prematurity/underweight. Illness. Inadequate diaper care. Malnutrition (difficulty with formula, sucking).	Thorough cleansing, antibiotic lotions and dressings. Encourage breastfeeding. Careful laundering of diapers. Prompt changing of soiled diapers. Intensive care for severe cases.
Narrowing or Blocking of Urinary Meatus	Scarring due to inflammation of glans after circumcision.	Surgical enlargement of the opening (meatotomy).
Loss of Penis	Cauterizing rather than stitching. Surgical accident (inexperienced operator).	Series of reconstructive operations. Raise as female.

The one nursing text which does mention the baby's cries during the operation, Fitzpatrick's *Maternity Nursing* (12th ed., Philadelphia: Lippincott, 1971) states: "This is due as much to the necessary restraints as to the discomfort." We doubt it. Perhaps when the operation was performed right after birth and the mother had been heavily sedated, the baby would be "benefiting" from the obstetric medications to the point that the circumcision was not very painful. When the baby has been born with minimal medication, though, the situation is quite different. It is an absolute

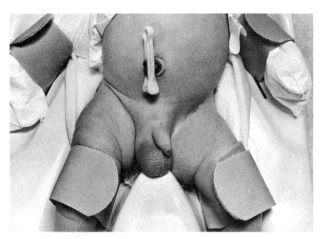

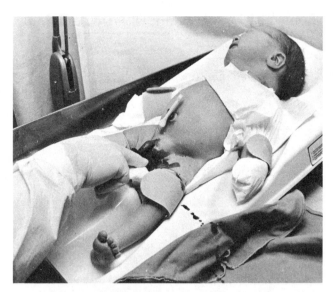

Above, *Close-up of uncircumcised penis.* Top right, *Immobilizing baby on circumcision board; painting on antiseptic scrub.*

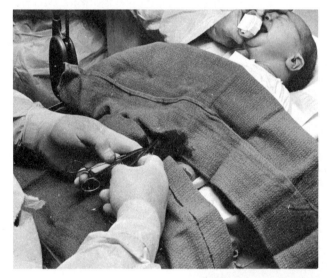

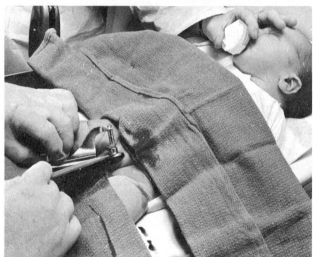

Above, *Cutting dorsal slit to permit retraction of foreskin; baby with pacifier to stifle cries.* Center right, *Removing Gomco clamp (foreskin rings shaft).*

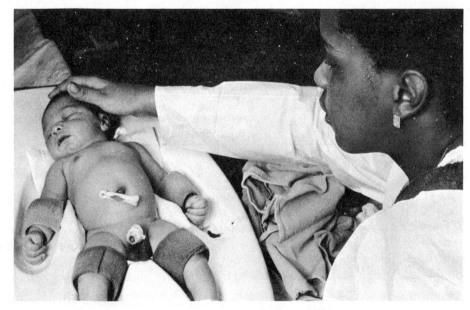

Comforting baby postoperatively.

Right from the Start

contradiction to marvel at the wondrous capabilities of the newborn (sight, smell, taste, reflexes, interaction potential) on one hand and then deny that the baby has any nerve endings in his skin on the other. Giving a small dose of local anesthetic seems the humane thing to do whenever circumcision is to be performed.

In Rosemary Wiener's forthcoming book, *Circumcision: The Painful Dilemma*, the point is made that sometimes babies do not cry a great deal during circumcision. Instead they seem to lapse into a state of "semicoma," presumably because of extreme trauma. The absence of crying in cases like this has led many parents and professionals to believe falsely that the operation did not hurt.

Immediately after the operation, you should nurse your baby to soothe him as much as possible. It is standard practice to then return him to the nursery for close observation for approximately 12 hours. The fresh wound may have a tendency to bleed or ooze. The nursery staff should report any undue bleeding to you and to the physician at once. Local pressure usually halts minor bleeding, but if the bleeding persists it may become necessary to place fine stitches through the edge of the wound or the bleeding blood vessels. The dressing applied to the penis and the diaper may stick to the raw area. Soaking these items with sterile water will help free them with less trauma and pain for the baby.

When you are responsible for changing your son's diaper and dressing post-op, ask the nurse to show you how to fold the diaper so only one layer of material covers the penis, thus allowing freer circulation of air to the wound and easier observation of any bleeding tendency. *No plastic pants should be used on the baby.* If your hospital provides only paper diapers, cut away the plastic except for the sections where the tabs are fastened, and place a rubber sheet under the baby to protect the mattress and bed linens. Finally, have the nurse show you how to hold the baby's ankles to prevent him from kicking the circumcised area while you change and cleanse him. Change diapers hourly to keep the wound as dry as possible. For more detailed instruction on care of the penis (circumcised and uncircumcised), see "A Quick Guide for Starting Right" in the Appendix.

There are some situations in which circumcision is completely contraindicated:

premature birth—These babies have enough to contend with, without having to try and overcome the aftereffects of surgery as well.

congenital abnormalities—Especially heart defects.

illness or infection—Where further complications are encouraged by added stress.

family history of hemophilia or bleeding disorders—The risks are obvious in such cases.

ambiguous genitals—Sex determination may require tests beyond mere examination of the genitals.

hypospadias—A developmental abnormality of the penis affecting 1 in 250 newborn boys, in which the urethra opens on the underside of the penis or on the perineum (not part of the penis at all). In this case, the foreskin is needed to reconstruct the urethra and any decision about surgery should wait until after you have had a consultation with a urologist about just what will be involved in your baby's case.

low Apgar rating—A baby with a low rating may need a longer period of time to recover after difficult birth.

Since many of these problems would not be discovered until a thorough pediatric examination of the baby was done, this is one more reason to wait *at least a day* before scheduling a medically indicated circumcision.

So far, we've been looking only at the medical rationales in the circumcision controversy. There is another facet to the circumcision decisions that are made each day, and it boils down to who you ask about the wisdom of having it done. By and large, obstetricians, who actually perform the operation (they are trained to do the surgery), continue to favor routine neonatal circumcision. Pediatricians and family practitioners, who have to deal with the aftermath, typically counsel against it. Several of the major articles on circumcision point out this difference of opinion, remarking that one could hardly expect the professional who gets paid for doing a routine service to find fault with the procedure.

And routine newborn circumcision is a big business in the United States. Conservative estimates (a million and a half operations at $50 per, plus hospital charges for equipment, use of a "circ" room, and extra days of hospitalization when infections occur) run around $150,000,000 a year. An editorial in the *British Medical Journal* (May 5, 1979, pp. 1,163–64), "The Case Against Neonatal Circumcision," comments on the vast amounts of medical and nursing time involved in caring for neonatal circumcision patients, terming removal of the foreskin within a few hours of birth "part of the North American way of life." As one would expect, the pediatricians may not be completely free of self-interest in the matter, either. "If the AAP [American Academy of Pediatrics] recommendations were put into effect," *Ob. Gyn. News* (December 15, 1974) asserts, "circumcision, when elected by parents, would not be done by obstetricians in the delivery room, but later by a 'specially trained' circumciser, probably a pediatrician." So, the recommendation you receive about your baby's foreskin may merely reflect the status of the fight for "turf" in your local hospital.

Ultimately, of course, the decision rests with us, the parents, and no matter what our consultants' viewpoints, it is our own good judgment that should prevail. Be sure to take the matter up with your obstetrician and pediatrician in the last month or two of your pregnancy, so everyone knows of your decision. If you do want your baby circumcised by the doctor, it is wise to sign a consent form that details the procedures to be performed, so that all parties are in full agreement. This is the same type of consent you would require if the operation were to be performed on yourself. It is also an excellent way of insuring that you will be allowed to be present for the circumcision, a point mentioned previously. If you decide against circumcision and are having your baby in an institution where circumcision is nearly universal, it may be worth it to request that a special card be attached to your baby's nursery cradle stating clearly that this baby is not to be circumcised. Your pediatrician's orders for the baby should state the same thing right at the top. Mention your wishes to the admissions personnel at the hospital when you go into the labor and delivery unit and again to the doctor during labor. It's easy for charts to get lost or interchanged, so taking a little extra measure of precaution on the day the surgery would most likely be performed makes sense.

Religious circumcision presents an entirely different set of considerations for parents, since the timing, methods, and circumstances of the procedure are at such variance with those of medical circumcision. In an interview with Rabbi Moshe Portnoy of Elmhurst (New York) Jewish Center, we were able to have many questions about religious circumcision answered which other sources slighted. Emphasizing that ritual Jewish circumcision is a requirement for formal entry into the covenant of Abraham, Rabbi Portnoy explained

circumcision as an initiation rite with every step imbued with spiritual significance:

The choice of the eighth day after birth as the time for circumcision corresponds to the medical observation that the baby's own store of vitamin K is usually in operation by then, but as far as Jewish law is concerned the eighth day is chosen because the number eight stands for the world of the spiritual. The law is also clear that any male product of conception must be circumcised, even if stillborn. The only exceptions to this rule are if the infant is not healthy on the eighth day, or if the mother has lost two sons from circumcision, or she has lost one and her sister has lost one, then the ritual should be postponed. This recognizes the hereditary patterns of many coagulation disorders.

A man specially trained in circumcision, a *mohel*, actually performs the surgery. Becoming a *mohel* is something of a family tradition, something to which one is "called." The legal minimum for entry into an "apprenticeship" as a *mohel* is that a young man must have completed his Bar Mitzvah, though most are considerably older than this. There is no classroom training for prospective *mohels*. The candidate accompanies a practicing *mohel* for two months or so, just observing. Then he will be permitted to assist with the postoperative bandaging. After he develops competence at that, he graduates to severing the foreskin after the experienced *mohel* has set the guard which protects the glans beneath. The final steps are learning to attach the guard and checking to see that it's in the right place, and learning to use the probe to loosen the foreskin before it is pulled forward and the guard placed. The *mohel* also must learn the ritual and benedictions that comprise the religious part of the ceremony. When his mentor is satisfied that the new *mohel* is competent, the Board of Rabbis notifies the State Department of Education and the State Department of Health (in New York State), who then issue him a certificate. This certificate is recognized even in hospitals where a *mohel* may often be called to perform a circumcision on an adult. The *mohel*'s fee for circumcision ($75 in New York City) compares very favorably with that charged by medical doctors, since the *mohel* also makes a precircumcision visit to the

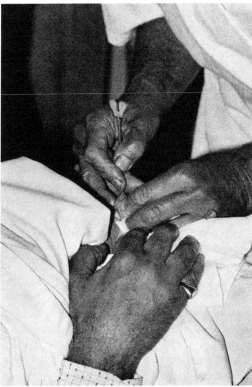

Left, *Prayers at the bris.* Right, Mohel *loosens foreskin with probe.*

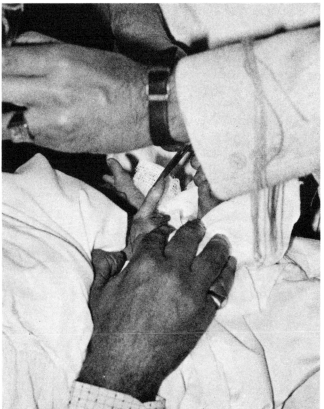

Loosened foreskin drawn over glans.

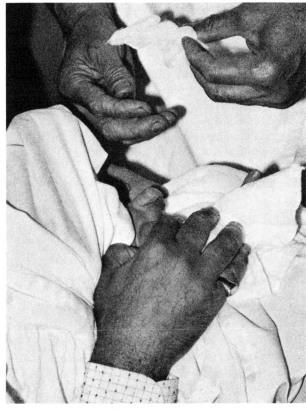

Circumcised penis (most of foreskin remains —glans not completely exposed).

Circumcision: Ritual Care

family to explain what to expect and to examine the baby, and a post-op visit 24 to 36 hours afterward to make sure the wound is healing properly.

Family and friends gather for the *bris,* after which it is customary to serve food and wine. The women remain with the mother during the brief time the ceremony lasts, while the men are present during the procedure. An honored man, the *sandek,* usually an elder member of the family, holds the baby in his arms throughout the circumcision. The baby is named during the ritual, usually after a deceased relative or revered person. As far as the surgery itself is concerned the baby is bandaged, diapered, and back in his mother's arms to be fed and comforted in a matter of minutes. (If a *mohel* takes more than 60 to 90 seconds to perform the operation, he's considered very slow!) The traditional pacifier given to the baby after the procedure is a drop of wine on the tip of the officiant's finger, but today the baby may suck on a pacifier filled with sugar water or dilute brandy. It is a happy time for family and friends, one of the high points for observant Jews.

According to experienced mothers, the best thing to do for yourself and your baby immediately after the circumcision is to lie down with the baby and nurse. Both of you will be calmed and reassured. It helps even more to have had a drink or two. The alcohol will go through to the baby (also a good idea a couple hours before the circumcision) and help with his discomfort. Then the baby may even sleep for a while before rejoining the party.

Overall, the religious circumcision seems far less traumatic a procedure for the infants than medical circumcision, and, since it is done fully a week later than most medical circumcisions and in the baby's home environment, the baby is generally stronger and less likely to develop an infection than in the hospital nursery. One study of 8,000 infants undergoing ritual circumcision in Israel showed that infection was almost unheard of, the most frequent complication being hemorrhage—and that occurring in only 10 boys (Shulman et al., "Surgical Complications of Circumcision," *American Journal of Diseases of Children,* 107:149, 1964).

If your son requires a circumcision for any reason at any time of life, you might want to contact a Jewish friend for the name of a *mohel* who will perform the surgery on non-Jews. The "free-hand" surgical technique results in less chance of post-op complications from retained plastic clamps or excess skin removal, both situations which can create a series of medical problems for your child. Be sure the *mohel* you contact does the "free-hand" procedure. Unfortunately, many *mohels* are now using the medical circumcision protocols (restraints, clamps, removal of entire foreskin), thereby rendering academic the difference between medical and religious circumcision. In the eyes of many rabbis, such circumcisions are invalid, since they do not follow Jewish law.

To summarize, unless you are observing a religious ritual, the indications for newborn circumcision are virtually nonexistent, and at this writing the disadvantages seem to outweigh any potential advantages resoundingly. For information on parents' circumcision information groups, see the Directory.

Chapter 8

Breastfeeding
Personal Care

Breastfeeding is the physical embodiment of the mother-baby relationship that continues after birth. The mother, as she did during pregnancy, gives of her own body to her child. The baby receives the nourishment for his/her body, the milk, and also nourishment for his/her spirit, the mother's loving presence. By the same token, the baby gives stimulation to the mother's body, and the mother receives the biological benefits of suckling she needs for a smooth return to the non-pregnant state and the emotional benefits of knowing she is doing something for her child no one else can.

Research into breastfeeding is at an all-time high. Biologists, physiologists, psychologists, anthropologists, sociologists, chemists, and ecologists are all getting into the breastfeeding counseling business, formerly the professional province of the nurse and the pediatrician. While all of these specialties have contributed interesting insights into various aspects of the lactation and child development processes, you still have to talk to mothers to find out the inside information on breastfeeding: what really works on a day-to-day basis, and what breastfeeding means to mother and child.

Joann Groman, mother of eight and author of a book on attachment, *Born to Love*, available from International Childbirth Education Association Bookcenter (see Directory) gets to the heart of why

ad lib breastfeeding best satisfies the deepest human nurturing needs:

> The growth of the child's capacity to make a deep and lasting attachment to anybody is allied to the constancy of his mother and to the appropriateness of her response. No human relationship carries with it a greater possibility for love and joy or for anxiety, sorrow, grief, and anger. So naked are these emotions in the young child that we scarcely have the courage to look upon them.

Jane and Joseph Jackson, in *Infant Culture* (New York: New American Library, 1979), discussing the frequently noted precocity of children in other cultures where breastfeeding is the norm, list several ways breastfeeding promotes this precocity.

- Breastfeeding on demand reduces a child's frustrations so there is more time to focus on events outside his/her own body.
- Constant contact with care givers stimulates message centers in the brain so they develop more quickly.
- Lack of restrictive clothing allows greater sense of being *with* others.
- The infant is kept in constant contact with care givers by being held and carried everywhere the adult goes, and by sleeping close

to the mother, thus developing a strong sense of personal security.

John Bowlby, the prime spokesman for the ethological theory of human attachment to which so many contemporary writers owe so much, notes that these are the behaviors upon which the very survival of our species has rested from the very start. How, then, did we go from the point where breastfeeding was essential to survival to the point where, until very recently, artificial formula feeding has been the norm? What happened to the innate, physiological process of lactation that turned it into a mysterious, mystical talent some women possess but others don't?

To start to answer these questions, let us return to the primitive couple we met in the Introduction to this book. Obviously, they have not attended prenatal education classes, nor have they read any of the popular books on child care. The mother follows her inborn feelings. She has also seen other mammals caring for their young. She knows, even if she cannot verbalize the principle, that creatures which bear their young alive also have the mechanism to ensure their young's survival—the lactation process.

If we observe a new mother holding her baby we are struck by the "rightness" of the position for nursing. The baby's head is cradled in the crook of her elbow, bringing the baby's mouth to the exact level of her breast. How convenient! How then, did something so basically simple get to be so complicated? To answer that we have to look at the effects that civilization has had on our biological processes.

Before this century, the choice of a feeding method was a relatively simple issue. One breastfed or employed another woman to breast-feed the infant. All other choices, from feeding the milks of other animals to feeding "pap," a mixture of gruel and water, were almost always fatal to the infant. As recently as 1897, Dr. Holt, the "expert" of his time, stated in his pediatrics textbook, *The Diseases of Infancy and Childhood*, that wet nurses (the term for a woman who nurses the child of another woman for pay) "are indispensable . . . as the perfect substitute for good breast milk is as yet undiscovered."

Unfortunately, at the same time that Holt was admonishing mothers to breastfeed, birthing was starting to move from the home to the hospital. Baby care moved with it. Because the hospital nursery had to run on a schedule, feeding

recommendations reflected regimentation. (See chapter 4.)

By the time the roaring twenties rolled around, bottle feeding was becoming the vogue among the liberated, educated women of the day. Whereas in 1897, Holt was recommending ten nursings a day, his 1924 tome, *The Care and Feeding of Children: A Catechism for the Use of Mothers and Children's Nurses* (10th ed.), recommended only seven. Without early and frequent stimulation of the breasts, lactation failure became rampant. Sadly, the cause of these failures was not recognized, and women blamed their own shortcomings for their lack of milk. Breastfeeding had started to become something only certain women could do. Bottle feeding became a growth industry.

Numerous books have detailed the psychological warfare wrought on the would-be nurser. Even Holt's *Care and Feeding of Children* placed this burden of responsibility on the mother.

> Uncontrolled emotions, grief, excitement, fright, passion, may cause milk to disagree with the child; at times they may excite acute illness, and at other times they may cause a sudden and complete disappearance of the milk.

With the medical profession lacking a clear understanding of the lactation process, the climate was right for the beginning of the subversion of breastfeeding by the formula manufacturers. A complete discussion appears in *The Promotion of Bottle Feeding by Multinational Corporations: How Advertising and the Health Professions Have Contributed*, by Ted Greiner (Cornell International Nutrition Monograph Series No. 2, 1975, Cornell University, Ithaca, NY 14853).

Artificial formulas have been on the market for over 40 years, but have been profitable for only about the last 20 years. This parallels the switch-over in teaching at the medical school level. Where doctors were formerly taught that "breast is best," those trained over the past 20 to 30 years were more likely to have been taught that "breast may be best, but bottle is easier."

Looking at formula ads that have appeared in the medical journals over these past 30 years, one is struck by the utter disregard for the dignity of women. One is also struck by the lack of alternative solutions to the problems that may lead to bottle feeding, especially if one assumes that a

TRU-BREAST

A revolutionary new method of infant feeding! It's ready in an instant! Less work for mother!

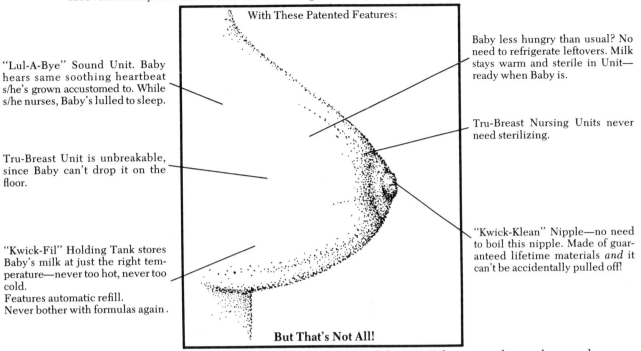

With These Patented Features:

"Lul-A-Bye" Sound Unit. Baby hears same soothing heartbeat s/he's grown accustomed to. While s/he nurses, Baby's lulled to sleep.

Tru-Breast Unit is unbreakable, since Baby can't drop it on the floor.

"Kwick-Fil" Holding Tank stores Baby's milk at just the right temperature—never too hot, never too cold.
Features automatic refill.
Never bother with formulas again.

Baby less hungry than usual? No need to refrigerate leftovers. Milk stays warm and sterile in Unit—ready when Baby is.

Tru-Breast Nursing Units never need sterilizing.

"Kwick-Klean" Nipple—no need to boil this nipple. Made of guaranteed lifetime materials *and* it can't be accidentally pulled off!

But That's Not All!

Tru-Breast Units solve the problem of storage of baby items until the next Baby comes along—they are decorative as well as functional! They come in all sizes, shapes, and colors, and outward appearance has nothing to do with ability of Units to function. Units come in pairs and improve with use. Tru-Breast makes traveling with Baby easier—the no-mess, no-worry way! **With Tru-Breast Around, Why Bother with Other Methods?**

Tru-Breast available as a flyer from: NAPSAC, P. O. Box 267,
Marble Hill, MO 63764
(ask for bulk order information)

medical journal is devoted to promoting better health for all.

Some quotes from formula advertisements (with our comments):

. . . Laboratory-made Breast-Milk
(False advertising.)
. . . When nature *is inadequate . . . recommend a* natural *replacement.*
(This tempts doctor to assume that all women are inadequate unless proven otherwise, when, in actuality, most lactation failures are caused by incorrect information given to the mother.)
. . . When traveling, the nursing mother need not be dismayed for lack of the privacy necessary for feeding her infant.
(We agree, but our solution is to find privacy or nurse discreetly, not a supplementary bottle as this ad suggests.)
. . . For doctors' convenience
(No comment necessary.)

. . . When supply can't meet demand
(It's easier to prescribe formula than to counsel mother about building up her milk supply.)
. . . To reduce the incidence of feeding problems . . .
(No mention here of the fact that human milk is for humans . . . and that the incidence of feeding problems such as allergy, poor digestion, and vomiting is higher in artificially fed babies.)

Now that the tide is turning and for the first time in many years more babies are starting out being breastfed than formula fed, drug companies are getting on the breastfeeding bandwagon. The idea seems to be—if you can't sell them formula and bottles, find something you *can* sell them . . . but don't make breastfeeding look too easy. Then perhaps most will fail and switch to our bottle-feeding products.

One popular alternative to the old bottle sterilizer/bottle brush kit is the new breast pump/

Breastfeeding: Personal Care

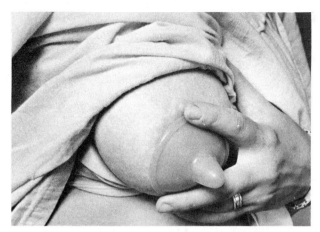

Breast shield, which is not recommended for sore nipples.

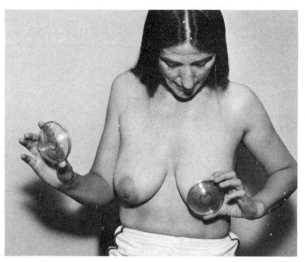

Milk cup helps correct inverted or flat nipples.

nursing pads/breast cream/nipple shield kit. Let's look at these devices and see how they, too, might be used to subvert breastfeeding.

Breast pumps are devices for removing the milk from the breast. It's far easier, as well as far more gentle, to use your hands. (See chapter 6 for instructions for hand expression.) But the underlying assumption in either method is that the baby needs your milk more than s/he needs you. This is an incorrect assumption. The process of breastfeeding cannot possibly be equated with the product, breast milk. Formula companies produce substitutes for the product, breast milk, but cannot produce a substitute for the process of breastfeeding. Breastfeeding keeps you and your baby together; breast pumps may be used to keep you apart.

The *breast shield* is a pliable plastic device that goes between your nipple and your baby's mouth. It is purported to prevent or cure cracked or sore nipples. In actuality, it *prolongs soreness and interferes with the stimulation of the nerves around the areola* that tell your body to manufacture more milk. They are often mistakenly recommended to women with flat or inverted nipples, to "draw them out." Many women are incorrectly told that their nipples are inverted. To check for yourself, follow the procedure on the accompanying chart and use *only* the correct device, a milk cup, as needed.

The *milk cup* is a rigid plastic cup which fits over your nipple and areola, exerting continuous, gentle pressure on the tissue surrounding the nipple. In response to the pressure, the nipple gradually extends. Over a period of time (several

months) with faithful use even the most resistant cases of inverted nipples can be corrected. The milk cup also collects the milk which dribbles from the breast in the process, so you aren't dampening your clothes constantly. Use only those milk cups which can be sterilized, since they should be thoroughly cleaned between wearings (a toothbrush and hot, soapy water can be used to remove any dried milk). Unfortunately, milk cups are often referred to as "breast shields," even by commercial manufacturers and some organizations providing counseling to nursing mothers. Be sure to check what's in the package before you order.

As for sore nipples, they can usually be prevented or treated in ways that will not interfere with your nursing relationship. Preventive care, which is based on adequate nutrition (the lactation diet is the same diet as for pregnancy), keeping mother and baby together, and nursing often from birth, avoids the need for devices like breast shields which only serve to put another barrier between the nursing couple.

The causes of sore nipples are myriad, but the treatment offered is almost always the same: *nipple cream.* Most professionals have abandoned the idea that nipples must be "toughened," and no longer advise drying agents such as tincture of benzoin or alcohol wipes. The "tough" nipple has a tendency to crack. The ideal nipple is supple and pliant. Since the quality of body tissue is directly related to diet, the foundation of good nipple care is an excellent diet. Nutrients help the nipple develop and heal from within; nipple creams

Inverted Nipples?

To diagnose: An inverted nipple is one that is "inside out." When stimulated, the normal nipple erects or stands out. When stimulated, the inverted nipple pulls further in. Some women have flat nipples which also make it difficult for the infant to latch on. Simply rub your fingers back and forth over your bare nipples. If they stay flat or retract, you need to correct them.

Treatment: For flat or mildly inverted nipples Wear milk cups inside bra three hours a day during the last four months of pregnancy.

For severely inverted nipples Start as early as possible in the pregnancy and wear as long as possible (up to eight hours a day). After birth, if inversion is still present or problem has not been diagnosed during the pregnancy, wear between feedings until baby is able to grasp nipple easily. After nursing leave the milk cups off for 15 to 30 minutes and allow nipples to air dry.

Warnings: Do not use any milk that collects in the milk cups. It is easily contaminated. Do not confuse the milk cup with the breast shield, a plastic device that fits over the mother's nipple *during a feeding.* When breast shields are used, baby becomes even less interested in sucking on the mother's nipple and mother loses stimulation essential to milk production. The milk cup does not intervene in the mother-baby relationship; the breast shield does.

To order milk cups: Nursing Mothers' Council Childbirth Education Association of Greater Philadelphia, 129 Fayette Street, Conshohocken, PA 19428, (215) 828-0131.

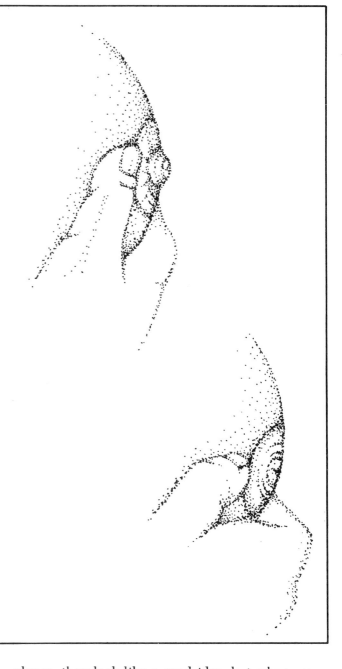

placed on the surface only soothe. In addition, many recommended creams contain perfumes which may irritate and alcohol which is a drying agent. This aggravates the problem. Beware! Read the label carefully and *never* use a product with alcohol as one of its ingredients. The most soothing cream is pure hydrous lanolin (available in small tubes at most drugstores). Many women swear by vitamin E rubbed onto the nipple.

Nursing pads are paper or cloth inserts for nursing bras. They absorb the overflow of milk that often comes just before or just after nursing. At first glance, they look like a good idea, but when we consider what we are doing to the nipple, we see that what a pad does is to keep the nipple wrapped in a wet bandage. If you'll recall what happens to your skin when you soak in water for a long time you'll see our point. When the nipple is constantly wet, which is likely to occur when pads are used in the first weeks after birth, it gets puckered, the skin sloughs off, and soreness and infection may follow.

Once you recognize the hazards in the standard advice given to new mothers you can appre-

Breastfeeding: Personal Care

ciate how one intervention in mothering leads to another. Let's consider just two more of these medically approved interventions, the *supplementary bottle* and the *pacifier*.

To understand why a supplementary bottle cannot possibly help successful breastfeeding, consider the process of lactation in the healthy, well-fed woman as a supply and demand phenomenon. Whether you decide to breastfeed or not, nature prepares you for nurturing your baby. Colostrum is present during pregnancy. If the mother nurses her baby at birth, and frequently thereafter, "mature" milk comes in, often within 24 hours. This is because the stimulation of the nerves around the nipple tells your body what your baby needs. The more frequent the stimulation, the greater the body's response. Other feedings, whether formula or juice, interfere with this delicate balance. In addition, sucking on a rubber nipple is far different from nursing. Some babies come to prefer the formula, which is oversweetened, and refuse to nurse. So any sort of feeding other than nursing in the early months should be viewed with suspicion.

For a discussion of pacifiers, see "A Quick Guide for Starting Right" in the Appendix.

If a baby is allowed to nurse at will from the well-nourished mother, s/he will get enough fluid as well as enough sucking. Note that this occurs in the well-nourished mother. There is a theory we like to call the "Magic Breast Theory" which states that the breast manufactures nutritious milk regardless of the mother's nutritional status. That theory is as outmoded as the idea that there is a "Magic Placenta," a concept which we discussed in chapter 1. The quality and quantity of breast milk is affected by how well the mother eats; and in the severely malnourished woman, lactation will virtually cease. The minimally nourished mother will produce some milk, but if her own diet does not contain the elements of good nutrition, her breast milk will be deficient in quantity as well as quality. The reason is the way the breast makes milk.

As Oliver Cope, M.D., for many years a surgeon and professor of surgery at Harvard Medical School, writes in his book *The Breast: A Health Guide for Women of All Ages* (Boston: Houghton Mifflin, 1978):

> The breast is an astonishingly complicated organ, an inseparable part of the whole intricate system of reproduction. It grows through-

out pregnancy, ready to do its job the minute the child is born. When no longer needed to supply the infant's nutrition, it recedes, to start all over again when called upon by another pregnancy. Man has nothing like it.

While anatomical diagrams of breast structure are readily available in books on breastfeeding, and the processes resulting in milk "letdown" or delivery to the nipples have been well described, Cope's book is the only one we've seen for the general reader that explains exactly how milk is formed. Referring to an article by Linzell and Peaker, "Mechanism of Milk Secretion," (*Physiological Review*, 51:563–96, 1971), Cope summarizes:

> Each [of tens of thousands of tiny cells] must absorb, *from the blood flowing by,* all the basic substances it needs to make colostrum and milk. The basic substances are water, salts, sugar, fats, and small nitrogen-containing molecules. These are put together inside the cell to make the complicated, life-building fluids. Colostrum, the glistening, clear fluid that is the first to be secreted . . . contains immunity-providing proteins that protect against measles and mumps and other infections until the infant can build his or her own immunities. Milk, appearing a day later, contains in addition a balanced amount of calcium, magnesium, and phosphorus to build the bones of the infant, and protein and sugar for the tissues to grow and live on. There is a full score of vitamins and cream in the right amount for the human infant.

In other words, milk does not appear out of nowhere. Nor is it automatically of high quality. *Only what's in the mother's bloodstream,* based on what's provided from her own daily food intake, is available to the milk-secreting cells to do their job.

Related to the bottle is another "whammy" that modern medicine throws at the nursing couple, the *"Introductory Take-Home Pack,"* thoughtfully furnished by the formula manufacturers. We asked the administrator of a large metropolitan hospital why, despite the fact that the hospital officially supported breastfeeding, all new nursing mothers were given a package containing a bottle and can of a popular artificial formula.

The administrator, himself the father of a new, breastfed baby, told us with a bit of embarrassment that the companies did not charge the hospital for the formula that they supplied. This saves the hospital administration a huge amount of money, since the company supplies regular formula for the nurseries and pediatrics divisions as well as any special formulas needed by a sick infant.

Of course, this is also a big convenience for the staff. The only stipulation made in exchange by the formula makers is that no mother should leave the hospital without a free sample of their product. The pack does not inform the mother of the circumstances under which it has been made available. So, the underlying implication is that *the hospital* recommends these products as being best for their littlest patients. We asked if the formula currently being given out was the best. The administrator said that, as far as he knew, there was little difference between them, and that "to be fair," the hospital rotated among the different companies.

He admitted that the presence of the bottle in the home could lead to mothers wrongfully believing that it was necessary "just in case," but opined that most women would probably want to supplement, anyway. Formula companies know from marketing surveys that a mother is most likely to continue using the brand she was given in the hospital whenever she decides to use the bottle. And from their advertising it's clear that after the "novelty" of breastfeeding wears off (a month or so), a few bottles a day will be a welcome addition to baby's daily routine.

What happens when the supplementary bottles begin? Too often, the untimely demise of breastfeeding. With the reduced stimulation, the increase in milk tension inside the breasts as they continue to fill and are unrelieved for several hours, and the gradual socialization of the baby to the bottle (perhaps given by someone other than the mother), the breasts gradually cut back on the amount of milk they produce. Then the supplementary bottle, instead of being a "convenience," becomes a necessity. The mother simply doesn't have enough milk any more to satisfy all her baby's rapidly increasing needs. She and the baby are hooked on the bottle, and if you're preparing three a day, why not just give six and be done with it? You're using that many, anyway, in the partial feedings that have now become necessary after each breastfeeding.

When mothers remark that they "lost their milk" after a few weeks, this sequence of events turns out to be a very common pattern. So, without wanting to sound paranoid, the little "introductory pack" isn't really as innocuous as it looks. Leave it sitting on the shelf—*in the hospital*—and concentrate on sustaining your own milk supply. (See chart.)

If you've already started down the supplementary bottle path, or if you have stopped breastfeeding altogether because you've begun to use the bottle, it's not too late to reverse the process. Even if you've adopted a baby (and have never been pregnant yourself), it is possible to lactate. The key is to keep the baby interested in sucking on a breast which, as yet, isn't producing anything—or producing far less than the baby needs for satisfaction. The best source of information about relactation is a series of well-researched monographs

---

"No Worries About Milk Supply" Checklist

1. My baby nurses at least every two or three hours, with, at most, one longer stretch at night.
2. I feed my baby as often as s/he seems to ask for it.
3. I have developed the "unbutton" reflex—when in doubt, I offer.
4. I allow baby to nurse as long as s/he wants to.
5. When baby slows down nursing on one side I offer the other side.
6. I alternate the side I offer first.
7. I do not offer a supplementary bottle of formula.
8. I do not offer a bottle of water.
9. I do not offer a pacifier.
10. I have not started offering solid foods or juice yet.
11. I am not taking birth control pills.
12. I am eating the same well-balanced diet I ate during pregnancy.
13. I am drinking plenty of water and nourishing liquids.
14. I get some rest and relaxation each day.
15. My baby has at least six to eight wet diapers a day.

from Resources in Human Nurturing, International (RHNI), P. O. Box 6861, Denver, CO 80206. The editor and co-author of the series, Jimmie Lynne Avery, is an expert on the subject of induced lactation, relactation, and the causes of untimely weaning. In the foreword to "Relactation After a Hospitalization-Induced Separation," Ruth Lawrence, M.D., of the pediatrics/neonatology department at the University of Rochester New York Medical Center explains:

> The subject of relactation is often misunderstood and almost totally neglected in medical writing. Many clinicians are totally unaware that it is physiologically possible to restimulate a milk supply in the human mother once the suckling stimulus has stopped. Experienced nursing mothers, however, have observed that they can express milk from their breasts weeks and months after their infant received his final feeding at the breast. In studying other cultures, sociologists have reported infants being nourished at the breast by substitute mothers who have not lactated for years when tragedy has taken the biological mother from the infant. Yet clinicians and breastfeeding counselors often find themselves ill prepared to assist a mother who wishes to relactate.

In other words, relactation may not be easy, but if the choice is hospitalizing your baby who can't tolerate anything but human milk, for example, it may be the easier of the alternatives. RHNI also markets a device to assist in keeping the baby suckling at the breast in order to stimulate milk production, the Lact-Aid. (See photograph.) Formula is placed in the bag attached to the necklace, and the soft plastic tube is laid alongside the nipple and into the baby's mouth so suckling is rewarded. Instructions come with the kit.

The primary rule for successful breastfeeding is to keep mother and baby together and nursing, regardless of what else happens. Let's say you manage to have your baby with you and nursing from birth on, and you are now settling into life as a nursing mother. What else can happen?

One of the most common problems women experience in the first few days is *breast engorgement*. Nature didn't know you were only having one baby—human mothers are equipped to feed two. This overabundance of milk is usually not a problem with ad lib nursing. But if there has been a separation of mother and baby, mother may find

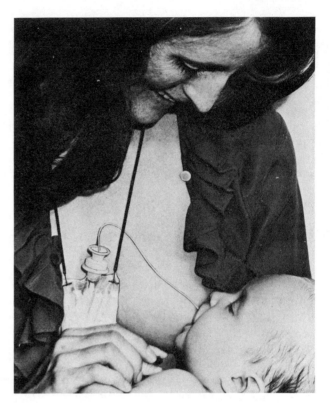

Lact-Aid Nursing Trainer assists in relactation.

herself with breasts that feel like hard basketballs. With engorgement, the nipple often becomes flat and difficult to grab. As with everything, an ounce of prevention is worth a pound of cure. Our pound of cure is these exercises adapted from the teachings of Asoka Roy, M.S., C.N.M., director of midwifery, Beth Israel Hospital, New York.

One of the most common complaints of new nursing mothers is nipple soreness. To prevent soreness from developing:

- Make sure baby is taking the whole areola in his or her mouth, not just chewing on the end.
- After each nursing allow nipples to air dry. Go topless or keep flaps down on nursing bra for part of the day.
- Change bra if it gets damp.
- Rinse bras in dilute white vinegar after washing to cut irritating soap residue.
- Avoid using anything on the nipples; use pure hydrous lanolin if you must, unless you are allergic to wool.

If *soreness or cracks* develop in the nipples, keep nursing and:

- Get the letdown reflex going with the

Relief for Engorged Breasts
Do each exercise six times.

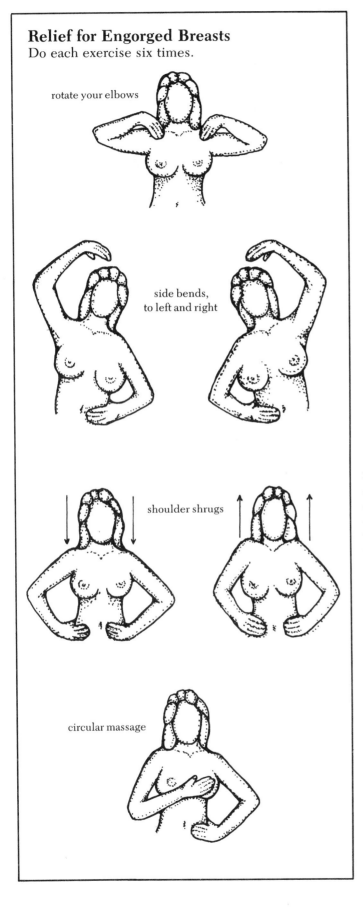

rotate your elbows

side bends,
to left and right

shoulder shrugs

circular massage

engorgement exercises and a bit of gentle breast massage.

- Nurse very frequently for shorter periods of time—start with a few minutes on each breast every one-half to one hour. Build up gradually, until baby is nursing ad lib and soreness is gone.
- Check baby's throat and mouth for thrush. It is a fungus infection that spreads to the nipples and causes soreness. Treatment consists of swabbing every hour with either a solution of one teaspoon of bicarbonate of soda to a glass of water or a drug prescribed by your doctor.
- Make an ice cap for your nipples—place a few ice cubes in a washcloth, close with a rubber band, crush ice with a hammer, and apply. This helps heal soreness and cracks.
- Check on your diet. Vitamin C helps rebuild cell walls, vitamin A helps prevent infection, and protein is necessary for repairs. Put your pregnancy diet sheet back up on the refrigerator and start checking off the portions every day.
- Do not resort to a breast shield. It only prolongs the soreness.

Many mothers who have had a healthy, well-nourished pregnancy and birth feel so good, they sometimes overdo housekeeping and outside activities. Usually all they suffer is fatigue, but occasionally a *breast infection* or *plugged milk duct* may result. It isn't important to differentiate between a plugged duct and an infection, since the causes and treatment are the same.

Some of the causes of plugged duct or infection are:

- general run down condition, poor nutrition;
- too-tight bra;
- baby not nursing regularly or often enough;
- using the same position every nursing so that all ducts do not have a chance to empty;
- hospital staph infection carried from baby to mother.

Even if a plugged duct develops into an infection, the most important treatment is to keep nursing as often as baby is willing. If the treatment is not followed, *a breast abscess,* which is a localized infection, may result. This needs to be surgically lanced. (It may be done in the doctor's office and breastfeeding may certainly continue. But prevention is better.)

Breastfeeding: Personal Care

To treat a plugged duct or breast infection:

- Go to bed and stay there. Let someone else do the cooking and housekeeping.
- Nurse at least every hour if baby is willing; this prevents infection from taking hold.
- Apply heat to the affected breast, either with a heating pad or towels wrung out in hot water.
- Offer the sore breast first so that it will stay relatively empty. *Do not stop nursing on the affected breast.*
- Change nursing position often to empty all ducts.

Beyond these rather routine situations which have always been obstacles for nursing mothers to overcome, breastfeeding your baby in our culture today has some unique problems. Great-grandma had it easier in many ways. Most important was the fact that all her female friends and relatives breastfed their babies, too. There simply was no other way to keep a baby alive. Today, on the other hand, your friends, your mother and mother-in-law, your sisters and cousins, the assistants in your doctor's office, your doctor herself, may never even have considered breastfeeding. You may find them unwitting sources of misinformation about what to do and when and why to do it.

If your mother or mother-in-law comes to help after your baby's born, *she* may want to take over the baby's care (complete with bottle feedings)—which is perfectly understandable. The smell and feel of a new baby, the cuddling and loving a new baby generates, may arouse in her a flood of fond memories of her own babies. However, no matter how gratifying for grandmother to give the baby a bottle, that's not the kind of help you need! If she's willing to help *you* as *you* mother your infant, that's wonderful. Make sure before she arrives. Suggest that she read this book and some of the others listed in the Bibliography. Having the support you need to breastfeed is one part of a complete family lifestyle geared to the best nurturing for the newest family member.

In order for a full breastfeeding culture to emerge out of today's token breastfeeding culture, women will need additional support from those outside our immediate family circles. This kind of support can only come when basic assumptions about mothers and babies, their needs and their roles, change in society as a whole. To a certain extent, this means adopting a much different view of the place of children as a group in our society.

Even since the famed turn-of-the-century pediatrician, Emmett Holt, issued the edict that the infant and young child are to spend 20 out of 24 hours a day in his or her own room, ideally presided over by a trained baby nurse who would not cater to the child's every whim, children of all ages have been banished from everyday adult society. Holt's rationales, that "babies need quiet surroundings for the regular, uninterrupted sleep essential to normal brain growth," that, indeed, "a great deal of harm may be done in this period of rapid growth by unduly stimulating and exciting the child" and that "infants should see but few people, should be left much alone and should never be romped or played with under six months of age—and the less of it at any time, the better for the infant" are seen today as absolutely without scientific merit.

Yet, the attitudes, for instance, about the appropriateness of nursing an infant in a restaurant or professional meeting, at a swim club or social gathering linger on. Nursing mothers, society still believes, belong at home in the nursery with their children. Since few families today can afford live-in help and most would reject the intrusion into their privacy such an individual's constant presence would mean, and *since there is no place in adult society for children,* mothers are expected to carry on their mothering functions apart from everyday grown-up life.

Virtually every advertisement for breastfeeding paraphernalia, or promotional materials for everything from cream to prevent stretch marks (it doesn't work) to baby soaps and powders, picture mother in immaculate negligee, every hair in place, every nail perfectly manicured. These are imaginary mothers who live in an imaginary world, a world comprised totally of themselves and their babies. We have never met one such mother. Real-life mothers, more than ever, are discovering what mothers in village markets the world over have always known—having a baby does not mean you must retire to an isolated chamber until the child is ready to wean. Babies can, and increasingly must, be integrated into the fabric of women's ongoing lives. To put it simply, where mother goes, baby goes until the time for weaning. No exceptions need be made.

Part and parcel of this attitudinal and values-shift, of course, has to do with de-eroticizing public display of the female breast. Whereas it is currently deemed acceptable to erect ten-story billboards of women in the flimsiest of resort attire, their nipples provocatively peeking through the fabric, to entice you to fly a particular airline to Miami, it is unacceptable for a woman dressed similarly at beach or pool to move aside the fabric and offer the breast to satisfy the hunger of her baby. Women's presumed sexual availability used to sell something (fine), women's natural response to child's need (not fine at all). How long it will take to accomplish this objective is impossible to predict, but the more we women assert our right to function as whole mothers in society, the quicker it will come.

Until then, nursing mothers will continue to need whatever support we can get from one another and from articles and books written by other contemporary mothers who have nursed successfully. In most parts of the country, nursing mothers councils are now being sponsored by local childbirth education groups who are awakening to the idea that breastfeeding is not a separate mothering function, but an integral part of the entire maternity cycle that reaches from conception to weaning. Many of these groups are modeled on the Nursing Mothers Council of the Childbirth Education Association of Greater Philadelphia which has been thriving for over 20 years on a direct mother-to-mother-basis. Mothers' centers also may sponsor nursing mothers' groups geared to the needs of today's woman. For information about such groups, or to find out how to organize one in your area, contact: International Childbirth Education Association, P. O. Box 20048, Minneapolis, MN 55420, or: Resources in Human Nurturing, International, P. O. Box 6861, Denver, CO 80206.

Books that give an up-to-date treatment of breastfeeding include:

- *The Pregnancy-After-30 Workbook: A Program for Safe Childbearing—No Matter What Your Age* (Emmaus, Pa.: Rodale Press, 1978), chapter 5, "Breastfeeding: Completing the Maternity Cycle" by Lynne Brody, M.D., and Margot Parsons, and chapter 6, "Pregnancy Means Parenting" by Jane and Jim Pittenger
- *Breastfeeding and Natural Child Spacing: The Ecology of Natural Mothering*, by Sheila Kippley (New York: Harper and Row, 1974. Paperback ed., New York: Penguin, 1975)
- *The Family Bed: An Age Old Concept in Childrearing*, by Tine Thevenin (self-published, P. O. Box 16004, Minneapolis, MN 55416, 1976)
- *The Continuum Concept*, by Jean Liedloff (New York: Warner Books, 1979)
- *Every Child's Birthright: In Defense of Mothering*, by Selma Fraiberg, Ph.D. (New York: Basic Books, 1977)
- *The Tender Gift: Breastfeeding*, by Dana Raphael, Ph.D. (Englewood Cliffs, N.J.: Prentice-Hall, 1973)

Breastfeeding your baby until the child decides to stop develops a uniquely personal bond between mother and child. This irreplaceable sense of personal caring and sharing stands against the endless interchangeability of people that typifies the world of human relationships today. On that basis alone, it seems a highly desirable way to mother.

Chapter 9

At Home
Skillful Care

Baby Amanda Jones, two days old, is on her way home from the hospital. Fed by her mother, diapered and dressed by the nursery nurse, and checked out by the pediatrician, she sleeps the whole way. As the Joneses' car pulls up in front of their home, some neighborhood children gather round to greet them and get a look at the new baby. After a minute or two, Mr. and Mrs. Jones break away from well-wishers, and, once inside, tenderly lay Baby Amanda down to sleep in her canopied, white wicker crib.

They stand by the side of the crib, gazing proudly at their daughter. Turning to one another, they smile contentedly and embrace. Home at last! Tiptoeing out, they close the nursery door part way and go to the kitchen to have a quiet lunch together. Mr. Jones has a special bottle of wine chilling in the refrigerator to celebrate the homecoming. Mrs. Jones' mother sent over a frozen casserole earlier in the day. All they have to do is warm it in the oven.

11:45 A.M.: Mother unwrapping casserole. Father setting table. Candles, flowers, the good plates. . .

11:46 A.M.: Cries of displeasure from the nursery. Mother quickly returns to nursery door, then hesitates. Hospital nurses warned her not to spoil the baby with too much handling. Amanda is not due to be fed until 2:00 P.M. Mrs. Jones returns to kitchen alone, puzzled.

12:00 NOON: Baby is still howling. Father recalls that nurse who taught feeding class at hospital recommended giving sterile water if baby cried between nursings. Father searches through take-home kit supplied by hospital, finds bottle marked "Glucose, 5%." Tries to remove cap, cuts finger. Mother takes bottle and hurries into nursery. Sits in rocking chair with baby and gives bottle. Baby sputters, but stops crying. Mother feels her milk let down, soaking the front of her dress. She puts baby back in crib and goes to bedroom to change, choking back tears.

12:30 P.M.: Father coaxes mother back into kitchen and sets a peanut butter sandwich before her. She says she's not hungry.

12:45 P.M.: Cries of misery from nursery. Father convinces mother to finish sandwich. He sneaks back to nursery, picks up baby, and rocks her gently until she seems to fall asleep again.

1:10 P.M.: Father returns to kitchen and eats his sandwich.

1:15 P.M.: Mother lies down, tries to nap. Cries from nursery. Mother resignedly unhooks nursing bra as father brings baby in. Baby latches on and nurses hungrily. Door swings open and neighbor marches in, gift in hand. Baby stops sucking, starts yelling.

1:30 P.M.: Father takes baby, attempts to get "burp" up. Baby spits up on father's back. Father hands baby back to mother and goes to change

Right from the Start

140

shirt. Neighbor is still sitting on bed. Mother starts nursing baby while neighbor tells her how she couldn't nurse her babies because her milk was too thin. Finally leaves when mother states for the third time she'd like to take a nap.

2:00 P.M.: Mother and baby fall asleep side by side, exhausted. Father attempts to remove baby to crib, baby wakes up, screaming. Returns baby to mother to diaper. Mother fumbles with pins, sticks herself, finally gets diaper on.

2:30 P.M.: Mother and baby nurse again, fall asleep. Father, exhausted, joins them.

5:00 P.M.: Mother and father wake up, discuss implications of baby sleeping with them, decide to put baby in crib. Baby wakes up, nuzzles for breast. Mother consults clock, decides to give water.

5:05 P.M.: Father holds crying baby while mother searches futilely for another bottle of glucose water. Mother takes baby, sends father to drugstore for bottle. Puts baby in crib.

5:10 P.M.: Father at drugstore. Baby crying in crib. Mother crying in kitchen while trying to clean up lunch.

5:15 P.M.: Father returns from drugstore with bottle. Boils water, boils bottle, burns fingers.

5:30 P.M.: Baby drinks water, falls asleep. Father puts baby in crib. Baby cries. Father curses. Mother cries, vows she will get baby on schedule tomorrow. Still crying, puts baby to breast.

5:45 P.M.: Baby is not nursing easily. Father attempts to "burp," gets spit-up on. Mother changes baby. Father changes himself.

6:00 P.M.: Baby still fretful. Mother getting desperate.

6:30 P.M.: More of same. Mother puts baby in crib with stuffed bear that plays "Rock-a-Bye Baby."

7:00 P.M. Father tries another "burp" with same results as before.

7:30 P.M. Baby is now howling at full blast. Neighbor rings bell to comment on the noise, asks father if baby is sick.

7:45 P.M.: Father calls pediatrician. Telephone answered by service. They will notify doctor of problem.

8:00 P.M.: Pediatrician calls and tells father that most new mothers don't have enough milk the first few days at home. He says to use popular brand of baby formula "until mother's supply increases."

8:15 P.M.: Amanda is served her first bottle of formula, the one from the hospital take-home pack. Father returns to the store for a few more cans, three more bottles, and a nipple brush.

For far too many of us, the first days at home with our new babies follow the preceding scenario. In the process we are robbed of much of the deep satisfaction and pleasure that should accompany the arrival of a new family member. With but a few modifications, this first day home and all days thereafter can be turned from frazzled to fulfilling. All that's needed is a clear understanding of how to translate the essential maternal and infant needs we have already discussed into a practical, continuing program for at-home care. The cornerstones of this care program are rest, privacy, equipment, and skills. None of the basics, despite massive propaganda to the contrary from the commercial baby industry, cost very much. The sine qua non, of course, isn't a commodity at all: it's you, the healthy, resourceful mother. No amount of gear can substitute for your loving attention, yet, as we shall see, most commercial items wind up trying to do just that, spelling disruption of mother-baby interaction as a result.

Let's retrace the steps the Joneses took leading up to bringing baby home, to pinpoint how this day could have been made less trying for everyone. First, the things they did right:

1. Coming home from the hospital as soon as possible—the Joneses' doctor would have preferred a four-day hospital stay, but Mrs. Jones felt she would get more rest at home.

2. Coming home to a well-stocked pantry— keeping meal preparations simple and nutritious reduces work while boosting energy.

3. Coming home to a private environment— making it known to relatives and friends that *you'll call them* when you're ready for visitors or need help and politely cutting short the visits of those who insist on dropping by, anyway. The overall approach is looking on the first week or so after birth as a "honeymoon" period for the new family.

4. Planning to rest a good deal (whenever baby naps)—respecting the fact that giving birth entails profound physical exertion for most women, but that it's easy in the flush of excitement that follows to ignore your body's signals of fatigue.

With all this going for them, what happened to the Joneses' best-laid plans? Failure to identify the "hidden hazards" inherent in the underlying assumptions of standard postbirth baby care. In other words, falling prey to some of the most debilitat-

At Home: Skillful Care

ing, but seemingly rational-sounding, advice of all. Examples:

preparing a separate room for baby—Just as the hospital is the fundamental modern intervention in birth, so is the isolation of babies in separate quarters the primary intervention in modern at-home care. Do couples take separate rooms on their honeymoons? Mother and baby are still an ongoing couple for months after birth, each with strong physical and emotional needs for the other that go unmet when they are separated. Other reasons against this method of baby care are the extraordinary sums of money it can take to furnish and decorate such a room (especially if everything is purchased new), and, most important, the tremendous drain on the mother's energy it imposes.

It makes no sense for anyone to have to get up three or four times a night in response to baby's cries (we mercifully faded out on our visit with the Joneses before they reached this part of their day), least of all you who are in such urgent need of rest yourself. This need is particularly acute if you've just returned home after spending a few days in a strange bed dealing with the continual interruptions hospitalization entails. Tossing off the warm covers, stumbling down the hallway, *turning on the light,* and numbly trying to see to the needs of your baby is hard enough. Add to this the fact that the baby will be *wide awake* by the time you get there, and it's no wonder each of these middle-of-the-night sessions can drag on for an hour or more. Mom's falling over in the rocker, but baby wants "to play." Not really. Baby just wants Mom to stay. The simplest ways of getting over this hurdle are to make, borrow, or invest in a baby carrier for daytime and a king-size mattress for nighttime (see details later in this chapter). This way, everyone's frustration level remains low and energy level high. Including Dad, who most commonly still has to get up and get off to work in the morning.

using crib or bassinet for baby—This is a smaller version of the previous pitfall. Babies in cribs or bassinets are still out of physical contact with other people. Being wrapped closely with blankets can give baby a "background feeling" of enfoldment and warmth, but it's still not the same thing as cuddling close to Mom. As you might expect, there are some commercial items that can provide a poor substitute for Mom's warmth and familiar sounds. You can lay a warm hot-water bottle wrapped in a receiving blanket next to baby in the crib, cradle, or bassinet and also stick in a "Beating Heart"—a bit of red velveteen that emits the familiar thump-thump-thump which it's been shown is soothing to babies. But what person in love would settle for a hot-water bottle in lieu of the beloved? Why should baby settle for anything less than the genuine mother?

The illusion that putting baby in the crib or bassinet next to the parents' bed is really going to save any effort in the night also needs to be exposed. You still have to toss off the covers, step out of bed (or lean out and get a tenuous grip on the baby in the process), sit across the room in the rocker to nurse so you don't disturb Dad, turn on some sort of nightlight to see what you're doing, put baby back in the box when feeding is done, climb back into bed, get comfortable once more, and hope against hope that the baby will settle down and fall asleep. Good luck. Honeymoons are seldom conducted in twin beds. Baby will often keep fussing until the desired outcome is obtained and everyone is tucked snugly together in the family bed. (The crib intended for use by the Brewers' third baby actually became a play spot for the older girls and their dolls. The baby never slept there. This time they didn't even put it up—a great time-saving decision.)

responding to baby as a "statistic"—The old ideas of how long between feedings, how much for each feeding, when there's been enough handling for one day, how fast baby should gain weight, when baby should meet certain developmental markers, how long baby should sleep, when baby should sleep, all are based on some abstract notion of an "average baby" who never existed. Your baby is a unique person, and, just as you should never expect a new adult acquaintance to conform to some absolute, preordained set of rules, so allowances must be made for each baby's temperament, pace, and style. The best way to stay in tune with your baby is to keep him or her with you so you can respond to baby's changing needs and developing personality; those things make your baby the individual s/he really is. The cues you pick up from the baby guide you in growing together, and the cues s/he receives from you help your baby learn what to expect from the world at large.

substituting objects for human contact—The standard mode of postbirth baby care, which involves substituting commercial products for mothering, can be hazardous to baby's and parents' health. As with all things in life, the substitute is never as satisfying as the real thing. Many of the devices used by the mother and father in our scene were outside the baby's range of needs, although they could conceivably be appropriate for an older baby. These substitutions have gained acceptance in our culture through the merchandising of them as the answer to mothers' and babies' needs. Some of the most hazardous substitutions are detailed below.

Expectant parents, wanting to do the best for their babies, are encouraged to believe that these items are essential to their baby's well-being. In this way, artificial environments are substituted for the mother—with complete social approval. The suggestion to a group of first-time expectant parents that a baby nursery is not only unnecessary, but actually undesirable, always results in looks of amazement.

There are several mechanisms in the newly delivered woman that support her need to be with her baby:

- The configuration of baby's chubby face, big eyes, and button nose serves as a biological "releaser" mechanism, trigger-

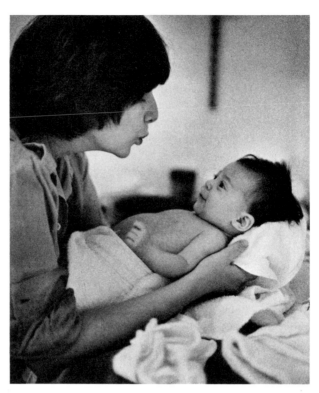

Baby's face is a biological "releaser" of maternal behavior.

ing the mother's desire to care for her baby.
- Mothers experience a heightened desire for skin contact. Babies are soft and cuddly.
- The letdown of the milk is often experienced as a tingly sensation in the breasts. Initiation of nursing fulfills this anticipatory feeling.
- New mothers experience hunger and thirst

Mother Substitutes

Commercial Item	What It Substitutes For
carriage, stroller	being held while mother is walking
crib, bassinet	sleeping with mother
infant seat	being tied onto mother with baby carrier
crib mobiles, wall decor	the outside world as seen from mother's arms
bottles, other feeding equipment	mother's breasts
walkers, jumpers, exercisers	playing with family
soft toys	cuddling with mother
pacifier	mother's breasts

as they nurse their babies. Fulfilling these urges insures adequate nutrition for lactation.

- The sound of a baby's cry makes the mother want to *do* something. Even if she believes that she should not pick up her crying baby she will experience the desire to do so, and may even feel guilty for giving in to this inborn biological mechanism. If she does not give in, she will usually attempt to soothe the baby with toys or a pacifier.

The parents in our homecoming scene made great efforts to care for their baby. They tried to follow rules designed for some mythical baby, not the one they really had, and succeeded only in exhausting themselves and frustrating their baby.

Almost all of us ask ourselves at times if we will be "good" mothers to the child we're carrying. The more we find out from other mothers and researchers the more we're sure that the exchange of pleasure-giving experiences is the essence of "good" mothering. Many people have commented that the baby's chief social developmental task in the early weeks after birth is developing a sense of trust in the world as embodied in his/her primary caretaker. As Ashley Montagu reminds us in *Touching: The Human Significance of the Skin* (New York: Columbia University Press, 1971), "The infant will develop a sense of trust or mistrust depending on his/her sensory impressions received primarily through the skin—whether they are gratifying or not." What we've discovered is that providing gratifying sensory impressions for our babies turns out to provide us with pleasurable experiences, too, once we establish being available to our babies as the top priority in the early weeks and months after birth.

Our prehistoric parents from the Introduction to this book couldn't help but notice the resemblance between a crib and a cage at the zoo. They would probably wonder how the security of crib bars could replace the security of mother's arms. Our visitors might admire the handiwork on the colorful coverlets but would probably assume that a mother's body warmth now dissipates after birth. And if the baby were being fed from a bottle attached to a stuffed plastic dog by an elastic band, they might just think that some alternative has been found for the natural process of lactation.

When we evaluated the hundreds of products being sold to new parents we found very few that could pass the test we established at the beginning of this book:

Does this object serve the urgent need my baby and I have to stay together?

In fact, this simple test eliminated just about everything in the local baby gear store. Our best advice—save your money and use it instead to hire some reliable cleaning/housework help during the first month after your baby's birth. You'll never miss the playpen, the educational mobile, or the baby-food jar organizer, but you may very well miss having a clean bathtub and folded laundry.

It turns out that the style of care that best meets the baby's most intrinsic needs is also the style of care that makes mothering most pleasurable. It is also the most economical. Here are some of the things experienced mothers do to make plenty of time for a new baby.

- Before the baby is born, stock up on non-perishable food items and nonfood items such as toilet paper, canned and frozen foods, cleaning products, and other foreseeable needs such as birthday presents. This cuts down on shopping trips.
- When you come home with your baby, go straight to bed and rest there together for several days. Get up to take meals, use the bathroom, and socialize with family to the extent you desire. Stay in nightclothes. If you're up and about and fully dressed, you'll be asked to do things you wouldn't be asked to do if you were in your nightgown.
- Arrange your bedroom, living room, and kitchen for your convenience. You'll appreciate a comfortable place to nurse all set up in each area, with a small table nearby to hold a diaper, tissues, beverage, snack, and other useful items.
- Assemble a wardrobe that is washable, comfortable, and easy to nurse in. You'll feel like going out in a week or so and probably won't fit into your usual prepregnancy clothes yet.
- Protect your privacy. Let your family answer phones and doorbells. When you are ready for company, don't be embarrassed to state exactly how much you want and to speak up when you need to rest.
- Whenever possible, have your mate sched-

ule vacation time to coincide with the "honeymoon" week. Any out-of-the-house trips are less difficult this way, and father gets extended experience with the new baby, too. If you have older children, they will benefit by having an adult "on call" for their special needs at this time when you may be very busy with the baby.

- Keep up the rest, exercise, and nutrition program you started during your pregnancy.
- When in doubt, nurse. Putting baby off with pacifiers, bottles, toys, and the like doesn't solve the problem if all baby wants is you. Using the breast as a pacifier *is* acceptable, quick, and efficient.

What changes in your household to expect, then, due to the baby's arrival? In the early months about the only new furnishings required might be a small dresser, set of shelves, or storage chest for baby's clothing and a rocking chair. Neither of these has to be a "baby design."

What goes into the storage container? Check our rock-bottom list for baby's layette and shopping guide.

While you're assembling these things for baby, also work on other things for yourself. Doting friends and relatives may want to buy you something special. See if you can interest them in helping with your personal layette needs.

Once you have the baby's layette, your layette, and your nurturing environment organized, you're in about the same position as the beginning cook in a well-stocked, well-designed kitchen. Now all you need are the skills to go with the equipment. With cooking, it's pretty easy to sign up for classes in whatever type of cuisine you choose. You get first-hand experience in cutting, chopping, glazing, and poaching. Naturally, you don't expect every dish to turn out perfectly the first time.

With babies, you may take a Red Cross course in how to give a bath, change a diaper, or burp a baby, but there's one real drawback: you only get to practice on a doll. When you have your own

The Rock-Bottom, Totally Basic List of Absolutely-Must-Have Baby Things

4 dozen diapers—fewer if you wash every day, more if you wash once a week. Gauze is most absorbent; prefolds are nice and worth the extra expense. Even if you decide on disposables or diaper service, buy at least a dozen. They're great over-the-shoulder cloths.

1 box disposable diapers—nice to have for emergencies. Manufacturers say they can be flushed down, but building owners say don't. Public health officials ask you to plastic-bag them before disposal to prevent possible contamination. Environmentalists say don't use them.

waterproof pants—these come in many different styles and sizes. One popular model has snaps down the front, other are pull-ons. Both are fine as long as the leg holes aren't scratchy. The expensive ones don't always last longer than the cheap ones, so buy a few different types and see what you like.

6 undershirts—get size One Year (or label may say 12 months). Most babies outgrow the smaller ones too soon.

4 receiving blankets—wash the flannel kind before you use it to remove excess fuzz. Add extra knitted or woolen blankets as the weather demands.

4 kimonos or gowns—kimonos open down the front and make diapering more convenient; gowns are longer and keep a kicker's feet covered. If you get gowns, remove the drawstring at the bottom and fold the mittens up so baby can explore. Either are preferable to stretchies for the tiny infant, because they make skin-to-skin contact easier.

outerwear—buntings, snowsuits, sweaters, depending on the season. Baby is happy in blankets, so don't rush to buy these.

2 towels—can be old, washed out, but soft adult size.

12 washcloths—one color for washing baby's face, another color for washing baby's bottom. Cheaper than disposable washers and less irritating.

diaper pins; baby scissors with rounded points; hair brush; fine-tooth comb; very mild, unperfumed soap such as Ivory; rectal thermometer and lubricant (like petroleum jelly or K-Y jelly); and it's so nice to have a rocking chair.

At Home: Skillful Care

Buying for Baby

1. Price of layette is not proportional to the amount of love parents have for their baby.
2. Babies don't care if it was borrowed or a hand-me-down. Boys can wear pink, girls can wear blue—saves you green!
3. Bouncers, walkers, jumpers, swings—who needs them? Baby prefers your arms.
4. Can you knit, crochet, sew? A yard of flannel, hemmed or pinked all around, makes a great receiving blanket. The same amount of terry cloth makes a fine towel.
5. Baby's feet are supposed to be cool, so baby shoes, socks, booties aren't all that necessary.
6. You'll get gifts, so don't overbuy before. Sweater sets, snowsuits, blankets are all popular items.
7. Bathe baby in the sink or on your lap in the big tub. You don't need a special plastic tub.
8. Oil, lotion, powder? Baby's skin has its own natural protection.
9. Diaper bags aren't all that convenient and are often too bulky. Try something you like for toting baby's things—an attractive shoulder bag, a flight bag, a shopping bag—whatever makes *you* happy.
10. Remember when you select baby's medical care provider that medical care is a consumer service. Get your money's worth by choosing early and using wisely. (See chapter 1.) And do consider the well-baby clinics run by your board of health.

New Mother's Layette

1. A sense of humor.
2. A kitchen stocked with nutritious, easy-to-prepare, easy-to-eat foods:
   a. Frozen homemade meals
   b. Canned protein—tuna, sardines, salmon, other fish, boned chicken
   c. Cheese—keeps well in the refrigerator
   d. Powdered milk for cooking and drinking when the milkman is late
   e. Eggs, fruits, vegetables
   f. Dried fruits, nuts and nut butters
3. Household help for first month (*not* a baby nurse!).
4. A living room with all the knickknacks and dust catchers put away.
5. A washing machine and a dryer.
6. Four nursing bras or soft-styled stretch bras that can be pulled aside for breastfeeding.
7. Nightgowns or pajamas that open down the front or pull up or down for easy breastfeeding.
8. Two-piece outfits for breastfeeding.
9. "Hospital-size" sanitary napkins (thicker than regular).
10. Sheets, pillowcases, blankets for the new king-size family bed.
11. Copies of some of the recommended books in the Bibliography.

child in your arms it may be the first time you've ever held a living, breathing baby, much less tried to diaper or bathe one! Finally assuming total responsibility for the baby's personal care is a moment most of us can remember as a mixture of elation and uneasiness. We are very hard on ourselves, wanting to do everything perfectly from the very start. This, of course, is highly unrealistic. Even if you've had several babies before, you've never had *this* baby. And every mother can tell you little differences (and big ones) she notices in the first few days with each of her babies.

Things to admit are likely to happen at some point or other, no matter how careful you are:

- sticking a pin into baby's skin or your finger;
- getting soap in the baby's eyes;
- cutting a nail too short or leaving it too long so baby's face gets scratched;
- baby crying for ten minutes while you're in the shower and don't hear the commotion;
- baby kicking off all the covers and sleeping that way for a few hours;

Right from the Start

- baby getting held awkwardly by a sibling who forgets to support the baby's head;
- baby wriggling around on the bed and winding up jammed against the headboard, screaming for help;
- losing grip on baby during bath, so baby goes under momentarily;
- baby having enormous bowel movement, soiling body, hair, clothes, and fresh bed linen—ten minutes after being bathed.

Alarming? Yes, for a minute or so, until you see that baby's okay. By the third or fourth time around, you are able to recognize these as just part of baby care—the equivalent of a sauce that didn't work out this time, but which doesn't ruin the whole meal. To the new mother, though, these events can assume disastrous proportions. You may worry for weeks that your baby will suffer permanent damage because you got the umbilical cord stump wet. Babies are not that fragile, but a mother's sense of self-confidence often is.

You will need reassurance and information to help you stop worrying and start relaxing a bit as you begin your new job. For that reason we provide "A Quick Guide for Starting Right" in the Appendix. While you're developing your skills, your baby will be working on skills of a different sort: starting to coo or make other sounds (noncrying), improving visual coordination, gaining some control over head movements, picking mother out of a crowd, becoming an expert nursling, gradually experiencing maturation of the central nervous system—all commonly take place in the first month after birth. This means that your repertoire of skills continues to expand in response to baby's changing needs and emerging abilities. You're both getting more accomplished every day!

At Home: Skillful Care

Chapter 10

Satisfactions

The One-Month Family Health Assessment

The end of the first month after birth marks the official end of your baby's neonatal period. It also marks the traditional time for your baby's first visit for routine pediatric care, a series of checkups and screening procedures that extend throughout childhood. Most often these visits emphasize physical development of the child, obviously an important consideration. We feel, though, that we owe it to ourselves, our babies, and our families to carry out a more extensive assessment of the health of all concerned at this time. This includes the physical, emotional, and social well-being of both mother and baby, in addition to their ongoing interaction and integration with the rest of the family. By now, certain basic care principles from the preceding chapters should be at work for you and your baby in day-to-day life. Otherwise, you're likely to be working at mothering too hard and enjoying it too little.

Mothering requires a great deal of stamina, creativity, and flexibility. If you feel below par yourself physically and/or emotionally it's virtually impossible to summon the energy you need to meet the demands of your new job. The one thing most of us overlook when we're feeling tired or short-tempered or overwhelmed is how we've been eating. Since all our body systems depend on our food intake for optimal functioning, doing a diet recall can bring our current food habits into focus quickly so we can see where improvements are needed.

To begin, write down everything you've eaten for the past 24 hours. Include all snacks and drinks (including water), as well as regular meals. In the next column, enter how much of each food you ate (½ cup, 3 ounces, for example). Next, write where and when the food was eaten. If someplace other than your own home, consider whether you'd have eaten better or less well at home. Notice if you fail to carry out your usual good eating habits when you're away from home or if you get busy during the day and skip meals. Beware of skipping breakfast—you'll feel like going back to bed all day if you don't eat a full meal in the morning. To find out if your diet is meeting your needs, compare your completed recall sheet with the SPUN Diet chart in chapter 1. Be careful to count each item in only one group; a serving of cheese, for instance, cannot count both as a meat substitute and as a milk substitute on the same day.

If you are lacking either specific types of foods (for example, a vitamin C source or salads with dark green, leafy vegetables) or adequate amounts of required foods (for example, if you're eating something from each group, but only half the protein or half the calories you need), make a shopping list that begins with these items. Plan your meals and snacks carefully for the next few days, being sure to include these foods and all the others on the diet chart. Make eating correctly a priority just as you did during pregnancy. The truth is that, as long as you are exclusively breastfeeding your baby, the quality and quantity of your baby's diet (your milk) depends on what you eat. In addition, food for yourself is the foundation of complete healing after childbirth, the factor upon which all other physical and emotional considerations are based.

Keep in mind that the SPUN diet chart is geared to average needs. You may need more of certain foods than the chart indicates if you are under unusual stress (getting ready to move, death in the family, other children ill, spouse out of work), if you are fighting a cold or other infection, or if your baby needs numerous night feedings and your sleep has been seriously undermined. The way you look and how you feel about yourself can also alert you to a possibly inadequate diet, lack of exercise, or a combination of both. Using the accompanying chart of wellness indicators, check where you think you stand on each item.

If the past few weeks have merged into a blur and you can't tell whether you're coming or going, you need to take stock right away and make changes in your daily care patterns that include your own well-being. As we've said before, this probably means that you're doing something you don't need to do—chores that burden you with extra work and no increased satisfaction or pleasure. Or you may be trying to go too fast in getting back into your accustomed prebaby lifestyle.

Under these circumstances, almost every experienced mother will advise you to do something she learned the hard way: *slow down!*

That movie will be playing at neighborhood theaters in a few months or at the drive-in next summer. You can shop the sales through the store catalogs. You can return the neighbors' dinner invitation next spring. You can finish painting the baby's room when s/he really needs it—about three or four years from now. You can have your mother or other relative/helper address envelopes for baby gift thank-yous. You can tolerate dust balls under the sofa and fingerprints on the coffee table

a few more weeks. You can wait another month or two to take the baby back for a visit to your old office. You can pack away your maternity wardrobe when you're really done with it—about nine or ten weeks from now. You can take an "incomplete" in that course, and finish the term paper next semester. You can opt to take your extra weeks of accumulated vacation time now to extend your maternity leave with pay. You can pay an enterprising 12-year-old to run to the market for you after school so you can nap, take a bath, read, or talk with your older children, rather than having the 12-year-old babysit while you go to the store.

After a few weeks of this, you'll become expert in the art of putting off most things at least until tomorrow. And the freedom that comes from really having time to yourself—maybe for the first time since you were a child—you may see as one of the most liberating things about having a new baby. There is a great feeling of maturity that accompanies the realization that you can finally be selective about what you do and when and with whom you do it. The contemporary compulsion to rush through every moment gives way gradually to an appreciation of the moments themselves. The life rhythms you felt so acutely during pregnancy continue to mark a steady counterpoint to the rest of the world's frantic beat. By staying keyed to them, you find you are well on your way toward setting your own pace as a mother.

More and more women schedule their own postpartum visit to the doctor or midwife for three or four weeks after birth, rather than waiting the traditional six weeks. With better nutrition, fewer drugs during birth, ad lib breastfeeding, and a more relaxed attitude about the minutiae of life, healing progresses faster, and women are eager to resume a full love life. Many want to switch their form of contraception in light of damaging reports about the Pill and the IUD. Must reading: Barbara Seaman's *Women and the Crisis in Sex Hormones*, (New York: Rawson, Wade, 1977). Others want their diaphragms checked to see if they need to be refitted. (Often a larger size is required in the first few months after childbirth until the vaginal walls return to their prepregnancy tone and alignment.) Obviously, an ill-fitting diaphragm is an unreliable contraceptive. This may also be the last chance you have to discuss any aspect of your pregnancy or birth experience with your doctor or midwife, to resolve any lingering concerns, or simply to express your thanks if you were pleased with their

Personal Wellness Indicators

Check where you feel you stand on each paired indicator. Add your score: 70 or more—keep it up!; 55 to 69—about average, make improvements where indicated; below 55—get the help you need right away to feel better.

	3	2	1	
energetic	—	—	—	fatigued
enthusiastic	—	—	—	apathetic
alert	—	—	—	lackadaisical
optimistic	—	—	—	pessimistic
pleasant	—	—	—	irritable
able to concentrate	—	—	—	easily distracted
erect posture	—	—	—	slumped
no backache	—	—	—	backache
no headaches	—	—	—	frequent headaches
good appetite	—	—	—	poor appetite
good digestion	—	—	—	stomachache, gas, cramps, heartburn, allergy
normal bowel movements	—	—	—	constipation, diarrhea, many movements each day, bloody stool
no hemorrhoids	—	—	—	hemorrhoids
normal urination	—	—	—	uncontrollable escape of urine, itching, burning, scanty urine
no infections	—	—	—	frequent infections
no vaginal discharge	—	—	—	spotting, bleeding, malodorous discharge
episiotomy scar healed	—	—	—	scar swollen, lumpy, painful
normal lactating breasts	—	—	—	sore spots, unusual lumps
soft, elastic nipples	—	—	—	cracked, sore nipples
clear, firm skin	—	—	—	greasy, scaly, dry skin
no dandruff	—	—	—	dandruff
shiny, resilient hair	—	—	—	stringy, dull, lank hair
healthy teeth	—	—	—	sensitive, decayed teeth
pink, firm gums	—	—	—	bleeding, swollen gums
pink tongue with normal papillae (bumps)	—	—	—	smooth, swollen, red or black tongue
pink mucous membranes and nail beds	—	—	—	pale mucous membranes and nail beds
strong nails	—	—	—	splitting, ridged nails
bright, clear eyes	—	—	—	itchy, burning, puffy, red, running, light-sensitive, bloodshot eyes
normal legs	—	—	—	swollen, tender legs
normal feet	—	—	—	swollen, cracked feet

Right from the Start

services. Of course, if you find you have a lot of checks on the right side of the Personal Wellness Indicators list you will want to follow them up at this time or else ask to be referred to someone else (such as a nutritionist, physical therapist, or breast-feeding counselor) for evaluation and treatment.

If you don't have these maintenance skills, now is the time to learn:

Breast Self-Examination (BSE)—Call your local unit of the American Cancer Society to find out when you can view their instructional films on BSE, and have them send you printed information in the meantime (some doctors have these available in their offices—ask the receptionist); or have your doctor or midwife demonstrate the techniques during your post-partum visit.

Vaginal Self-Examination—Purchase a clear plastic speculum (you can order one from: Feminist Women's Health Center, 6411 Hollywood Boulevard, Suite 202, Los Angeles, CA 90028, or your local medical supply store), flashlight, and hand-held mirror, and use them a few times a month to view your cervix and vaginal walls—a self-help technique pioneered by the Feminist Women's Health Center and now recommended by state health departments across the country. Reason: to spot any abnormalities early (cervical inflammation or erosion, polyps, infections, tumors, unusual discharge, site of irregular bleeding) so you get treatment early and to become acquainted with your normal cycles relating to fertility; as Carol Downer,

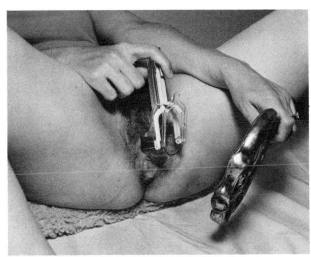

Vaginal self-examination (inserting speculum).

originator of vaginal self-examination, comments, "Once you get the hang of it, it's no more complicated than looking inside your mouth. Men are accustomed to inspecting themselves casually all the time, since their organs are in full view. There's no reason women shouldn't take advantage of the same opportunity." Many childbirth educators, midwives, and personnel at women's health centers are familiar with vaginal self-examination now and are available to help with any questions you may have. Other mothers in your postpartum group may also be willing to give you some assistance. The Childbirth Education Association of Westchester County (New York), for example, includes vaginal self-examination as a routine part of post-partum class information and provides each mother with a speculum as part of the course fee.

Pelvic Floor Exercise Program—Essential to restitution of your internal organs to their pre-pregnancy location and as a preventive against prolapsed bladder and/or prolapsed uterus later in life, these simple exercises also result in your vaginal walls toning up after childbirth to increase sexual pleasure for yourself and your partner. For detailed instructions see Elizabeth Noble's *Essential Exercises for the Childbearing Year: A Guide to Health and Comfort Before and After Your Baby Is Born* (Boston: Houghton Mifflin, 1976) or the exercise chapter by Helene Yocum, R.P.T., in *The Pregnancy-After-30 Workbook* (Emmaus, Pa.: Rodale Press, 1978). Every few days do these bare-bottomed in front of a mirror so you can see your progress.

Exercise and Rest Program—Every day from now on get at least one-half hour of brisk walking, jogging, swimming, rope jumping, or other activity that gets your heart pumping and your skin glowing, plus something for maintaining flexibility (dance, yoga, *t'ai chi*, special limbering exercises) two or three times a week or whenever you start to feel tense, tight, or sore. By the same token you also need deep relaxation (the kind you learned in your childbirth class) and refreshing sleep, so continue to use your relaxation practice daily when you have a few minutes to rest (resist the impulse to switch on television or read a magazine). Just lie down on your sofa and let all your muscle groups release. Repeat at night just before you go to sleep or whenever you're nursing. (Do as much nursing as possible lying down, taking the time before you start to prop your back, legs, and arms so every joint is bent and every joint supported—just as in labor—for true relaxation.) Nap when your baby naps as much as possible in the early months. It won't make the slightest bit of difference five years from now if you finished making that afghan or not! Enroll in a special Noble technique postpartum exercise class (many childbirth groups offer these as an adjunct to their postpartum mothering support groups) that welcomes you and your baby— you'll meet mothering colleagues and get away from the house once or twice a week; keep up the massage you learned for labor and expand your skills with your partner. Pregnancy may have made you more sensually aware of yourself, and there's no reason why the pleasure giving and receiving has to stop after the baby's born.

How Are Your Spirits?

We've all been made aware in recent years of the important connections between physical and emotional health. To find out if your spirit is doing as well as your body at one month postpartum, answer the following questions with a Yes or No:

1. Do you have at least one friend you can call when you're feeling stressed, just to say how you feel? _____

2. Do you have some time each day (at least 30 minutes) completely to yourself to do whatever pleases you? _____

3. Do you get out of the house every day with the baby, weather permitting? _____

4. Do you feel motivated to get basic housework done each day (laundry, dishes, quick pickup, meals)? _____

5. Do you fall asleep easily and sleep soundly? _____

6. Do you feel comfortable nursing your baby away from home? _____

7. Do you feel your mate approves of your mothering of the new baby? _____

8. Do you feel ready to plan an occasional social activity with friends? _____

9. Do you feel secure in your relationships with your parents, children, mate? _____

10. Do you feel your baby responds to you in a positive way? _____

11. Do you get out of sleepwear for most of the day? _____

12. Do you feel a sense of partnership with your baby's medical care providers? _____

13. Do you have time each day to spend with your mate quietly discussing the problems and joys you're experiencing? _____

14. Do you feel a renewed interest in lovemaking? _____

15. Do you feel renewed tenderness toward your other children? _____

16. Do you have at least ten minutes each day alone with each of your other children to speak privately or to pursue some activity particularly enjoyed by the child? _____

17. Do you allow yourself to cry when you feel like it, even if you're not sure of the reason? _____

18. Do you have the feeling that you're gradually surfacing after a month of total immersion in the new baby (getting interested in the newspaper, neighborhood events, other children's activities, and so on)? _____

19. Do you feel financially secure for the time being? _____

Right from the Start

20. Do you feel you have integrated your birth experience (what really happened as compared with your plans)? _____

21. Do you know other mothers of new babies with whom you can meet for fun and support? _____

22. Do you feel personally necessary for your baby's continued well-being? _____

23. Do you feel increasing confidence in your ability to meet your baby's needs? _____

24. Do you feel increasing confidence in your ability to meet your own needs? _____

25. Do you feel an increased sense of personal worth as the result of your experiences in having this baby? If you had the choice to do it over again, knowing what you do now, would you? _____

If you answer No to five or more of these questions, you may be facing a bout of depression. According to Barbara Ciaramitaro's outstanding and practical book, *Help for Depressed Mothers* (Independent Printing Company, 640 Tolman Creek Road, Ashland, OR 97520, 1978), clinicians recognize three distinct levels of postpartum depression:

- the after-baby "blues," experienced by 50 to 80 percent of women in the United States two to ten days after birth and attributed to a combination of changing hormonal levels and the aftereffects of routine hospital procedures—no treatment of "the blues" is indicated and recovery is generally considered to be 100 percent;
- mild to moderate depression, affecting one in five mothers somewhere before the sixth month after birth and lasting several months to a year or more—characterized by the classical symptoms of depression (fatigue, difficulty in concentrating, insomnia, weight loss, gloomy thoughts, tearfulness, and/or feelings of hopelessness, loss of interest in sex, social withdrawal, lack of pleasure in activities previously enjoyed, anxiety attacks, guilt)—70 percent of people with depression recover within six months whether they receive treatment for the condition or not—researchers cite four factors contributing to depression: genetics, nutrition, stress, and sleep deprivation—clearly, many new mothers are in danger of falling behind on all the last three unless they take special care to avoid it;
- postpartum psychosis, a severe psychiatric illness, requiring hospitalization within six months after childbirth for 3,000 to 9,000 women in the United States each year with

a diagnosis of delirium, a manic episode, severe depression, or schizophrenia—20 percent recover within a month, 40 percent take more than six months, and 15 percent remain chronically ill—in half the cases, it remains an isolated event in their lives.

Ciaramitaro, herself a survivor of an incapacitating period of postpartum depression, provides a detailed, step-by-step self-help recovery program for women in the mild to moderately depressed stage. The book is indexed to the medical literature, but written in a straightforward manner directly to the mother. Extensive reading resources are provided in addition to the program itself, and the author knows when to recommend outside help for problems that are beyond the program's design. You need the help of a psychiatrist or other mental health worker you can trust, she writes, if:

a. you cannot do anything on behalf of your own recovery;
b. your depression has led you to become dependent on alcohol or drugs or has caused you to attempt suicide or to abuse your child;
c. you are afraid that you might harm yourself or others as your energy returns;
d. you lost a parent through death or divorce when you were a young child or you had a cold or abusive parent; or,
e. you and your husband need help in coping with the problems that parenthood and your depression have made in your marriage.

Noting that even mild postpartum depression in the mother can have a severe impact on the entire family unit, and that up to 690,000 families are so affected each year, Ciaramitaro draws attention to the tremendous impact postpartum depression has on our entire society. She asks, "How many divorces could be avoided, how many homes kept together by timely recognition and treatment of a mother's depression? How many children would be spared the scars of parental neglect and abuse? How many women could avoid long years of hospitalization or alcoholism or drug addiction? It is time we found out. Postpartum depression is not only a women's problem—it is a social problem as well."

Her recommendations for prevention of postpartum depression and its attendant problems for women and families read like a mini-index to this book: taking good care of your body, getting appropriate help in assessing your physical and psychological needs, learning to mother yourself and your baby, and taking actions that increase your sense of self-respect and feelings of competence. It is impossible to cherish your child without also cherishing yourself.

Other aspects of the one-month health assessment relate to the family as a whole.

- Are your other children free from sleep problems, nervous tics and/or habitual nail-biting, bedwetting, excessive crying and/or whining, school problems, eating problems, recurring infections, ongoing bickering and fighting, or communication problems with you and your mate? If not, and the children seem receptive to the idea, an open-ended invitation to join the family bed (we set up their mattresses next to ours on the floor) has worked wonders in reducing the jealousy younger children especially feel when the new baby gets to sleep with Mom and Dad and they don't—in the Brewer house, the arrangement lasted three months and cured bedtime arguments/stalling even now that the older children have moved back to their own beds (a decision they made in honor of the six-year-old's birthday!).
- Does your mate have an extended period of physical contact with the new baby each day (at least a half-hour)? If not, perhaps bathing the baby or taking the baby for an outing in the baby carrier after supper could become father's time with baby while you attend to the other children or your own needs.
- Does the family do something together, apart from watching television, at least once a week? Setting aside this time when they are young goes far toward keeping lines of

communication open when children reach adolescence.

- Does anyone smoke in the home? Elimination of all smoking materials greatly reduces the incidence of respiratory infections for the children and adults, as well as the long-term, debilitating, and death-dealing diseases such as emphysema or lung, throat, stomach, and bladder cancer. If you want to be around long enough to enjoy your grandchildren, stop all forms of smoking.
- Do you have a primary medical care provider for the family with whom you are satisfied? Review checklist in chapter 1 if you're thinking of making a switch.
- Are you keeping a family health care chart for everyone with all immunizations, illnesses, medications, growth charts, and developmental milestones recorded? Baby books are fine, but they have a way of getting misplaced—and most stop after five or six years of age. The March of Dimes chapter in your area can provide a good chart free of charge—call your local chapter and request one. Take the record with you each time your child visits the doctor or clinic, and take notes of all measurements and any allergies or other findings. You may think you'll remember every detail of your child's medical history, but it's highly unlikely—especially after another child is born and you're keeping up with two or more. Of course, you can keep a more detailed account of your child's progress than just medical appointments, observations which may be very important to a diagnosis sometime in the future or just fun to re-read and reminisce over.

What to expect at your baby's one-month pediatric checkup? Basically a repeat of the newborn physical evaluations done in the hospital or after birth at home by your family doctor, but with an eye toward certain advances in baby's growth, coordination, and behavior patterns. Also, if a different doctor (a hospital resident, for example) performed your baby's examinations in the hospital, this visit gives your own doctor or nurse-practitioner a chance to get to know your baby and establish a baseline for future development.

Specific questions you may be asked include:

- Approximately how many hours a day does your baby sleep?

- Has your baby established regular day and night activity/sleep cycles that are in harmony with the rest of the family?
- How many minutes/hours a day does your baby cry? Any tears?
- Does your baby stop crying when you pick him/her up? When you offer breast? When you change diaper? When you rock or walk about? When you give massage?
- How many times does baby nurse in 24 hours? Is suck strong? How long at a feeding? Does baby seem satisfied after nursing? Does baby choke, gag, or vomit a great deal?
- How often does your baby have a bowel movement? What about its color and consistency?
- How often does your baby urinate (at least six to eight wet diapers a day)? What is its color?
- Has your baby smiled?
- Does your baby make sounds—cooing or humming?
- Does your baby focus his/her eyes on you when you talk? When you nurse?
- When you hold your baby, does s/he relax in your embrace, or does baby seem resistant to cuddling?
- When you kiss your baby, do you notice a salty taste on baby's skin?
- Do you have any questions about your baby's development or behavior? (Come with a list prepared in advance—just jot things down as they come to mind in the week before the visit.)

You may also be asked to assist directly with the physical examination by holding baby's arms in such a way that the infant's head is restrained and the examiner can view the tongue and throat more easily. Alternatively, you may be asked to keep holding the child on your lap through most of the examination, restraining the arms by holding them firmly across the abdomen when necessary.

Generally speaking, the one-month pediatric exam follows the basic format of any well-person checkup. The more easily tolerated procedures are done first, the less pleasant toward the end. You will be asked to disrobe the baby, leaving on just the diaper. If the room is chilly and you must wait for the examiner, wrap the baby in a receiving blanket and keep holding him/her until the exam gets underway. After taking measurements of the baby's temperature, pulse rate, respiratory rate,

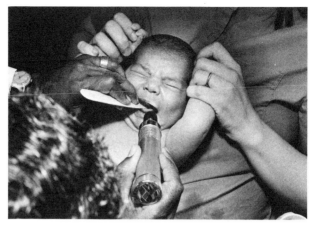

Restraining arms and head during tongue and throat exam.

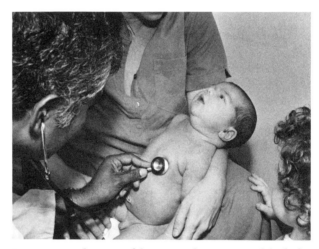

Listening to lungs and heart is often easier when baby is held by mother.

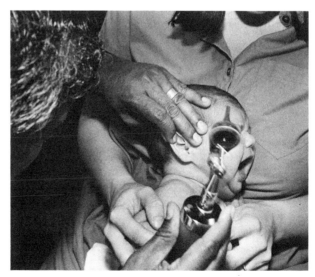

Mother holds arms while doctor examines with otoscope.

Satisfactions: The One-Month Family Health Assessment

height, weight, and (sometimes) blood pressure, the infant's head and chest circumference will also be checked. Growth in length, weight, and head and chest size are good indicators that baby's nutrition is adequate and his/her digestive system up to par. The general appearance of your baby will be noted, as well as the baby's cry, positioning, types of movements, state of nutrition, body odors, skin (color, texture, turgor, bruises, eruptions, or lesions), fingernails, and hair. Next, body systems are evaluated: head and neck, the chest, the abdomen, the genitals, extremities, the spine, joints, and muscles. Finally, a neurological examination is performed which checks the baby's reflexes and general responsiveness to the examination. An experienced examiner may complete the procedures in 10 to 15 minutes, after which there should be a time for discussing the exam with you.

To read in depth about the pediatric examination, and to learn how to perform many aspects of it yourself as your child gets older, buy, read, and use again and again Dr. Mary Howell's *Healing at Home: A Guide to Health Care for Children* (Boston: Beacon Press, 1979). Former director of the Family Evaluation Unit at Massachusetts General Hospital and a former dean at Harvard Medical School, Howell is the mother of six children and a practicing pediatrician in Boston. Her perspective on mothers reflects her own experiences, both professional and personal, and is an encouragement to all of us to learn more about skillful home care of our children of all ages, both in sickness and in health.

She writes in the foreword to her book:

I am convinced that any useful information presented to mothers about healing at home must begin with an understanding and recognition of what it is like to be a mother in this society, to act as agent for one's child in relation to medical experts, and to carry out the responsibility of caring for one's children when they are ill or injured. . . . The information and skills that you can learn for healing at home are, for the most part, fairly simple to use. This is a well-kept secret of the experts. But your store of information about your child is unique and irreplaceable. Your child's trust in you is an invaluable ingredient in healing assistance. And your ability to teach your child about healthiness and healing—from your intense desire that your child be well—is one of the most precious gifts of your mothering.

So, in the end, we find ourselves back where we started—to you, the new mother—your special qualities, your strengths, your skills, your storehouse of worldly wisdom, all the things you have done and felt that have made you the person you are today. There will never be another baby exactly like the one you're caring for now. There will never be another person just like you to provide that care. Nurturing this baby will be one of the most personal things you ever do. Much of the way your child goes through life, meeting challenges, facing adversity, experiencing pleasure, will be learned from the early care you provide. If this book has made giving that first care easier and more enjoyable than it otherwise would have been, we will be well pleased. Applying these basic strategies to your own situation is what sets your mothering apart from all others. Best wishes!

Appendix

A Quick Guide for Starting Right

Right from the Start

Baby Carriers

Baby carriers are a time-honored way of keeping mother and baby together by making baby portable, yet allowing mother's hands to be free for whatever other work she is doing. Different styles can be found all around the world, but the basic feature, a slinglike support for baby attached in some way to the mother, is universal. Whether your family originated in Italy or Guatemala, Nigeria or Polynesia, Alaska or Bolivia, there existed some form of baby carrier. The reason is simple: women had too much else to do to just stay home and mind the children. There was bread to be baked in the community oven, clothes to be washed in the river, land to be farmed, meals to be prepared, goods to be readied and taken to the village market, ceremonies to be attended. Children, down to the very smallest, were part of these life activities by virtue of being taken there by their mothers.

Appendix

Traditional baby carrier, South Africa.

Though today's activities may have changed somewhat, women are still busy outside the home, and the baby carrier facilitates our ongoing community involvement. It also gives the child a chance to have matchless sensory stimulation while at the same time enjoying the closeness and security of mother, father, or another person. Nurses at the Denver Children's Hospital, for instance, *wear* the babies in their care rather than tend them in cribs whenever the mother is unable

Contemporary baby carrier, North America (Andrea's Baby Pack).

to care for her own baby. In most cases, then, a baby carrier replaces the stroller or baby carriage—at least until the baby is older and can sit up alone. Yes, the baby does get a certain amount of stimulation (more than lying in a crib, for example) when riding in a stroller or carriage, but the human body contact is lost when these devices are used. This contact, as ecologist Jean Liedloff and others maintain, is essential during the phase of development she terms the "in arms" period, roughly from birth until the baby can crawl away from mother under his or her own steam.

Numerous brands of baby carriers are available commercially today, even in department stores. This was not the case when we began having babies ten years ago. We had to make our own. The best buy (at half the cost of the best-known brand): Andrea's Baby Pack, unbeaten for versatility, quality workmanship, and *comfort*. If your local store doesn't carry it, you can order by mail. (See Directory.) Used carriers are often available through thrift shops or mothers' exchanges. (Check your local childbirth/mothers' groups.)

Baby Nurse

Just what you don't need after giving birth. The ultimate intervention in mother-baby interaction. You need someone to take care of *you*, while you take care of the baby. The best person for this, if you have a good relationship, is your own mother. Next best, some other relative. Hiring a nurse to come into your home and look after baby only stalls the moment of truth: the day she leaves and you're on your own with baby (with part of your maternal fine tuning already disabled by the lack of contact with your baby over the past few days or weeks). An extended period of hired help may be necessary for the mother who's had a Cesarean, but it's *household* help that's needed—not someone to take over your child.

The major complaint of women who have employed baby nurses: they often insist on doing things *their* way—even to the point of disparaging remarks about breastfeeding (feeding the baby is part of what you're paying them for), complaints about the food served (they expect *you* to provide the meals), enforcing a reign of absolute silence in the house (baby must sleep), and criticizing everything about baby's room (this pitfall commonly leads an exhausted mother to hire a nurse in the first place). Who needs this sort of aggravation and invasion of privacy?

Through your childbirth class or mothers' center you may be able to arrange a swap of services with another mother whose baby is due two or three months before or after yours if your own family is not close enough to help out. This "homecoming service" is also provided, for a fee, by some childbirth groups as a source of income for the organization. The key is that the service is two or three hours a day (not a live-in arrangement) and covers whatever you need to have done—

everything *except* baby care! In other cultures, anthropologist and lactation authority Dana Raphael explains in *The Tender Gift: Breastfeeding* (Englewood Cliffs, N.J.: Prentice-Hall, 1973), this helping person is called a *doula*. Having an adult around during part of the day can also be a good way to break the walls of isolation that all too often set apart the new mother and baby from the rest of the world. This isolation can become especially acute after your mate returns to work and

---

Sponge Bath, How to Give

Especially for use before the cord stump has fallen off.

You need:	a basin of warm water
	a bath thermometer if you're unsure of your ability to judge what warmth is best (95° to 100°F)
	a soft washcloth
	2 large, soft towels or receiving blankets
	mild, perfumed soap—only when baby seems really dirty (lint accumulated in body creases, for example); soap can dry baby's skin
You don't need:	lotions and oils—a clean baby smells wonderful all by itself! Mineral oil-based products should never be used, because they are absorbed through the skin and cause fat-soluble vitamins such as A and E to be lost.
	cotton-tipped swabs—which can damage tender tissues (especially ears) and force debris back into nasal passages.
Preparing yourself:	Dress in comfortable clothes and have a comfortable chair ready.
Getting baby ready:	Undress baby and wrap him or her in a towel or receiving blanket.
Then:	Using a warm, wrung-out washcloth, wash each part of the baby separately, starting with face and head, then body, arms, legs, and last the diaper area. Dry each part well after it's washed, and keep it covered. The other towel or receiving blanket can be used if the first one gets too damp.
Now:	You're ready to dress the baby. You don't need a dressing table because you can do it with baby on your lap. To put shirts on, seat baby on your lap with his or her back against your front. This gives you two free hands with which to ease on the shirt. For diapering, put baby on your lap with his or her feet nearest your body. This gives you one hand to lift baby's legs up with and one to slide the diaper under baby's bottom. Pin the diaper, wrap a receiving blanket around him or her, get comfortable, and play and/or nurse.
Alternative:	On a warm, sunny day you may want to give bath outdoors or take baby out just wrapped in blanket for some sunshine (see Sunbath) that's so good for baby's skin. In winter, find a warm, sunny spot indoors to sit holding naked baby for a few minutes to obtain same benefits of sunshine.

Appendix

161

your mother goes home, and there you are, just you and baby from now on—seemingly forever. Making this "adjustment" is not only unnecessary, it's unhealthy. Going from a full work life surrounded by colleagues to a life of solitary confinement with your baby (no matter how much loved or wanted) is not normal for human beings. Having appropriate helping hands in the early weeks, then staying active in a mothers' group or resuming your other work on a part-time basis at home, can prevent serious problems, such as depression and marital squabbles from coming on. (See "How Are Your Spirits?" in chapter 10.)

Baths

How often? Whenever baby seems to need it. In summer, a few quick once-overs a day can help keep baby cool and refreshed. In winter, every two or three days may do. Always rinse bottom with clear water after each wet diaper, and wash with soap and water after each bowel movement. (See Diapers, How to Change.) This is the best preventive measure for diaper rash, coupled, of course, with speedy removal of soiled diapers.

Bowel Movements

Like so many other things, bowel movements are widely variable. Some breastfed babies have several movements a day, after almost every feeding; other babies go for days with nothing, then produce a massive movement that flows out of diapers and clothes, inundating everything in range (including you). Baby may signal that it's about time by screwing up face, turning red, and fussing, or crying until effort is over. Remember, baby has no control over this event—there's just this sudden feeling that comes over him or her, and the bowels and abdominal muscles automatically squeeze and bear down. Learning to recognize this feeling is the first step toward becoming toilet-

---

Baths, Family Style

You need:	2 adults, one of whom wants a bath a bathtub in a warm room lots of towels 2 washcloths mild shampoo mild soap rubber ducks, plastic boats, floating toys as desired
First:	Fill the bathtub with warm water to whatever level would be comfortable for one adult. Undress the "wet" adult, keeping the "dry" adult armed with towels. Also have a change of clothes ready for the baby and the "wet" adult.
Then:	Undress the baby and put "wet" adult in tub. "Dry" adult hands baby to "wet" adult, who places baby in lap. It works better if "wet" adult is the mother, since baby's head fits between mother's breasts, which are also available should baby desire a snack.
The bath:	Wash the baby, face first, then downward with a washcloth. Soap

	is usually unnecessary. Use your wet hands to massage and love every inch of your baby.
The shampoo:	Many newborns have very little hair. In that case just wash the scalp with a cloth. For the baby with a full head of hair, take a washcloth and first wet the hair, being careful not to drip in baby's eyes. This is where the advantage of the family bath comes in. You can lean back and be the baby's reclining chair. Then take the washcloth with a little bit of shampoo on it and rub into baby's head. Rinse the same way with another clean washcloth.
Next:	Here is the advantage of having two adults. "Wet" adult hands the clean baby to "dry" adult and can get washed and shampooed while "dry" adult dries and dresses baby.
Now:	All get together and take a family nap!

trained, but most children don't attain that long-awaited skill much before two years of age (the cold, cruel facts).

The consistency of breastfed babies' stool ranges from almost watery (no, it's not diarrhea) to a soft paste, usually golden to deep mustard in color. Constipation is almost never a problem with these soft bowel movements (unless the baby is not being fed often enough [see chapter 8] or it's extremely hot and a great deal of body water is being lost through perspiration). The other advantage to breastfeeding: the bowel movements usually have a mild smell, reminiscent of a tangy yogurt, rather than the stronger odors associated with stool from a diet of formula and solids. A breastfed baby's diapers are also easier to wash, since the stains from these bowel movements come out much easier than the other kind.

Times to wonder if all is well: if bowel movements of breastfed baby take on strong, foul odor, or you notice baby straining to move bowels and nothing comes out for a day or two. (See Constipation and Diarrhea.) You may want to consult your medical care provider in either case. (See Pediatrician, How to Call.)

Burping

Most babies will self-burp if gently turned over on their stomachs after a nursing. If this doesn't happen, the baby most likely doesn't have a "bubble" to bring up. Breastfed babies take in much less air, as a rule, while nursing, than bottle-fed infants, since the baby's lips and tongue form a seal against the breast and the breast itself contains no air space as do most artificial feeding systems. If baby has been an avid nurser and emptied both breasts quickly, s/he may have taken in more during this oral orgy than the stomach can hold. Result—a little regurgitation accompanies the burp. Our advice: always place an absorbent cloth (diaper or cotton receiving blanket) under baby's head when you place him or her on the stomach, or lay the cloth over your shoulder if you prefer to hold baby this way after nursing. This protects your shirt from spit-ups (assuming they're small ones). One drawback to the baby-over-the-shoulder position right after nursing is that pushing hard into the baby's stomach with your shoulder may cause a *big* spit-up that runs all the way down the back of whatever you're wearing. This can really make the laundry pile up fast! If baby throws up constantly in considerable quanti-

ties, or if the milk travels out several feet from where you're nursing (projectile vomiting), you need to have baby checked to see what's wrong.

Car Seats

Recommended for car travel, especially when you're the driver and there's no other adult (in seat belt) to hold baby in the back seat. In the biological continuum, probably humans aren't "supposed" to travel any faster than we can run, but in today's world, that's a specious observation. We travel in automobiles, boats, trains, and airplanes—all of which present their own unique hazards to human life that exceed traveling by foot. We have no "built-in" protection against high-speed impact, the chief danger in auto accidents, so if we intend to use this form of conveyance, we have to use some additional form of protection as well. All of us, not just babies. The problem here is that car seats *do* separate mother and baby—often for prolonged periods of time if it's a long journey—but the consequences of not doing so may be far worse. Another difficulty: baby may want to nurse before dropping off to sleep. (The jiggles of taking a drive have been known to send many babies off to Dreamland when nothing else works.) When mother attempts to move sleeping baby from her arms into the car seat, baby may protest (loudly). It's the same problem you'll have if you use a crib. Sometimes baby will settle down, anyway; sometimes it won't work and in the interests of getting where you have to go (do you really have to go there?), baby cries the rest of the way—or until fatigue wins out. This doesn't make for a pleasant trip through the countryside. You'll have to weigh the merits of each situation on your own as it unfolds. For information on car seats and auto safety for babies and young children contact: Action for Child Transportation Safety. (See Directory.)

Clothing

1. Complete layette information can be found in chapter 9.
2. Baby does not need to be dressed any warmer than you are. Extra sweaters, hats, and blankets are unnecessary.
3. The best way to tell if baby is too cold or too hot is to feel the back of his neck. If it is hot and sweaty, baby is overdressed. If it is icy cold, baby is underdressed.
4. Natural fabrics (cotton, in particular) are most

absorbent and therefore most comfortable for baby. Avoid synthetics. They trap moisture and heat, can contribute to rashes, and often don't launder as well (they pill, pull out of shape, and retain stains far more commonly than natural fibers). Natural fibres are well worth the extra money.

5. Preowned baby clothes are presoftened. If you don't have a good source for hand-me-downs, try secondhand stores, bazaars, rummage sales, garage sales, or flea markets.

6. Factory outlets often have the same products as expensive stores but at a no-frills price. A directory of factory outlets may be consulted at your local library. Some sell by mail order.

7. Be sure baby's clothes are large enough. Tight, confining garments can cut off circulation (check baby's skin for deep marks left by elastic bands) and restrict baby's range of movement.

Colic

The medical dictionary says, "acute paroxysmal abdominal pain." To parents and all within earshot, it's never-ending crying and seeing one's infant double up in pain and expel large amounts of gas by rectum or by mouth, often for two or three months. You feel helpless. Nobody knows what causes it. You feel resentful. Why your baby? You feel driven to the wall. Will it ever stop?

Some possible causes cited in various medical references:

> **inability to digest formula**—Sometimes the problem can be solved by switching to one not made with cow's milk, such as a soy-based product, or, better yet, relactating so baby has the benefits of the easily digested breast milk.
> **immaturity of certain segments of the intestinal tract**—As food travels through the gut, it slows down at the immature places, forming gas accumulations which then make their painful way through the system.
> **excessive swallowing of air, overexcitement, nervous tension communicated from anxious mother**—All these raise the chicken-or-the-egg controversy; are these causes of colic or the results of it?
> **overfeeding**—Forcing or enticing baby to "finish" a certain prescribed amount of formula or solids is a real hazard of artificial feeding, since baby is not permitted to self-regulate intake or feeding interval—some researchers feel this may interfere with the

ability to appraise one's appetite accurately in childhood and adulthood, leading to permanent obesity.

For the breastfeeding mother, a complete dietary recall is in order to make sure that your milk is providing enough of the nutrients baby needs for good digestion. (See chapters 1 and 10.) Some midwives also suggest that digestive enzymes and brewer's yeast (to provide B vitamins necessary for proper digestion) may be added to the baby's diet until the colic subsides. For proper dosage levels, consult a nutrition therapist familiar with treatment of colic. Frequent, small feedings of the baby are recommended (that's the normal pattern in the completely breastfed infant) to prevent the introduction of large amounts of food all at once to the irritable gut.

Other writers mention that keeping baby warm, picking baby up, and moving around with baby to ease the passage of gas are sometimes helpful. Using your baby carrier in these circumstances is most appropriate. Some have even theorized that leaving baby in a crib for most of the day, particularly in the early months when baby can't make his/her own way about, may lead to such a buildup of nervous tension that a baby goes into a colic episode to discharge the tension—another reason for "wearing" your baby most of the time. As a last resort, some physicians prescribe antispasmodic medication for baby and a glass of wine for mother. While we are not in favor of drugging babies, this may be one instance where medication gets the family through a very tough spot.

Most sources assure parents that, even with colic, most infants do well as far as growth is concerned, and that the problem usually tapers off by the third month. Small consolation if you're only in your first month of it, but we hope we've provided some clues about what may work in your situation.

Constipation

Hard, difficult-to-pass feces may result from:

- supplementary formula given (sometimes without your knowledge) in hospital nursery—even if your baby was supposed to have been exclusively breastfed;
- too little fluid intake (nursing ad lib, assuming the mother has a good milk flow, should prevent this—baby doesn't need supplemental bottles of any other fluid, including

water, if mother offers the breast whenever baby fusses or cries);

- hot weather causing excessive perspiration with no increase in fluid intake to offset loss through skin.

A breastfed baby may be considered constipated when s/he strains trying to move the bowels for a day or two and nothing comes out. Contact your medical care provider with details, but read Bowel Movements, above, before you do. Simple lack of a bowel movement, even for days at a time, in a completely breastfed baby does not always indicate constipation.

If your doctor prescribes a glycerine suppository, be sure to buy the infant size, and only insert it until it's just out of sight. To insert, follow procedure for taking temperature. (See Temperature, How to Take.) Suppositories lubricate the rectum and stimulate bowel contractions. If the suppository slips back out before the baby is successful, gently reinsert it. It need not dissolve completely to achieve the desired effect. If nothing happens in an hour, call the physician back for further directions. S/he may want to examine the baby.

If your baby was born at home and hasn't begun to pass meconium by the next day, contact your doctor or clinic. The baby will need to be checked for possible bowel blockage.

Coughing, Choking, and Gagging

All are successful strategies for clearing baby's airways of mucus, stray particles in the air, or fluids that "go down the wrong way" (enter the windpipe instead of the esophagus during nursing). Most babies have strong gag reflexes at birth, and their snorting and coughing during sleep are signs that the baby is performing well in the new waterless environment. Sometimes, as your milk lets down in copious quantities, baby may not be able to keep up with the flow. Pausing a minute to allow the excess to drip onto a lap cloth or hand-expressing until the gush is over can save baby a few choking episodes. Other tips:

1. Keep the room humid in cold, dry weather to prevent drying of mucous membranes. This can be done with a steam vaporizer or by hanging wet towels in front of the radiator.
2. Wipe mucus away from nose gently. If nasal tissue becomes irritated, apply soothing ointment, such as plain petroleum jelly.
3. Snoring is common in babies. Just cuddle up and go back to sleep.
4. Nose drops are helpful for liquefying mucus. You can make your own out of a half-teaspoon of salt dissolved in eight ounces of tap water. Use one or two drops in each nostril every few hours. These drops are kinder and gentler than commercial preparations, rubber syringes, and cotton swabs, though baby will probably protest the insertion of the drops, too. It may cause baby to sneeze, dislodging the entire offending mucous plug.

Crying

Crying is your newborn's only way of telling you s/he needs something. Your prompt response to your baby's cries is the only way baby has of learning that you're reliable and trustworthy. All baby's needs are *right now*!

What to do:

1. Try nursing again, even if you just stopped a half-hour ago. You may be going through a "frequency" day which will boost your milk supply in response to baby's growing needs.
2. Is baby's life too hectic? Try a quiet, darkened room.
3. Baby feels lonely? Bring him or her into the family circle.
4. Is the room too hot or too cold, too humid or too dry?
5. Check that diaper again. Does baby cry before, during, or after a bowel movement?
6. Does baby have a bubble of air in the stomach? Gently rocking in a rocking chair with baby's head on your shoulder is just as effective as pounding the back.
7. Walking the floor or swaying back and forth recreates the gentle rocking of prenatal life. A baby carrier makes it easier on you. Take a walk for a change of scenery.
8. Is it too quiet? Try singing or turning on some soft background music. It doesn't have to be a lullaby as long as it's consistent in rhythm and volume.
9. It's highly unlikely, but it could be an open diaper pin or threads from seams wrapped tightly around tender toes.
10. *Take steps to prevent crying by keeping baby close at hand and starting your comforting while baby is merely fussing or smacking lips (in preparation for feeding).* These may be the

only sounds you hear in the night, for example, when you have baby sleeping with you, so your mate doesn't even wake up, nor does baby get fully revved up as is the case when loud crying is necessary to attract Mom's attention from another room.

11. If all else fails and crying is persistent, medical attention may be necessary. (See Colic.)

Diapers ... The Great American Diaper Controversy

Back in a simpler time there was very little choice of what to cover baby's bottom with. One used cotton diapers which came in rectangles measuring about 21 by 40 inches or squares which were about 27 by 27 inches. Either way, mother or her helper had to soak them, wash them, boil them, dry them, fold them, and one expert even recommended ironing them. Of course that "expert" was a male doctor who probably never changed a diaper, much less ever ironed one!

The invention of the automatic washing machine marked a great milestone in the history of diapering, and, for those who had no access to one, commercial diaper laundries were a boon. Of course, this still left the folding. Throughout the years, clever mothers had made the discovery that they could eliminate the repetitive task of diaper-folding by doing it once and stitching the folds. The idea caught on, and prefolded diapers became a marketable item.

The next great advance in diapering came in the early 1960s, coincidentally during the dawning of the antipollution movement: the invention of the disposable diaper. Disposable diapers had been in use in Europe for several years but were basically unsatisfactory. They consisted of a pad that fit into plastic pants. Absorbency was poor, and they were considered an emergency measure for long journeys. The American disposable, however, was a one-piece pad plus plastic cover with a liner that allowed the baby's urine to pass through to the padding. Over the past years several improvements have been made in the basic model. Diaper pins are no longer necessary as most brands now have self-closing tapes (but the tapes can get stuck to baby's skin causing reddened, sore spots). There are even elastic-legged disposables which

Diapers, How to Change

You need:	an underpad (waterproof) a clean diaper or two a washcloth a source of water Caldesene powder, if desired
First:	Place baby on back on underpad (preferably on floor). Remove the soiled diaper by unpinning it and removing from front before back. Wipe away feces from front to back as you remove back of diaper.
Then:	Use the washcloth to wash baby's bottom. Wash from front to back to avoid contaminating the urethral opening or girl's vaginal opening. Then turn the washcloth around and rinse with clear water. Apply Caldesene powder if bottom is red or irritated (pour onto your hand first, then rub onto baby).
Now:	Select one or two diapers.
Goal:	You want a snug, comfortable fit for baby.
First, ask yourself:	What kind of diapers do I want for my baby?
Choice:	27″ x 27″ birds-eye 21″ x 40″ gauze 13″ x 21″ prefolded gauze stretch or fitted style disposables
How to fold:	27″ x 27″: Fold in half, then in thirds. Turn the diaper so that the narrow sides are on top and bottom, and lay the baby on the diaper with the top of the diaper at the top of baby's waist. Bring the front up and pin at the sides. To pin, lap back corner over front corner and slant pin down and back. The best pins have a sliding lock head. The

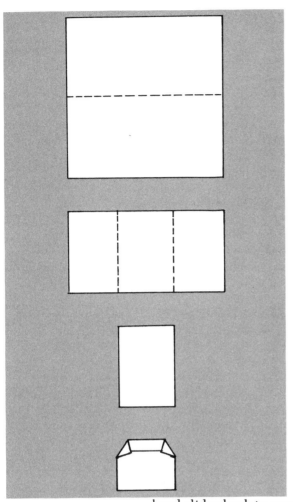

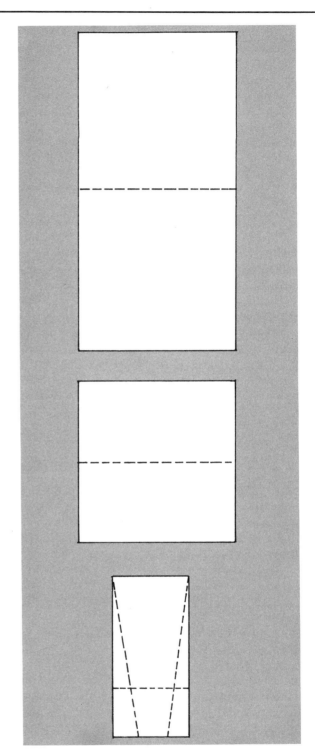

head slides back to open the pin. After pinning, slide the head back.

21″ x 40″: Fold in half, then in half again. Turn so that narrow sides are on top and bottom. Fold in a wedge on each side. Fold up one-third from the bottom. This gives an extra thickness in front which works well for boy babies.

13″ x 21″ prefolded gauze: Follow directions as above from folding the wedge onward.

Stretch, fitted, or disposables: These vary, so follow directions given with product.

To complete the job:	Slip on or snap on rubber pants.
Place soiled diaper in:	covered pail containing soapy solution and washing soda (after rinsing in toilet).

give a better fit around baby's legs (but cut off air circulation to bottom, promoting more rashes). There is a wide range of sizes to fit the wide range of babies. So what's a mother to choose?

Disposables get lots of advertising, so most mothers are aware of the claims made for them: nice smell (but perfume may irritate baby's skin), ease of diapering, no danger of pins sticking baby, keep baby drier, easier to dispose of, especially convenient when traveling.

In the interest of fair play, here's equal time for the old-fashioned method. Cotton is a natural fabric. Mothers find it soft and comfortable and so do babies. The part of the disposable that goes next to baby's skin is made of nonwoven fibres, virgin wood fibres (we were assured by an executive of the American Paper Institute that baby could not get a splinter from these wood fibres), and synthetics, such as nylon. These make the liner feel smooth, but most mothers find that cotton diapers are softer.

Cost is a big factor for most families. An independent study furnished these surprising figures:

Disposable diapers	9.3¢/use
Home-laundered diapers	12.3¢/use
Diaper service diapers	9.8¢/use

Use cost depends on the number of diapers put on at one time. The average cotton diapering was figured to be 1.4 diapers, as many mothers use double diapers for an older baby or at night. The average disposable cost 9.3 cents for 1. The man from the institute explained the surprisingly high cost of home-washed diapers this way: they figured on *paying the mother* to wash the diapers—7.56 cents per diapering! So if you do your baby's diapers for love instead of money, it works out to 4.74 cents per diapering (of 1.4 diapers). That's about 3.33 cents a diaper. Also, they added in the price of the washer and dryer which you probably find other uses for, energy to run them, and detergents and extras that you might use. For additional savings which the study didn't consider, here are some tips:

1. Try line drying. Sunshine is free, clothesline is cheap.
2. Do a full load. Add in towels, sheets, other whites for more economy per piece.
3. Try cooler water. Today's detergents work in lower temperatures, saving on heating bills, but some babies (and grownups) react with skin

rashes to some of these stronger compounds. You'll just have to experiment to see what your baby and other family members can tolerate.

4. The average home diaper washer uses bleaches, fabric softeners, bluers, and other additives. Find a soap or detergent that works without the expensive extras. A bonus here is that diapers will be less likely to irritate and will be more absorbent. Plain Ivory Snow plus chlorine bleach in the wash water (you should use hot for best results) and a half-cup of vinegar in the rinse water (cold) has stood the test of millions of loads of diapers.
5. Put the baby in your carrier and be close while you do laundry. Get paid in cuddling!
6. When you're finished with diapers, you still have them to use for household cleaning cloths.

Diarrhea

Diarrhea is the rapid movement of fecal matter through the intestine, resulting in poor absorption of water into the body tissues, poor absorption of nutrients and electrolytes needed to keep body tissues and fluids in balance, and repeated elimination of watery, foul-smelling stools. Potassium is especially depleted by diarrhea and can produce acidosis (a fall in blood pH) as well as dehydration. The stool may contain mucus and be streaked with blood due to local irritation of the intestine by infectious agents. The abdomen may be very crampy, and the baby may appear very weak and listless.

Diarrhea is a symptom of disease, not a disease itself, but in severe cases intravenous treatment to relieve the dehydration, nutritional deficiencies, and disturbances of electrolyte balance caused by diarrhea may be given in the hospital. Antidiarrhea drugs may also be used in extreme cases to decrease the flow of fecal matter through the intestine and alleviate cramps.

The normal soft or liquid stool of the breastfed baby is not diarrhea. (See Bowel Movements.) Even if a baby has mild diarrhea due to infection, the best treatment is breast milk, since it contains anti-infective agents. *Severe diarrhea is a medical emergency in the small baby.* Severe diarrhea occurs when any of these other symptoms are present: vomiting, temperature over 101°F, pus or blood in the stools, very dry skin, or sunken eyes or fontanels. Seek medical care *immediately* in severe diarrhea, as a small baby can get into life-threatening problems quickly as the result of dehydration that follows.

Washing the anal area, legs, and abdomen after each bowel movement is essential to preventing the baby's skin from becoming "scalded" by the caustic feces. Applying petroleum jelly as a protective coating in this case can be helpful.

Ears

Except for an otoscope for diagnostic purposes, never put anything into baby's ears. Ear wax that accumulates can be dissolved (if it's excessive) by mixing a solution of hydrogen peroxide (the same preparation people use to bleach hair) and water, half and half, and putting two or three drops into baby's ear. Hold baby on side for a few minutes, then turn him or her over and do the other side (if it needs it).

The outside of the ear can simply be washed as part of the regular bath. Do check *behind* baby's ears for encrusted milk that can dribble back there during nursing, and look closely at the tiny folds up toward the top of the outer ear which also tend to trap lint and skin oil, forming little crusts. A cotton swab for these *external* ear cleansings is okay. Using a swab for the ear canal can impact wax against the eardrum or even puncture it.

Ear shape can change dramatically as the child matures. Ears are often flattened or pushed outward from months of being squished in the womb, but most gradually flatten out and lie back. The only way to correct ear shape is through surgery, best postponed until adolescence when the child can decide for him/herself if it's warranted.

Eyes

A small amount of crusty yellow material may be present in your baby's eyes when s/he awakens. This is normal. It's just the result of defective drainage of tears which are continually produced by the eye. Using a clean washcloth or cotton ball moistened with warm water, wipe carefully from the inner corner of the eye outward. Use another part of the washcloth or a fresh cotton ball for the other side.

If you see a clear, watery discharge flowing out of the baby's eye, the tear duct which drains tears into the nose may be clogged. Notify your baby's medical care practitioner who will probably recommend cleaning as described above and applying gentle pressure from the inner corner of the eye toward the bridge of the nose. Repeat four to five times, and then do the whole massage again several times each day until the duct opens.

A very inflamed eye may mean the baby has gonorrheal conjunctivitis or some other infection (especially if the eyes have not been treated with silver nitrate or an antibiotic ointment). See chapter 4 and get *medical attention at once.*

Feet

The bones in your baby's feet are very malleable, as each has soft spots to allow further growth. During the first month after birth, the feet and ankles should straighten out (they've often been cramped in the last weeks before birth and may stay in peculiar positions for a few days) and the legs become less bowed. At the one-month pediatric checkup (see chapter 10) the legs and feet will be carefully checked to make sure there's no abnormality (which is sometimes hard to determine right after birth) such as club foot or *metatarsus varus* (where the foot itself angles inward from the instep, but there's no ankle involvement).

Should your baby have either of these problems, correction may take many different forms, since there's a great deal of dispute among reputable orthopedists about treatment. Much, of course, depends on the degree of the deformity. For some infants, a cast from toes to thigh may be advised for months (with several recastings to allow for growth). Others may be fitted with special shoes and a bar to hold the shoes at the angle needed for correction. For milder cases, wearing hard shoes on opposite feet or no treatment at all may be needed. Usually, the pediatrician would refer a moderate to severe case to an orthopedic specialist who would then carry out the course of treatment. Club foot and *metatarsus varus* are very common foot problems in babies, and they usually respond nicely to appropriate therapy. The orthopedist may also demonstrate and ask you to carry out foot massage a few times a day designed to lengthen the tendons and ligaments of the baby's instep. Let the physician or nurse-practitioner know at your baby's one-month checkup if you've noticed that the child holds the feet in a peculiar position.

Baby's feet may look a bit bluish until circulation to them is 100 percent. Baby's feet are typically a bit cooler than the rest of the body for this reason. If you use booties, try to pick fabrics such as cotton or corduroy rather than the knit variety which can entangle baby's toes, especially if they have a design with open spaces. All booties look cute, but most of the time they wind up lost because baby kicks them off. Don't use rubber bands or tight lacings to prevent this: that cuts down on vital circulation to the feet. As you'll notice at bath time, booties also contribute fantastic amounts of lint that you have to remove from in between those tiny toes! An alternative: an older child's elasticized crew socks can serve as knee socks for the baby.

Fever and Convulsions

A temperature over 100°F in a baby indicates fever; over 104°F is a high fever. How to take a temperature is presented in a later section. Fever accompanies so many illnesses, it's impossible to give a list. The important point is that fever in a baby under three months of age should be viewed as a serious sign. Your doctor or clinic should be notified. They will want to know what other signs of illness your baby shows and probably will want to see the child in person as soon as possible. The numbers do not necessarily indicate the severity of the disease causing the fever, so a thorough examination is in order. Do not just administer aspirin and wait. You may be able to lower the temperature, but the underlying problem will not be treated.

Occasionally, a baby with fever will have a convulsion. This is particularly true when the child's temperature rises sharply in a short time. A baby who has convulsed is in need of emergency care even if s/he seems almost back to normal after the seizure has passed. While the convulsion is occurring, know that there is nothing you can do to hasten its conclusion, but you should hold the infant to one side, with the head down to facilitate drainage from the mouth, throat, and nose and to prevent the baby from choking and cutting off the supply of oxygen. A convulsion due to sudden high fever is not a sign of a chronic disease such as epilepsy, and the episode is unlikely to recur. After a convulsion, the child is usually quite unresponsive (a great discharge of electrical energy from the nervous system has occurred) and often sleepy. The baby should be transported immediately to an emergency room or other facility as per your doctor's orders.

Fontanels (soft spots)

The "soft spots" of your baby's skull require no special care. They are covered with quite a tough membrane (the scalp) which protects the tough coverings encasing the brain (the dura). There's no reason to be afraid to touch the fontanel

as you wash or brush the baby's hair, for example. The brain itself is very well protected.

Going Out with Baby

One of the joys of having a nursing baby is that you can go anywhere together without having to pack a suitcase full of formula, bottles, bibs, baby food, spoon, dish, feeding chair, etc., etc., etc. A basic rule of thumb for short trips is, bring one diaper for each two hours you will be away, plus one extra, and one change of clothing for each four to six hours you will be away. For example, let's assume you are going to visit your great-aunt who lives two hours away. That's four hours of travel time. Now let's say you plan to spend three hours there. That makes seven hours. Bring five diapers and two changes of clothing. That's probably more than you will actually use, but it's good to have extras. Don't forget the washcloths, receiving blanket, and additional warm clothing if the weather warrants. On your way from house to car, a knitted shawl loosely draped over the baby's face warms icy air before it reaches baby's lungs.

If you will be taking car trips, see Car Seats. Current information on auto safety devices can be obtained from Action for Child Transportation Safety. (See Directory.)

Some favorite places to go with nurslings:

- movies (young babies usually nurse and sleep through the show);
- drive-in movies (even if baby is awake, no one is disturbed);
- visiting, especially other new parents;
- parks, zoos, and gardens (new sights and fresh air!);
- the beach or pool (be sure to use a sun block, and keep baby under an umbrella and well covered in thin clothing);
- any place else you enjoy.

Hands

Babies like to keep their hands in tight little fists. The only problem this poses is cleaning in between the fingers where lint is likely to accumulate as baby picks at blankets and clothing. The nice part about this trait is how sweet it feels to have that little fist grip your finger. It's baby's first handshake. As we've mentioned about feet, circulation to hands may not be perfect yet, so they may be cooler than the rest of the baby's body. Many babies are born with the ability to suck their thumbs, fingers, and whole hands. It's perfectly normal, though in Holt's heyday, mothers were admonished to slip mitts over the baby's hands to prevent sucking or to bind the arms to the baby's sides altogether in those who persisted. Babies use their hands from the earliest moments after birth to explore this new place, so please don't encase them by turning down the ends of their gown or kimono sleeves. If it's scratches you're worried about, trim baby's nails. (See Nails, How to Cut.)

Head Control

Baby gains control of his/her body from the head downward. At birth, some babies can lift their heads completely off the surface on which they're lying stomach down. Almost all who are born full weight and full term can turn their heads from one side to the other when they're on their stomachs. In a few weeks (sometimes by the end of the first month in the strong ones) your baby will begin to pull his/her head back a bit from your shoulder as you hold baby upright against you. In the beginning, these experiments may catch you off guard. Baby's head is quite heavy and may cause the whole body to pitch backward away from you and out of your reach if you're not holding on tight. The little efforts usually end with baby's head bumping back onto your shoulder. A rest. Then, another try. Such hard work (imagine trying to move your head if it were one-quarter of your adult height!), but so essential to later developing voluntary hand movements, sitting, standing, and, much later, walking.

Helpers

Helpers can be relatives, friends, or neighbors, paid or unpaid. Obviously, grandmothers, aunts, sisters, and brothers are closest to the baby's continuum. Other sources can be visiting nurse services or homemaker and housekeeping services, often available through state or county employment services and private "baby nurse" agencies. (See Baby Nurse.) Prenatal contact with childbirth education organizations or breastfeeding support groups can help with peer support.

Each individual potential helper should be evaluated on his/her own merits. A relative with whom you have had a long-term good relationship may theoretically be closer to your continuum, but a visiting nurse or childbirth teacher who has had recent experience mothering new mothers may be better for you. How to tell:

Grandmother and baby nap while you shower!

- When the two of you are present with the baby, who appears to be mothering whom? A helper who tries to show you how to mother your baby may just be playing the "see what a good example I am" game. A cute baby is easy to mother. A newly delivered, tired out, stringy-haired woman with hemorrhoids and the weepies is hard to mother. The test is, how does she mother *you*?

- Does she say things like, "Oh, let me do that for you," when you start to diaper or dress your baby? Does she imply that she will cause your baby less stress? Let her hold the pins while you do the diapering.

- Who holds the baby more? Does she encourage you to have constant physical contact with baby or does she suggest that the crib be near *her* bed, that *she* take baby out, that *she* be in charge?

- Can she cook? *Will* she cook? Make a specific list of the work you need to have done, and show it to the prospective helper or the agency *in advance*. Hopefully, she'll tell you what she "doesn't do."

- If there are older children, does she use the opportunity to ease their adjustment to the new baby? (This is especially important to consider where grandparents are the potential helpers.) Or does she constantly warn them "to be careful" around the baby, tell them not to talk too loud "because of the baby," forbid them to touch the baby, and similar injunctions? Even the youngest child will react negatively to this sort of treatment, and the baby will get the blame.

Housework

Food, a clean bed, and getting the laundry done. If you manage these, you're doing better than most! Things to absolutely forget for a few months:

- dusting knickknacks (store them), bookshelves (you won't be doing much reading), or windowsills;
- polishing silver (no formal dinner parties);
- rearranging the furniture;
- dusting under beds (who's checking?);
- vacuuming (unless you discover its steady whirr sends your baby off to sleep);
- window washing (you'll be too busy to look out);
- sweeping the basement (save your energy);
- defrosting the freezer;
- redecorating (baby won't be able to tell the difference);
- cleaning the oven;
- beating rugs (what's another year?).

A once-through-the-house anticlutter pickup first thing in the morning will do wonders for your spirits for the rest of the day, as will getting dirty dishes off the dining table and into a sink full of suds to soak (so what if you don't actually get around to washing them until 4:30?). What not to put off? Anything that makes you feel wretched if it's not done (this may be cleaning the bathroom for some—others just can't stand to see a fireplace with old ashes standing in it). Be sure your helper understands your priorities and follows through. It might be a small thing, but if it bothers you, it

---

Laundry

You need: a washing machine with *hot* water
a dryer or clothesline
liquid detergent or boxed soap
dilute bleach, if desired
white vinegar

First the wash: Diapers and cotton clothing can be washed together with sheets, towels, and your nursing bras. Liquid detergent is best if your family isn't allergic to it, because it is phosphate-free and doesn't remove the fireproofing from infant wear. Or, use plain soap such as Ivory. Wash as usual. If you use bleach, dilute it (¼ cup bleach in 1 cup water) or you may find your diapers full of holes. Don't use fabric softeners, which lessen the absorbency of clothes and diapers and may cause rashes or skin irritation. Add ½ to 1 cup of white vinegar to the final rinse cycle. It cuts soap or detergent residue and helps clothes rinse cleaner. (There is no vinegar odor left after the rinse.)

Now the dry: If it's a sunny day and the air is fresh and unpolluted consider yourself lucky, and hang the wash out to dry. If it's raining, you live in a high-pollution area, or you're just too busy, use an automatic dryer. The high heat also kills germs that escape the detergent and vinegar. Snaps on clothing should be fastened if you use an electric dryer, since they get extremely hot and can burn holes in other items.

Putting clothes away: This is something even the smallest child can help with. Ask each child to find his or her own clothes in the big pile and put them in his or her own pile. Then, the bigger ones can help the little ones fold or at least stuff the items back in their own drawers so they're out of sight.

Right from the Start

ought to be taken care of, so you don't feel obligated to do it yourself.

Humidifiers/Vaporizers

Important equipment for any house with children, humidifiers preserve mucous membranes during heating season and when kids or grownups are sick. Vaporizers perform a similar function, but they are constructed so that the moist air can be aimed directly at the patient. The old hot mist/cool mist question has been answered; it doesn't seem to make a bit of difference. These items can often be purchased at considerable savings on sale. They vary widely in price, so shop around for the best buy.

Illness, Serious, Signs of

Your baby needs **immediate** medical attention if s/he displays any of these signs:

1. Loss of consciousness
2. Labored breathing
3. Fever (temperatures over 101°F)
4. Decrease in urine output or very dark, strong-smelling urine
5. Blood or mucus in stool or foul-smelling stool
6. Repeated vomiting
7. Refusal to nurse
8. Lethargic appearance
9. Convulsions
10. Bleeding you can't control

Lotions, Oils, and Creams

Leave them on the store shelf. A clean baby smells terrific without any perfumes added. Many lotions contain alcohol, a drying agent, thereby insuring their own continued need. Baby's skin is fine and tender—why risk irritation from chemicals in the lotion (just read the labels)? At least one major baby lotion is widely known to doctors to cause tiny blisters all over the skin of babies who happen to be sensitive to it (a fairly large percentage). Use no lotions, oils, creams, or emulsions unless there is some medical need (as an antibiotic preparation for an eye infection or a cut). Saves a bundle over the years, too.

Lovemaking

Baby doesn't mind a bit. Parents the world

Nails, How to Cut

You need: a pair of baby scissors with rounded points

The best time: After a bath when the nails have been softened by the water, or any time baby is quiet and relaxed (asleep is fine).

The position: Hold baby in your lap, and if s/he is squirming or seems to be impatient, take special care to prevent an accidental kick to your cutting hand.

The cutting: Hold the exposed hand in your left hand (right if you're a lefty), spread the fingers gently, and trim straight across just below the top of the finger. Reverse for other hand, and do toenails similarly.

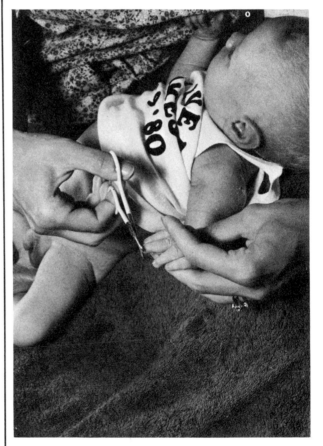

Cutting nails.

over live in one- or two-room accommodations with their children and yet the United States, where adult lovemaking is carried on behind closed doors, has one of the highest rates of sex-related crime anywhere. If having your baby present inhibits you or your partner, you can use another room or move baby temporarily. Most of the time baby just snoozes through the grand passion, though, so you needn't worry about the noise (see Noise), the candlelight, or the music (if you're so inclined).

Remember that it's possible to become pregnant even though you're breastfeeding, so if your plans include intercourse, have your mate use a condom until you've consulted your doctor or midwife about your own form of contraception. (See chapter 10.) Unless, of course, you're prepared to have two babies within 10 months' time.

Massage, Infant

A massage is a nice adjunct to a bath that some babies find very relaxing. Of course, if your baby is being held and carried a great deal, the stimulation may not be as necessary as for the baby who is primarily crib-bound. Baby massage is widely performed in native cultures around the world and Frederick Leboyer's book, *Loving Hands: The Traditional Indian Art of Baby Massage* (New York: Knopf, 1976), gives a step-by-step guide to the form practiced in India. Your best local source of information is a physical therapist who works with infants and young children, or a massage therapist with similar experience. The basic principles of massage, for children and adults, are well presented in George Downing's *Massage Book* (New York: Random House, 1972).

Navel

Once a day, until the umbilical cord stump falls off, swab the stump with rubbing (isopropyl) alcohol to promote drying and to reduce the chance of local infection. Wait until the stump has fallen off (anywhere from a week to three weeks) before giving a tub bath. Sponge baths are fine until then. (See Baths.) Keep the front of baby's diaper and rubber pants turned down far enough to prevent moisture from softening stump. When the cord falls off, you may notice a few spots of blood on baby's shirt or gown and the new skin may look very tender (it is). You may discontinue the alcohol swabs at this point, but keep the navel clean with simple soap and water.

If the area around the base of the stump or the navel itself becomes red, has a discharge, or smells offensive, contact your baby's doctor or nurse-practitioner. You will probably be advised to use another antiseptic lotion, cream, or powder until the condition clears up.

The size and appearance of the navel in the beginning has little to do with what it will look like as the child grows older. The new navel is often quite prominent, but gradually flattens out as the skin of baby's abdomen becomes more taut. Sometimes navel prominence persists and the baby is found upon examination to have an umbilical

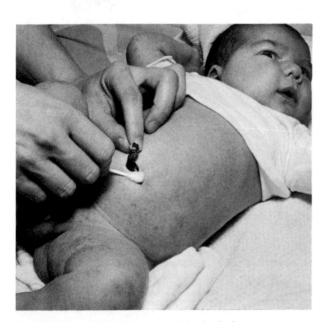

Swabbing umbilical stump with alcohol.

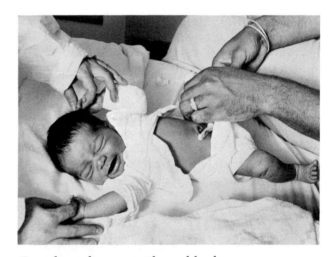

Turn down diapers until navel heals.

Right from the Start

hernia. Most of these out-pouchings of intestine through the abdominal wall close on their own, with no treatment whatever. They may range from one-half inch to three inches in diameter, the larger ones causing parents to worry about clothing that fits snugly about the waist. Some pediatricians recommend an abdominal binder for very large hernias, just as a comfort measure for the infant. Follow your doctor's recommendations.

Noise

Babies will sleep when they are tired no matter where they are. There is no need to tiptoe around for months every time the baby is napping. Some infants do react with a full-body startle in response to certain sudden, loud, sharp sounds (a door slamming, the doorbell, dropping a heavy pot in the kitchen, a basketball being bounced against the side of the house), but they usually fall back asleep even when this happens. Otherwise, they were close to waking up, anyway. Many mothers report that their babies are soothed by monotonous, steady-volume sounds, like the vacuum cleaner or the dishwasher running, and that they awaken when these sounds turn off. You'll soon find what your baby likes best. The point is that baby doesn't have to spend hours a day in a "quiet" room in order to get the sleep s/he needs.

Nose

Baby's nose is like baby's ears—don't stick things into it. The tissues are very delicate. Babies don't learn to breathe with their mouths for several weeks after birth, so if nose is stuffy (those passages are very small) baby may become quite fussy trying to get a good breath. To soften and loosen mucus in baby's nose, see Coughing, Choking, and Gagging.

Pacifiers

Mother is the best pacifier of all time. Keeping baby close prevents much fussing. You have two breasts that will usually calm the most frantic infant. An artificial pacifier is just a substitute for them. About the only situation in which a pacifier might be warranted for a few hours is in the early days of breastfeeding when nipples are very tender and you've been nursing the baby for hours off and on and you just have to have a break to put on an ice pack, but baby still wants more sucking. Some babies will gum and suck on your finger (Dad can take over here), a wet, clean washcloth, or their own fingers if the breast is not available. Others only accept something that's as close to the real thing as possible. If your baby has exceptional sucking needs and your breasts need a break, choose an artificial pacifier that imitates the shape of the compressed real breast (the Nuk models are designed this way). Use it only until your breasts have recovered. In just a few months, baby will start to drool, and for our money there's nothing less appetizing than a sloppy piece of plastic stuck into baby's mouth on a more-or-less permanent basis. Overreliance on a pacifier can thwart the normal expansion of your milk supply, too, since baby's suckling at the breast stimulates milk production. Save it for a real crisis when there doesn't seem to be any alternative.

Pediatrician, How to Call

1. In an emergency, do not waste time calling the pediatrician's office. Notify the emergency room at the hospital s/he practices at (find this out before your first visit) and get your child there right away.

2. Write down symptoms, problems, and/or observations you have made so that you do not leave out important information.

3. Have available pencil, paper, phone number, and hours of business of local drugstores, so doctor's office or clinic can telephone prescription, if needed, and you can pick it up or have it delivered as soon as possible.

4. Keep pediatrician's telephone number in a handy reference spot (written on front of telephone book or on a special list hung on your refrigerator door), so you don't have to waste time looking through the directory every time you phone.

5. If it's not an emergency, and the doctor has a "call hour," try to call at that time. You know how frustrating it is to be waiting in an examining room with your half-dressed child for 10 or 15 minutes while the doctor is called away to the telephone on a nonemergency matter.

6. If you notice something early in the day, don't put off calling about it on the assumption that it'll probably get better by itself pretty soon. Baby's illnesses (minor and major) have a way of seeming much more critical around 10:00 P.M. than they did at 10:00 A.M.—and making the trek to the office or hospital during the night can be so wearying and *expensive*. Also, unless you live in a major city, it's awfully difficult to find

Naps, Mother and Baby

Can't do without these. Two a day minimum for first two weeks after birth.

Napping and nursing.

You need: one bed or mattress, made up
at least four pillows

The position: You should be on your left side, baby on his/her right side, both of you with a pillow at your back. This prevents baby from rolling onto his/her back after nursing. (Just in case s/he should spit up, the milk will flow onto cloth, not get caught in windpipe and cause choking as might happen if baby were on back.) It also saves you from very tight back muscles which can result from holding still in the nursing position until baby falls asleep. You also need one pillow placed between your head and shoulder. (Don't put your shoulder up on the pillow because that strains your neck muscles.) Another pillow goes between your legs so they are not resting one on the other (each leg is supported). Some people also like to have a pillow across their middle to rest their upper arm on. The goal is to have every joint bent and every joint supported. (True muscular release can only happen when there is *no work* being done by the muscle.)

Getting the baby on the breast: Offer the left breast first (one closest to the surface of the bed) by drawing baby and baby's pillow close to it, then use your right hand to introduce the nipple to the baby's mouth. Both breast and baby are lying directly on the bed, no pillows under either one. Do not try to support the baby's body with your left arm. (This is always shown in drawings of nursing but is impossible in real life—your arm goes to sleep—and the baby always wakes up again when you try to remove the arm support later.) Draw up a sheet or blanket and let baby snuggle close. You remain as still as possible.

If baby wants more: Switch to second breast by breaking suction on first with right hand. Then just lean your torso toward baby

a pharmacy that's open late at night. Call as soon as you think you have a problem. (See Illness, Serious, Signs of.)

7. If you want your child examined, don't be put off with a telephone consultation. Simply ask what time it will be best to bring the baby in.

Penis, Care of

Uncircumcised

First: Undress the baby.
Last: Wash his penis—just the outside.

a bit more until right breast is within baby's range. Use right hand to introduce nipple as before. Advantage—you change breasts without having to move baby. Result—baby more likely to drift off to sleep after a few more minutes of suckling. This time, you won't have to break suction. Baby's jaw will just relax as sleep overtakes him or her and the nipple will be released.

To move away: Tuck sheet or blanket snugly around baby as you pull your body away. This gives baby the continuing sensation of enfoldment and warmth. You can then roll over and sleep on your own pillow or, if you're already rested, you can get up to do something else. Baby takes nap right there—no need to transfer to any other place.

Recommendation: Do as much of your breastfeeding as possible in this position for greatest relaxation and least fuss when you want to get something done while baby sleeps. If you accustom baby to this position, baby will be extremely portable and go to sleep wherever you lie down with him or her. Baby will be tuned to you, not to a crib.

That's all. Just wash it. Don't try pulling back the foreskin. It won't move easily for a few years. Don't force it back. It may get caught there and cause the glans to swell painfully. Just wash as any other part of the body.

T. D. Swafford, M.D., of the Group Health Medical Center, Seattle, Washington, wrote in support of this approach in the *Canadian Medical Journal* (January 28, 1967):

> What has been largely missing in North American literature is information on the proper care of the foreskin in babies and young children. This lack of information has in fact produced complications in uncircumcised children which is unfortunately due to ignorance rather than lack of circumcision. . . . Every casualty department is well used to seeing babies with paraphimosis, which results from the mother's efforts to retract the foreskin on someone's wrong advice.
>
> Since the young child is able to bathe himself (if given a chance) by the age of four or five, retraction of the foreskin can be put off until the child is able to take care of it himself, in the same way that girls gradually learn to take care of personal hygiene.

Circumcised

1. There will usually be a length of petroleum jelly gauze covering the wound. Leave it in place for a day.
2. Observe wound carefully at each diaper change. If bleeding occurs, notify whoever did the circumcision.
3. Change baby's diapers as soon as they are wet or soiled. If baby seems uncomfortable, leave diaper off. Just slip it under baby's bottom and place a rubber sheet under baby to protect mattress.
4. Do not place baby on his abdomen for at least 24 hours.
5. After the dressing falls off or is removed, a sterile gauze pad with ointment may be placed over the wound after each diaper change until complete healing has occurred.

Photographing Baby

1. It is considered safe to use flash photography with babies.
2. Take pictures of the everyday events in baby's life. These are usually more interesting than the posed kind.
3. Be wary of salespersons who try to get you to sign a contract for "a picture every month," or other deals that look too good to be true. When in doubt, call your local Better Business Bureau or Chamber of Commerce.

Picking Up Baby

When to:	Whenever baby cries, pick him or her up.	To hold over shoulder:	Position baby's cheek at shoulder level, still keeping steady hold on back of neck and supporting baby's weight with your other hand under the buttocks. This allows baby to see over your shoulder. Some babies like to be held even higher, almost draped over the shoulder. Experiment to find your baby's preference.
To support head:	If baby is on back, cup hand behind baby's neck before you begin to lift body. Place other hand around and under baby's hip farthest from you, then lift head and buttocks at the same time. This prevents undue strain on the spinal column and gives you control in case baby should make any sudden moves.		

Never lift baby by holding under arms. Head can flop and spinal column bears full weight of infant.

Playing with Baby

1. Avoid the practice of tossing, shaking, or bouncing the tiny infant. Babies are very susceptible to whiplash injury, because their heads are so heavy.
2. In the first month baby receives visual stimulation from looking at mother while nursing and by being put in a baby carrier while you do your daily work.
3. Singing and talking to baby aid in the development of verbal abilities.
4. Human presence is always preferable to an inanimate object, no matter how expensive or "educational."

Powders

Avoid all baby powders containing talc. The dust can settle in lungs. Best powders are Caldesene and plain old cornstarch. Caldesene is antibacterial and antifungal. Both are very absorbent.

To apply, shake powder into your own hand first, then rub onto baby's skin, making sure to get it into all the folds and creases (sometimes quite a feat!). Don't overdo—just a light film will make baby comfortable, especially in hot weather. Use it under your breasts, too, if they are heavy.

Rashes, Spots, and Sores

1. The most common rash in young babies is diaper rash. If you follow the directions for washing diapers, change the baby frequently, and are breastfeeding with no additional foods or liquids given, you may never see diaper rash on your baby.
2. If diaper rash occurs:
   a. Air baby's bottom as long as possible during the day. Place diaper under baby's bottom, but don't pin on. Put baby on a rubberized sheet.
   b. If you must put a diaper on, leave off the rubber pants so air continues to circulate to the skin.
   c. Use a protective ointment such as Balmex A and D or an antiseptic powder such as Caldesene.
   d. Double-check your diaper-washing techniques, or, if you have been using disposables, switch to cotton diapers. Your baby may be sensitive to the perfumes in paper diapers, or the plastic covering may be so tight that air is prevented from circulating and heat builds up inside the diaper.
3. A fiery red, sharply defined rash that doesn't respond to above care may be a thrush (*Candida* or *Monilia*) infection which requires medication, so call your baby's health practitioner.
4. Prickly heat (tiny pumps or blisters) is a sweat rash commonly found around neck and shoulders and in the folds of baby's skin. Be sure baby isn't overdressed for the weather. A diaper alone may do in summer.
5. Other rashes, spots, and sores in the very young

baby should also be evaluated by the doctor or nurse-practitioner. Some are perfectly harmless; some are signs of disease or injury such as insect bites, poison ivy, impetigo, or seborrhea.

Receiving Blankets

How to make:

You need:	one yard of 36″ or 45″ 100% cotton knit for each blanket
	needle and thread, or pinking shears, or a sewing machine, if you prefer
First:	Cut the material into 36″ lengths.
Then, either:	Trim around the four sides with the pinking shears or hem around the four sides with needle and thread, or by machine.
How to use:	as lightweight blanket
	as towel after bath
	as a shoulder cloth
	to swaddle baby

Rocking Chair

This is the only new piece of furniture you really need. To test for comfort and usability, sit in it at the store and place your arms in the position for nursing. Can you rest your elbows on the armrest? Is the chair wide enough for you, the pillow on your lap that holds baby at breast level so your back doesn't get tired, and the baby? Do your legs reach the floor comfortably, or will you need a footrest, too? Is the chair edge rounded so it doesn't dig into your thighs? Can you easily fit a small pillow behind your neck? (You can relax while nursing if you select the right chair.) Is it built sturdily to last through hours and hours of rocking? Does it squeak? Any chair that doesn't pass these tests isn't right for you. You'll just be uncomfortable every time you use it—or you won't use it at all, a waste of money at today's furniture prices.

Rubber Pants

Choose the nylon type with the padded edges over the plain plastic with the exposed elastic even though the former may cost three times as much initially. The plain plastic pants can't take repeated washings (they split, harden, and discolor), and the elastic is almost always too tight on baby's legs and abdomen in the size recommended for your baby's weight. The result: you keep buying the plastic ones over and over, so you don't save a penny, and baby is always uncomfortable (just run your finger along the elastic edge to feel how rough it is).

As far as style goes, slip-ons and snap-ons each have their admirers. With slip-ons you have to lift the baby by the legs to pull them under baby's bottom. With snap-ons you have to fiddle with all the snaps.

To launder, just put in with the diapers. Air-dry, since the high heat of dryers can weaken the elastic, and pants wear out much sooner.

Safety Pins

The most reliable are those with an enamel "cap" over the head. After fixing the shaft of the pin in the head, you slide the "cap" down which prevents the sharp point from accidentally opening and sticking baby. Many varieties have decorative plastic heads which are also pretty reliable, but they can splinter or fall off, leaving a naked pin. Don't use ordinary safety pins from your sewing box. They're not heavy enough to go through four thicknesses of cloth and withstand baby's kicking and twisting without eventually getting pulled apart.

Scalp

1. Wash scalp several times a week (see Baths), even if baby is virtually bald.
2. Cradle cap is crusty, greasy, yellow patches on the scalp. It's the result of overactive glands that produce sebum, a skin lubricant. It is not dangerous, though it is not pretty. It's the equivalent of dandruff. To treat, oil the scalp (olive oil is fine) and leave on for an hour. Comb through with a fine-tooth comb to loosen scales, and follow with a mild shampoo or soap to remove them and the excess oil.

Siblings, as Helpers

Far from getting in the way during the early weeks with a new baby, your older children can be a great help. Store supplies like diapers and rubber pants, baby's clothes and blankets in a low chest or on low shelves of an open bookcase so even a three-year-old can reach them. Do your diaper-changing on a mattress on the floor protected by oilcloth or an old shower curtain and a fitted sheet. This way, the youngest child can watch while baby gets changed, or hand you a washcloth or a bar of soap and babble to the baby. (This can come in handy if your baby hates to be changed and the older child is skilled at making faces and sounds that intrigue the baby.) It makes baby care something the older children participate in, not something they start to resent for taking you away from them so many times during the day. And it's a natural way to teach hygiene, sex education, and concern for others all at once. Another point—other little ones can't be getting into too much mischief if they're at your side, whereas when you leave them to themselves for ten minutes to change the baby you never know what you'll find when you get back to them!

What else can siblings do to help? Depending on their ages:

- learn to set and clear the table
- learn to sort clothes for the laundry
- learn to sort clothes by owner for putting away (a clothes party)
- learn how to hold baby (use the changing-area mattress for this—even if baby is dropped, it's only a few inches and it's onto the soft surface, not the floor)

- learn how to tie or buckle their own shoes
- learn how to button and zip on themselves and on smaller brothers and sisters so you don't have to
- read to younger siblings
- take younger ones to play outside and have a picnic lunch
- learn how to make simple sandwiches and how to pour cereal from box or jar, milk and juice from containers, how to reconstitute frozen juices, how to cooperate in spreading a large cloth for picnic
- learn to operate a cassette tape recorder so they can amuse themselves while you nap or rest on the couch
- learn to keep toys out from underfoot (station a basket or large cardboard box in each room so they can do this even if they're very small and can't lug a truck upstairs yet)
- learn how to make their own beds
- learn how to dial their own telephone calls

Kids will want to learn these things if they're presented as new, fun things to do—not something they *have* to do because you're too busy. (That means it's really your work, not theirs.)

Sleeping Arrangements

Mattress on the floor. Mom in the middle, baby on one side, Dad on the other. Other kids on

another mattress close by. Everybody happy. No more sleepless nights, no more bad dreams, no more protests at bedtime, no more black bags under the eyes from nervous exhaustion. Added benefit: you can turn your thermostat down—more people in room equals more warmth!

To nurse—you hear baby clucking and smacking lips (no loud crying to contend with). You roll over and offer breast. (See Naps, Mother and Baby.) Baby nurses, goes back to sleep. You, too. Sleep, sleep, sleep. . .

It's called the family bed. Get the book: *The Family Bed: An Age Old Concept in Childrearing,* by Tine Thevenin (self-published, P. O. Box 16004, Minneapolis, MN 55416, 1976.)

Sleeping Patterns

Don't expect baby to develop one for a while. Some researchers think that mother and baby who stay close in postbirth period remain in body-mind harmony (as during pregnancy), even to wake and sleep cycles. (See Gay Gaer Luce's book, *Body Time,* New York: Bantam, 1973.) Many mothers say they could sense when their baby was about to wake up, or that they and the baby just seemed to rouse about the same time in the night. You will read that babies "sleep all the time" in the early weeks. Some do; others don't. If you have an alert, active baby, just follow the same pattern of keeping baby with you and baby won't get bored and cranky. If your baby is placid and restful, just enjoy the golden moments.

Smiles

Smiling is a uniquely human form of communication. It's not just "gas pains," no matter what you've heard otherwise. Smiling is one of the infant's most powerful ways of promoting others' attachment to him/herself. By two weeks, according to Jackson and Jackson in *Infant Culture* (New York: New American Library, 1979), your baby can discriminate between you and all others by sight, and by three to four weeks, your voice alone can elicit a smile. Your baby's smile, plus eye-to-eye contact, makes you feel baby really reciprocates your attention. *You* make the difference.

Storage and Changing Area

The old double-bed mattress you had before you got the king-size family bed does wonderfully for a baby-changing/play area. Here's one with

Baby-changing/play area.

everything right at hand. See also Baths; Diapers; Lotions, Oils, and Creams; Siblings, as Helpers; and the layette list.

Sunbath

A sunbath is a real boon to baby's skin. Sunshine for just five minutes a day, and baby's skin produces all baby's vitamin D requirements. Can be done in window or outside when weather's warm. Be careful in summer not to do it between 11:00 A.M. and 2:00 P.M., though, as sun's rays are extremely intense at that time, and babies can sunburn so easily.

Temperature, Room

Baby does well at room temperatures that are comfortable for other family members. Do not overdress, or heat rash ("prickly heat," "sweat rash") can occur, making baby very uncomfortable. In hot weather, dress baby lightly; just a diaper and undershirt will do most of the time. In winter, a diaper, undershirt, gown, or stretch suit and maybe a receiving blanket should be enough (unless you keep your house at less than 60°F). You won't even want the blanket if you use your baby carrier most of the time—your body will produce lots of heat that baby will receive. Babies who are riding in heated cars don't need to be bundled up in heavy snowsuits. Ditto for shopping. Unzip outerwear at the very least so baby doesn't get overheated and sweaty.

How the temperature affects body functions is related to the humidity of the atmosphere as well. During the heating season, use a humidifier at

Temperature, How to Take

You need: a rectal thermometer (can also be used to take temperature by mouth, but an oral thermometer has too pointed an end to be used safely in the rectum)
petroleum jelly, K-Y jelly, or a similar lubricant

First: Shake the mercury down by holding the thermometer firmly in your hand and snapping your wrist downward. Lubricate the bulb end of the thermometer.

Position of baby: Place baby on his or her abdomen, on your lap, with baby's legs between your knees.

Then: Insert the lubricated end of the thermometer into the baby's rectum gently, for about an inch—NO FURTHER. Hold the buttocks gently together, with the thermometer held loosely between your index and middle fingers.

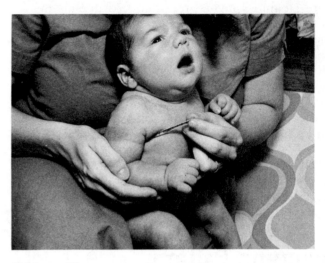

Taking axillary temperature.

    Keep it in for two to three minutes. Remove gently.

Or do it this way: Place an unlubricated thermometer in the baby's armpit (axilla). Hold arm gently over thermometer for five minutes.

Reading the thermometer: Wipe the lubricant off with a tissue and rotate the thermometer between your fingers until you see the end of the column of mercury. The number next to this level is the temperature. Write it down, cleanse the thermometer with soap and water, and return it to its case.

When reporting temperature to doctor, always tell *how* it was taken.

What's normal: by rectum—99.6°F
by mouth—98.6°F
by axilla—97.6°F

See Fever and Convulsions.

    Don't take temperature right after a bath or after baby's been yelling a lot—both can cause temperature elevation.

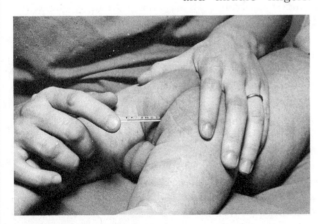

Taking rectal temperature.

least in the room where baby sleeps. Keeps nasal passages and throat from becoming dry and sore.

Thrush

Caused by *Monilia* or *Candida* (yeast) fungus, thrush appears as a thick, white coating or white patches inside baby's cheeks and tongue that cannot be wiped away with a washcloth or by gentle rubbing with your fingertip. Baby's mouth may be sore, so s/he may be disinclined to nurse.

Thrush is most commonly contracted from the mother's vagina during delivery, but it can also be transmitted to baby from anyone else who has an infection and doesn't wash hands properly before caring for the infant.

You can pick up thrush via your nipples when your baby has an infection, creating very sore nipples that make *you* disinclined to nurse. You and baby both need treatment. (Some sort of antifungal medication, usually a mouthwash that you squirt into baby's mouth, is the typical prescription.) Call your doctor or clinic for specifics of treatment.

Urine

Baby's should be very pale and there should be plenty of it (at least six to eight wet diapers a day). Urine contains water and waste products which have been filtered from the system by the kidneys. Changes in the urine can be an important warning sign of illness. Blood-tinged, dark, or very

---

Twins . . . It Goes Double!

During your pregnancy:
> Double-check your diet.
> It's twice as important to have medical care you're comfortable with.
> Cook double batches of nutritious food—eat one, freeze one for after the birth.
> Take it twice as easy—rest twice as often and twice as long.
> Double-check your posture. It's twice as important with a twin pregnancy, because the added weight can be a strain on your back. (See Elizabeth Noble's *Essential Exercises for the Childbearing Year* and *Having Twins*, Boston: Houghton Mifflin, 1976, 1980.)

Concerning labor:
> Double-good nutrition makes you twice as prepared to withstand the stresses of labor, but twins make it twice as likely you'll encounter "traffic problems" in birth, so be prepared, be educated, be relaxed. Even if a Cesarean is necessary, you'll heal twice as fast with double-good nutrition. (See chapter 1.)

Postpartum:
> Two babies + two breasts = twice the benefits of breastfeeding. Each baby can be nursed on his or her "own" breast, or they can be switched back and forth. There are two basic positions for nursing two at the same time.
> Hospital meals are usually inadequate for a

nursing mother of two, so order double: two eggs, two containers of milk, two glasses of juice, and so on.
> Make it twice as easy to eat well in the hospital by ordering what you like from the hospital menu and having visitors bring additional highly nutritious foods.
> Be doubly insistent about feeding both babies *yourself*—no supplements. Virtually all well-nourished mothers can feed two—just nurse early and often.

At home:
> You don't need two cribs, two bathinettes, two infant seats, two sets of bottles, just twice as many diapers, extra shirts and receiving blankets, and another baby carrier.
> You'll need twice as much help with the chores—meal preparation and laundry are the most important tasks someone else can do for you.
> Most nursing mothers feel the need for a glass of water, juice, or milk during each feeding—you may want two glasses if babies feed at the same time.
> Don't even try to keep their clothes separate as infants—just get everything big enough for the bigger twin. Some Mothers of Twins Clubs lend extra baby clothes to twin mothers. Write to their national office at: 5402 Amberwood Lane, Rockville, MD 20853, for the address of your local chapter.

---

concentrated urine (strong-smelling) needs to be evaluated by a medical practitioner. Medication you're taking, such as penicillin, can travel through your milk into baby and cause changes in baby's urine. Remember, as long as you're breastfeeding, you and baby continue to be a biological unit and things that affect you will affect baby, too.

Vulva, Care of

In the early days, girl babies may have a pink, mucousy discharge due to the fall in hormones after birth (a mini-period). No special treatment other than ordinary hygiene is necessary. Girls have myriad creases and folds that boys don't. Using soap and water (after a bowel movement) or plain water (after urination) and a lightweight washcloth (a thick one won't fit into the creases very well), follow the creases and folds with a fingertip to make sure they are thoroughly cleansed. Otherwise, inflammation and diaper rash can follow quickly. Occasionally, a girl baby will have adhesions on the outer vaginal lips. Don't try to stretch them, and don't permit a medical care provider to do it, either. These are vestiges of the differentiation of the genitals from surrounding tissues and the adhesions will gradually loosen over a period of time just as those on a boy's penis do. After washing, rinse from front to back, just as you do for yourself, and towel dry.

Walks

A good restorer of your spirits. Just put on your coat and baby's outerwear, slip baby into baby carrier, and you're off! Alternatively, if you have a poncho, put on carrier in front-carry position, then slip poncho over both you and baby. Save strollers and carriages until baby is ready for them—about six months of age.

Water, Need for

Baby gets all the water s/he needs from your milk if:

- you eat well enough and take enough fluids to sustain a good milk flow;

- you offer the breast *first* when baby fusses or cries;
- baby is having six to eight wet diapers a day;
- you're getting enough rest and have developed a relaxed attitude about nursing.

Water in bottles is absolutely unnecessary in the completely breastfed baby under these conditions. In extremely hot weather, when both you and baby are losing a great deal of body water in perspiration, baby may want a few minutes of nursing every hour or so just for thirst. This is perfectly normal—all you have to do is remember to drink more to replenish your own body fluids and keep your milk production up. (See "No Worries About Milk Supply" Checklist in chapter 8.) Your milk supply is not favored for fluid over your other body needs, so if your intake is not adequate, milk production will fall.

Weight Gain

Babies who are breastfed ad lib seldom lose the traditional half-pound hospital workers assume to be "normal." If your baby isn't gaining weight, you must thoroughly evaluate your diet and lifestyle to see if your breastfeeding is as it should be. Baby's mouth and tongue action in suckling should be checked. If you're using a pacifier, cut it out—baby may be sucking on it so much that s/he is tired when put to the breast or confused by the two different sucking styles. A very thorough monograph, "Management of the Slow-Gaining Breastfed Baby" (1978) written by two pediatricians, Ruth Lawrence, M.D., and Paul Fleiss, M.D., and a pediatric nurse-practitioner, Kittie B. Frantz, R.N., is available for $3.00 from Resources in Human Nurturing, International, P. O. Box 6861, Denver, CO 80206. It is referenced to the medical literature and suitable for sharing with your medical care provider if you encounter this problem.

If baby is gaining weight "too fast" (it's hard to fit right into the statistical model), don't worry if all the baby's getting is breast milk. Many breastfed infants are roly-poly as babies and reed-slim as children and adults. The charts are "averages" and your child isn't average!

Directory: Useful Items and Services for the Family

Some of the gaps that exist in contemporary health care have been filled by manufacturers and volunteer self-help groups, acting alone or in concert with health care professionals. We have attempted to compile as extensive a list of these as possible without being judgmental as to their worth. Most groups have free catalogs or pamphlets describing the range of their services.

Baby Carriers

Andrea's Baby Pack
2441 Hilyard Street
Eugene, OR 97405
(503) 345-1324

Sarah's Creations
24 Beaupre Crest NW
Calgary, AB T3B 2S8, Canada

Birth and Health Care Supplies
(mail order/free catalog)

Cascade Supplies Center
718 16th Street SW
Corvallis, OR 97330
(503) 754-6184

Childbirth Education Supplies Center
10 Sol Drive
Carmel, NY 10512
(914) 225-7763

Circumcision Information
Parents' Groups

Circumcision Hotline
1939 E Street
Hayward, CA 94541
(415) 537-3948

Intact
Box 5
Wilbraham, MA 01095

Paul Zimmer, M.S.
P. O. Box 48
St. Peters, PA 19470

Slide Set and Information Sheet Showing Neonatal Circumcision—Suitable for Use in Childbirth Classes
Rosemary Wiener
Prepared Natural Childbirth
6294 Mission Road
Everson, WA 98247

Mail-Order Books and Supplies

Birth, Family, and Health Bookstore
3440-B West Orange Avenue
Anaheim, CA 92804

International Childbirth Education Association
  Bookcenter
P. O. Box 20048,
Minneapolis, MN 55420

Pregnancy and Parenting

Action for Child Transportation Safety
#15P, 400 Central Park West
New York, NY 10025

American Academy of Husband-Coached Childbirth (Bradley Method)
P. O. Box 5224
Sherman Oaks, CA 91413

American Academy of Pediatrics
1801 Hinman Avenue
Evanston, IL 60201

American College of Nurse Midwives
Suite 801, 1012 14th Street NW
Washington, DC 20005

Association for Childbirth at Home, International
1675 Monte Cristo Street
Cerritos, CA 90701

Cesareans/Support, Education, and Concern
66 Christopher Road
Waltham, MA 02154

Consumer Product Safety Commission
Bureau of Information and Education
Product Safety Information Center
Room 745-A, 5401 Westbard Avenue
Bethesda, MD 20014

Couple to Couple League
(natural family planning)
P. O. Box 11084
Cincinnati, OH 45211

Eastman Kodak Company
(free pamphlet AD-12, *Movies of Babies and Children*)
Dept. 841
Rochester, NY 14650

Home Oriented Maternity Experience
511 New York Avenue
Takoma Park, Washington, DC 20012

International Childbirth Education Association
P. O. Box 20048
Minneapolis, MN 55420

National Association of Parents and Professionals
  for Safe Alternatives in Childbirth
P. O. Box 267
Marble Hill, MO 63764

National Organization: Mothers of Twins Clubs
5402 Amberwood Lane
Rockville, MD 20853

Poison Control
(consult your local telephone directory)

Resources in Human Nurturing, International
(breastfeeding information and publications)
3885 Forest Street
P. O. Box 6861
Denver, CO 80206

Sex Information and Education Council of the U.S.
1855 Broadway
New York, NY 10023

Society for the Protection of the Unborn through
  Nutrition
Suite 603, 17 North Wabash Avenue
Chicago, IL 60602

Special Situations

Association for the Help of Retarded Children
200 Park Avenue South
New York, NY 10003

Children in Hospitals
31 Wilshire Park
Needham, MA 02192

Closer Look
(federal programs)
Box 1492
Washington, DC 20013

Easter Seals Foundation
2 Park Avenue
New York, NY 10016

Juvenile Diabetes Foundation
23 East 26th Street
New York, NY 10010

National Foundation/March of Dimes
1215 Mamaroneck Avenue
White Plains, NY 10605

National Rare Blood Club
164 Fifth Avenue
New York, NY 10010

National Save-A-Life League
(suicide prevention)
815 Second Avenue
New York, NY 10017

Parent-to-Parent
(prematures and others in NICUs)
NICU Follow-Up Clinic
San Francisco Children's Hospital
3700 California Street
San Francisco, CA 94118

Recording for the Blind
215 East 58th Street
New York, NY 10022

Women's Health

Boston Women's Health Book Collective
P. O. Box 192
West Somerville, MA 02144

The Federal Monitor
(publisher of a periodic news alert on legislative
    and regulatory activities relating to the health of
    women and children)
Drawer Q
McLean, VA 22101

Feminist Women's Health Centers Federation
Suite 202, 6411 Hollywood Boulevard
Los Angeles, CA 90028

Healthright
175 Fifth Avenue
New York, NY 10010

Montreal Health Press
P. O. Box 1000, Station G
Montreal, PQ H2W 2N1, Canada

National Women's Health Network
Suite 105, 2025 I Street NW
Washington, DC 20006

Resource Center on Women
National YWCA
600 Lexington Avenue
New York, NY 10022

Widow's Consultation Center
136 East 57th Street
New York, NY 10022

Glossary

A

afterbirth the membranes (*amnion* and *chorion*), placenta, and umbilical cord, expelled after the birth of the child.

afterpains uterine contractions that assist in returning the uterus to its prepregnant size. Usually more noticeable during breastfeeding, but rarely last more than 48 hours.

AgNO₃ chemical symbol for silver nitrate, often used to prevent eye infection in the newborn. Argyrol (silver vitellin) is a common substitute.

amenorrhea the absence or suppression of the menstrual flow, normal during pregnancy and lactation. It is not synonymous with infertility; therefore if pregnancy is unwanted during the lactation period, contraception is necessary.

amniocentesis puncturing the amniotic sac to remove amniotic fluid for diagnostic purposes.

amnion the inner of the two fetal membranes, the bag of waters enclosing the fetus and amniotic fluid.

amniotic fluid the transparent fluid contained in the sac that protects the fetus from injury. Complete exchange takes three hours.

amniotic sac formed by the fusion of the *amnion* and the *chorion* at the end of the second month, it may rupture spontaneously with the beginning of labor or during labor.

amniotomy artificial rupture of the amniotic sac.

amphetamine a central nervous system stimulant, "diet pills," "uppers," "speed." They produce devastating mental and physical changes including increase in blood pressure, heart rate, fatigue. They increase dehydration and malnutrition. Sold as: Desoxyn, Obetrol, Benzedrine, Dexamyl, Preludin, Dexadrine, Ritalin, Biphetamine, Darbid, Combid, Eskatrol, and others. The counterculture phrase of the sixties was "Speed Kills." This is an accurate assessment, especially for the pregnant woman and her baby.

analgesia loss of sensitivity to pain, usually drug-induced, by an analgesic such as Demerol, aspirin, Acetominophen, codeine, Empirin, Fiorinol, Nisentil, Percodan, Darvon, and others.

anoxia deficiency of oxygen.

antenatal occurring or formed before birth.

antepartum occurring before the onset of labor.

Apgar score a system of scoring the infant's condition one minute and five minutes after birth, based on heart rate, respiratory effort, muscle tone, reflex irritability, and color. Range is zero to ten. Named for Virginia Apgar, M.D., who developed it.

apnea cessation of breathing, usually temporary.

areola the dark area surrounding the nipple. During breastfeeding, the baby's lips compress this area, causing the milk to be ejected into the baby's mouth. During pregnancy a secondary areola forms around the areola, extending the pigmented area of the breast.

asphyxia deficient respiration leading to increased carbon dioxide and decreased oxygen. May be caused by insufficient prenatal oxygen supply, premature placental separation, or overdose of drugs, especially narcotics.

auscultation the process of listening to body sounds, commonly with a stethoscope. A fetoscope, a specially constructed stethoscope, may be used to listen to the fetal heart.

B

bag of waters the common name for the amniotic sac and fluid.

bilirubin an orange yellow-colored pigment produced from the hemoglobin in broken-down red blood cells. Its presence in the baby's blood may indicate the normal reduction in red blood cells that occurs after birth, or may be the abnormal destruction of red blood cells as in *erythroblastosis fetalis*.

birthmark a skin discoloration present at birth, a mole.

blood pressure the pressure exerted by the blood on the wall of the blood vessel. As commonly measured with a sphygmomanometer or blood pressure cuff, blood pressure is expressed as two numbers such as 130/80, pronounced 130 over 80. The top number refers to systolic pressure or pressure during the contraction of the left ventricle of the heart. The lower number refers to diastolic pressure or pressure during the rest time between heartbeats.

bradycardia slow heart rate. In the fetus, below 120 beats per minute; in the newborn, below 100 beats per minute.

Braxton-Hicks contractions mild uterine contractions that do not dilate the cervix, and increase in frequency toward the end of pregnancy. They may be confused with true labor, and are then called false labor.

breast the mammary gland, which secretes milk for the young.

breast abscess closed pocket of infection in the breast. May be avoided by proper treatment of simple infection or inflammation.

breast engorgement congestion of the breast, with swelling.

breast infection usually painful, sore swelling or lump, or red, tender area of breast. May be caused by overfull breast, cracked nipple, tight bra, low resistance, poor nutrition. Treatment consists of frequent nursings (at least every hour or two), heat, rest, nutritionally complete diet.

breast pump mechanical device for removing milk from the breast. May be manual or electric.

breech delivery birth of baby, buttocks or feet first. Occurs in approximately 3 percent of births.

C

caput the head.

caput succedaneum fluid-filled swelling of the baby's scalp during labor.

caudal anesthesia an anesthetic solution injected into the space around the spinal membranes. The needle is inserted between the bones in the lower back. There is loss of sensation in the lower part of the body.

cephalhematoma swelling on the baby's head containing blood, which may not begin to appear until several days after birth. A frequent consequence of forceps delivery, it usually disappears in a month or two.

cervix the neck of the uterus, about one inch long. During birth, the labor contractions cause it to be pulled up. See *dilatation* and *effacement*.

Cesarean section birth of the baby through an incision in the abdomen and uterus. Performed for reasons of fetopelvic disproportion, slow progress of labor, or fetal distress. Currently 10 to 40 percent of all births are performed this way, the percentage varying with the hospital.

chorion the outer of the two membranes forming the amniotic sac. It gives rise to the placenta.

chromosome the carrier of inherited characteristics. Each parent contributes 23 chromosomes, one of which determines the sex of the baby (a chromosome of the father).

circumcision surgical removal of the foreskin of the penis.

cleft lip, palate a congenital division in the lip or palate. It is correctable by surgery and is not, as commonly thought, a contraindication to

breastfeeding. Often associated with prenatal malnutrition.

clitoris organ of sexual pleasure in the female.

colostrum the first milk, which contains protective factors for the infant. Every baby's birthright.

congenital present at the time of birth.

D

delivery expulsion of the child, placenta, and membranes from the mother. Birth.

dilatation expansion of the cervix to allow the baby to pass into the birth canal. The labor contractions cause the cervix to dilate to approximately four inches or ten cm, the approximate diameter of the newborn's head.

diuretic a medication which increases the secretion of urine. Causes profound reduction in the amount of blood circulating and therefore contraindicated in pregnancy. Sold under many names such as: Lasix (furosemide), Aldactone, Diamox, Dyazide, Edecrin (ethycrinic acid), Diuril, Hygroton, Hydrodiuril, Thiomerin, Mercuhydrin, and others.

Down's syndrome a variety of congenital retardation caused by abnormality in the chromosomes. The eyes appear slanted or Oriental, the nose is often flat, the ears set low.

E

eclampsia the convulsive and/or coma stage of metabolic toxemia of late pregnancy.

edema a condition in which the body tissues retain fluid, marked by swelling. Most healthy pregnant women have some edema in all body tissues. It may be especially noticeable in the feet and ankles at the end of the day.

effacement refers to the thinning and shortening of the cervix in labor.

episiotomy an incision made in the perineum during the second stage of labor to enlarge the vaginal opening.

F

fetal distress condition of fetus during labor characterized by periods of apnea. Diagnosis is difficult, but fetal distress is presumed by a heart rate under 100 beats per minute by auscultation or electronic fetal monitor.

fetal monitor electronic device to measure and record strength and duration of contractions and fetal response to the contraction. May be external, via belts around mother's abdomen, or internal, via electrode inserted into fetal scalp.

fetopelvic disproportion condition in which the diameter of the presenting part is too large to pass through the bony pelvis. Also termed cephalopelvic disproportion (CPD) when the head is the presenting part.

fetus in humans, the developing child from the third month of pregnancy through birth.

fontanel the "soft spots" on baby's skull that allow molding during the birth. The anterior fontanel (in the front, just above the forehead) closes at about 12 to 18 months; the posterior fontanel (triangular, in the back) closes at about 2 to 4 months.

forceps pincers for holding and/or extracting. There are many different varieties for different situations.

foreskin fold of skin covering the head of the penis. See *circumcision*.

full term refers to the normal end of pregnancy when the baby weighs over 6½ pounds and is over 18 inches long.

fundus the large upper end of the uterus.

G

genitalia the reproductive organs, internal and external.

gestation the period from conception to birth.

gland an organ that secretes a substance such as oil, mucus, or hormone. The mammary gland (see *breast*) secretes milk and is actually a modified sweat gland.

gravida a pregnant woman. Also refers to the number of pregnancies a woman has had.

H

hematocrit the percentage of total blood volume that consists of red blood cells, the carriers of hemoglobin.

I

impetigo highly contagious inflammatory skin disease, easily transmitted from baby to baby in a central nursery.

intramuscular injection (IM) hypodermic injection of drug into a muscle.

intravenous (IV) solution or drug injected or infused into a vein.

involution the return of the uterus to prepregnant size and position in the pelvis following delivery. Complete involution takes about six weeks and is aided by breastfeeding.

isolette apparatus for isolating premature baby. Contains some life support systems.

J

jaundice a condition characterized by yellowed skin, due to higher than normal levels of bilirubin in the blood.

K

kernicterus a form of jaundice where the bilirubin is deposited in areas of the brain and spinal cord. Retardation and death may occur if not treated.

L

labor parturition, the process by which the fetus is expelled from the uterus.

lactation the period, beginning at birth, when the mother suckles the baby. The process of producing and letting down milk.

lanugo the downy hair that covers the fetus.

letdown reflex also called milk ejection reflex. The baby's suckling causes more milk to let down and become available. The baby's jaws then milk out the sinuses under the areola and the process is repeated.

lochia the discharge from the uterus during the puerperium.

M

malnutrition lack of necessary foods or nutrients in the body or the body's inability to use them correctly.

manual expression removal of excess milk from the breast by hand massage and milking. See *breast pump*.

mastitis breast infection.

meconium the newborn's first bowel movement, black and sticky like tar.

milia rash caused by obstruction of sweat glands, common in the newborn. No treatment is necessary.

molding the shaping of the baby's head as it is propelled through the birth canal. Made possible by the flexibility of the baby's skull.

mongolism see *Down's syndrome*.

Montgomery's tubercles small glands on the areola of the breast which enlarge during pregnancy and secrete a natural lubricant.

N

natural childbirth childbirth without medication or other intervention.

navel the umbilicus, popularly called the belly button. It is the scar where the umbilical cord was attached before birth.

neonatal the period from birth through the fourth week of life.

nevus birthmark.

nipple shield these are of two types, the Woolwich type and the protective type, often prescribed for sore nipples. Use of the protective type usually results in a severe decrease in milk supply due to inadequate stimulation.

O

ophthalmia neonatorum severe pus infection of the eye in the newborn. Gonorrhea-causing organisms are responsible for most cases. $AgNO_3$ is required by law in many areas to prevent this disease.

ovary the female gonad, where ova are stored and female hormones manufactured.

ovulation the maturing of the ovum and its release from the ovary.

ovum egg, or female sex cell.

oxytocic a drug which stimulates uterine contractions, given to accelerate childbirth or to start involution after birth. Sold as: Ergotrate, Methergine, Pitocin, Syntocinon, Tocosamine, and others.

oxytocin a hormone produced by the pituitary gland that stimulates the uterus to contract. It also stimulates the release of milk. Nipple stimulation during breastfeeding causes release of oxytocin.

P

parity the number of children a woman has borne, expressed as para; for example, para 0 = no children; para 1 = one child.

parturient the woman giving birth.

parturition labor.

perineum the area between the vulva and the anus in the female, or the scrotum and anus in the male.

peritoneum the membrane covering the intestines and lining the abdominal cavity.

PKU abbreviation for phenylketonuria, a disease of amino acid metabolism caused by a defect in body chemistry. A blood test for it is done at birth.

postpartum after childbirth.

premature born before full term or weighing under 5½ pounds at birth.

premature rupture of membranes (PROM) the spontaneous rupture of the amniotic sac prior to the onset of labor.

primigravida woman during her first pregnancy.

primipara woman who has given birth to her first child.

prolactin hormone produced by the anterior pituitary gland which stimulates lactation.

puerperium the period from birth through completion of involution, which takes about six weeks.

R

resusitation the act of bringing one back to full consciousness, as in artificial respiration.

Rh factor a blood factor found in about 85 percent of the human population, called Rh+. The other 15 percent are called Rh−.

Rhogam a solution of a protective factor containing anti-Rh. When given to an Rh− mother who has just delivered an Rh+ baby, it prevents an Rh immune response, and prevents Rh disease in future babies.

rooming-in the practice of having mothers and babies cared for in the same room, preferably beginning immediately after birth and continuing through discharge. Many modified forms are incorrectly referred to as rooming-in, such as having baby and mother together four hours per day. Rooming-in is of great benefit in establishing breastfeeding.

S

small for gestational age (SGA) any baby weighing less than 6½ pounds at the end of a full-term pregnancy.

smegma thick, cheesy secretion found under the foreskin or between the vaginal lips.

sonography a medical speciality concerned with assessment of maternal/fetal conditions by use of sound waves and image-reproducing equipment.

stat immediately.

T

tachycardia abnormally fast heart rate.

thrush a fungus infection of the mouth or throat. Can be transmitted by the nursing baby to the mother's nipples.

toxemia, metabolic a disease of liver dysfunction and reduced blood volume caused by malnutrition during pregnancy.

U

umbilical cord the attachment connecting the fetus with the placenta. Two arteries and a vein are within the cord and serve to exchange nu-

Appendix

191

trients and waste products with the mother's body.

umbilical cord prolapse if the cord is in front of the head or breech after the membranes have ruptured, it is said to have prolapsed. Pressure on the cord often causes asphyxia in the newborn.

V

vernix caseosa protective creamy covering on the fetus during the period of gestation.

viable capable of living outside the uterus.

vulva the external, visible female genitalia.

W

Wharton's jelly a jellylike substance found within the umbilical cord. It surrounds and protects the vein and arteries within.

"witches' milk" the milk secreted by the breast of the newborn baby. It is due to the mother's hormones of pregnancy, and is normal in either a male or female child.

womb uterus.

Bibliography: Parents' Annotated Reading List

Annas, George J. *The Rights of Hospital Patients: The Basic ACLU Guide to a Hospital Patient's Rights*. New York: Avon, 1975.

A reference work written for the medical care consumer. Chapters particularly relevant to pregnancy and birth decisions discuss informed consent, children, and women.

Bean, Constance. *Labor and Delivery: An Observer's Diary*. Garden City, N.Y.: Doubleday, 1977.

An on-the-scene account of what really goes on in labor and delivery in various hospitals, told by an experienced childbirth educator. A must for first-time mothers.

Boston Women's Health Book Collective. *Our Bodies, Ourselves*. 4th ed., New York: Simon and Schuster, 1979.

The grandmother of women's self-help books. Should be a part of every woman's library. An excellent introduction to the politics of women's health care as well as clear explanations of anatomy, physiology, sexuality, and psychological responses to pregnancy.

Brewer, Gail Sforza, ed. *The Pregnancy-After-30 Workbook: A Program for Safe Childbearing— No Matter What Your Age*. Emmaus, Pa.: Rodale Press, 1978.

An overview of pregnancy, breastfeeding, and parenting with special emphasis on preventing pregnancy complications. Chapters contributed by experts in the field they write about focus on reducing the risks of childbearing to the absolute minimum—no matter what your age. Numerous charts, diagrams, illustrations, and photographs.

Brewer, Gail Sforza, and Tom Brewer, M.D. *What Every Pregnant Woman Should Know: The Truth About Diets and Drugs in Pregnancy*. New York: Random House, 1977. Penguin paperback, 1979.

Why pregnant women should not follow low-calorie, low-salt diets or take diuretics or appetite suppressants, and how these practices became established in American prenatal care. How inadequate diets are responsible for toxemia of pregnancy, low birth weight, and neurologically impaired babies. Menus and recipes for insuring high-quality nutrition.

Corea, Gena. *The Hidden Malpractice*. Jove ed., New York: Harcourt Brace Jovanovich, 1978.

A carefully documented look at how the medical profession treats women as patients and professionals, with wonderful insights into the history of obstetrics/gynecology as a male-dominated specialty. If you think your doctor has your best interests at heart—you may be right, but you need to be *sure!* Read this book.

Fraiberg, Selma. *Every Child's Birthright: In Defense of Mothering*. New York: Basic Books, 1977.

How contemporary child care practices thwart the normal psychological development of children. Why infants and young children require personal (one-to-one) mothering and the issues surrounding making this kind of mothering available to every child. Impassioned analysis of current day care programs by a leading child psychotherapist.

Holt, John. *How Children Learn*. New York: Dell, 1970.

A set of first-person accounts of interactions with children from infancy through grade school by a perceptive and caring observer. Exceptional in helping us understand and respect our children's drives to learn and gain our approval. A classic.

Howell, Mary, M.D. *Healing at Home: A Guide to Health Care for Children*. Boston: Beacon Press, 1979.

A thorough, engaging, how-to book that de-

Appendix

mystifies the care of healthy and sick children and encourages/instructs mothers to learn how to do much routine pediatric evaluation on their own. Especially designed for ages six months to 12 years, with detailed information about conducting the physical examination and checking for common illnesses.

Kippley, Sheila. *Breastfeeding and Natural Child Spacing: The Ecology of Natural Mothering.* New York: Harper and Row, 1974. Penguin paperback, 1975.

The why and how of ad lib breastfeeding with complete investigation of one of its side effects for many women: suppression of ovulation. Determining your own fertility using the mucus assessment method.

Kraus, Barbara. *The Barbara Kraus Dictionary of Protein.* New York: New American Library, 1976.

The best guide to protein and calories we've seen. Foods are described in common measures with brand names used where necessary. Recognizes the importance of protein-calorie interrelationships. A great help in making sure your diet is adequate in these essential nutrients.

Leboyer, Frederick, M.D. *Loving Hands: The Traditional Indian Art of Baby Massage.* New York: Knopf, 1976.

Mothers and babies enjoying the primal language of touch and sensation, as depicted in photographs captioned with Dr. Leboyer's poetry.

Liedloff, Jean. *The Continuum Concept.* New York: Warner Books, 1979.

Conventional baby care conditions us for a lifetime of loneliness, according to the ecologist-author. Based on her own observations and the research of others, she proposes a form of baby care in which the infant's "in arms" phase is recognized and happier, better-adjusted people are the result. A landmark book.

Montagu, Ashley. *Touching: The Human Signifi-* *cance of the Skin.* New York: Columbia University Press, 1971.

An exploration of our largest and most basic sense organ, with special concern for the sensory lives of infants during the human "18-month" gestation period (the 9 months prior to and after birth). Stunning interconnections between sensory experience and physical health/disease and emotional health/disease in people of all ages.

Neill, A. S. *Summerhill: A Radical Approach to Child Rearing.* New York: Hart, 1960.

One schoolmaster's pioneering philosophy and experience in raising children without the use of force by encouraging self-determination. A book that's likely to make you rethink your own school experiences as you help your child grow up with a respect for the continuum of life. Devastating reevaluation of concepts of discipline and authority.

Nilsson, Lennart. *A Child Is Born.* New York: Delacorte, 1977.

Photojournal of prenatal life by a master photographer. The text, however, is replete with inaccuracies: beware of statements about nutrition, weight gain, toxemia, breath control, pushing, postpartum care, all of which are very out-of-date.

Noble, Elizabeth. *Essential Exercises for the Childbearing Year.* Boston: Houghton Mifflin, 1976.

The best all-around exercise program for pregnancy and postpartum, including complete Cesarean recovery sequence. Illustrated. Skip the controlled breathing exercises, though. Noble is revising this section in light of recent research on respiratory considerations in labor and birth.

Noble, Elizabeth. *Having Twins.* Boston: Houghton Mifflin, 1980.

Everything you ever wanted to know about having twins—including how to have full-size, full-term ones! Excellent on nutrition, body mechanics, and natural mothering of multiples.

Right from the Start

Rich, Adrienne. *Of Woman Born: Motherhood as Experience and Institution.* New York: Norton, 1976. Bantam paperback, 1977.

Revelations about the nature of becoming a mother written with grace, intelligence, and fury by a reknowned feminist poet. A book to read, assimilate, and use as a foundation for making the institution of mothering more congruent with real life.

Rugh, Roberts; Shettles, Landrum B.; and Einhorn, Richard. *From Conception to Birth: The Drama of Life's Beginnings.* New York: Harper and Row, 1971.

Again, beautifully detailed pictures of fetal development, combined with some disappointing points in the text: "baby is a parasite," etc. Excellent appendices on the effects of medication and maternal disease on the developing baby, plus a helpful glossary.

Seaman, Barbara. *Women and the Crisis in Sex Hormones.* New York: Rawson, Wade, 1977.

Before you choose a method of family planning, read this book carefully. A sobering investigation of the aftermath of the epidemic of hormone-pushing by American physicians. Thoroughly referenced.

Stewart, David, and Stewart, Lee, eds. *Twenty-First Century Obstetrics Now!.* (2 vols.) Marble Hill, Mo.: NAPSAC Press, 1978.

An expanded set of papers presented at NAPSAC's 1977 national conference on safe alternatives in childbirth. The range of subjects gives an introduction to the controversies in childbirth today: nutrition and prenatal care, childbirth law, midwifery, obstetrics: home and hospital, birth centers, interventions in childbirth, family bonding, and breastfeeding. Papers contributed by people active in the field, not just journalistic assignments.

Thevenin, Tine. *The Family Bed: An Age Old Concept in Childrearing.* Self-published, P. O. Box 16004, Minneapolis, MN 55416, 1976.

Interviews and studies of family sleeping. How sleeping with children until they are old enough to want their own beds creates closer bonds within the family and increases the child's feelings of security and love, plus reducing wear and tear on parents (especially mothers) in the night by cutting down on the number of children's night wakings.

Wallerstein, Edward. *Circumcision: An American Health Fallacy.* New York: Springer, 1981.

Many physicians and nearly all parents are unfamiliar with the facts about circumcision. Here is detailed information based on a review of medical and popular literature. This unique book challenges the practice of routine circumcision, except for religious reasons, as not only unnecessary and devoid of health benefits, but also potentially harmful and traumatic.

Williams, Phyllis S. *Nourishing Your Unborn Child.* New York: Avon, 1975.

A basic introduction to the science of nutrition as it affects pregnancy. The nutrients are discussed by their functions in the body and practical suggestions for how to choose foods with optimal nutritional value are included. Menus, recipes, and a resource list.

Index

Medications. *See also* Drugs
    after delivery, 102
    during labor, 36, 55–59
    for newborn, 115
    refusal of, 58
Membranes, rupturing of. *See* Amniotomy
Mental health, during pregnancy, 15–17
Men Who Control Women's Health: The Miseducation of Obstetrician-Gynecologists (Scully), 45, 47
Meperidine, dangers of, 56
Mepivacaine, dangers of, 56
Meprobamate, dangers of, 56
Methergine, dangers of, 57
Methoxyflurane, dangers of, 57
Methylergonovine, dangers of, 57
Metycaine, dangers of, 56
Midwifery, decline of, 40
Midwives
    in hospital, 45
    versus doctors, 43
Milk cup, for inverted nipples, 132
Miltown, dangers of, 56
Monitoring, electronic, during labor, 59–62
Morphine, dangers of, 56
Mothering, unconditional, 16
Multiple pregnancy
    daily menu for, 8
    management of, 25, 36, 183
    signs of, 25
    ultrasound to detect, 48

N

Naps, postpartum, with baby, 176
Narcotics, dangers of, 56
National Association of Parents and Professionals for Safe Alternatives in Childbirth (NAPSAC), 44
Natural Childbirth Institute (NACHIS), 44
Navel, infant's, care of, 174–75
Nembutal, dangers of, 56
Nesacaine, dangers of, 56
Newborn, care of, 87–105
    forced fasting by, 97

heat loss in, 75, 95
in intensive care, 106–19
nursing of, 80–83
separation from mother, 39, 76, 81, 93–95
Newborn Child, The (Vulliamy), 97
Nipples, inverted, 132, 133
Nisentil, dangers of, 56
Nitrous oxide, dangers of, 57
Noise, infant sleeping through, 175
Non-stress test, before delivery, 49
Nourishing Your Unborn Child (Williams), 10
Novocain, dangers of, 56
Nose, infant's, care of, 175
Nupercaine, dangers of, 56
Nursery, in typical hospital, 87–92
Nursing. *See* Breastfeeding
Nursing pads, 133
Nutrition
    during breastfeeding period, 148–49
    during hospital stay, 99
    during pregnancy, 2–12, 41

O

Of Woman Born (Rich), xi, 46
One-month health assessment, 148–56
Orgasm, as uterine exercise, 20
Our Bodies, Ourselves, 47
Oxygen
    for newborn, 113
    newborn's blood and, 73
Oxytocics, dangers of, 57
Oxytocin, dangers of, 57
Oxytocin challenge test, dangers of, 48–49

P

Pacifiers, need for, 175
Pediatrician. *See* Medical caretaker, baby's
Pelvic floor exercises, postpartum, 151
Penis, care of, 176–77
Pentazocine, dangers of, 56
Penthrane, dangers of, 57

Pentobarbital, dangers of, 56
Pesticides, avoidance of, 12
Pharmacologic Basis of Therapeutics, The
     (Goodman and Gilman), 12, 98
Phenergan, dangers of, 56
Phenobarbital, dangers, of, 56
Photographs, of baby, 177
Phototherapy, for jaundice, 109, 114
Physical contact, importance of, xiii, 15, 16
     for bonding, 75–80
Physicians Desk Reference, 12
Picking up, of infant, technique for, 178
Piperocaine, dangers of, 56
Pitocin, to induce labor, 53
     dangers of, 57
Placenta
     chemicals passing through, 12
     contractions and, 24
     function of, 3–4
     hormones made by, 18
Placental insufficiency, nutrition and, 49
Placenta praevia, ultrasound to detect, 48
Pontocaine, dangers of, 56
Postmature syndrome, in newborn, 54
Powders, for infant, 178
Pregnancy, 1–21
     bed rest during, 50
     last month of, 17–21
     mental health during, 15–17
     nutrition during, 2–12
Pregnancy-After-30 Workbook, The (Brewer), 20,
     69, 139
Premature Delivery of Medical Technology, The
     (Banta), 59
Prickly heat, 178
Prilocaine, dangers of, 56
Procaine, dangers of, 56
Prochlorperazine, dangers of, 56
Progressive relaxation, for labor, 59
Prolapsed cord, 55
Promazine, dangers of, 56
Promethazine, dangers of, 56
Propiomazine, dangers of, 56
Propoxycaine, dangers of, 56
Pulse rate, of newborn, 72

R

Rashes, on infant, 178
Red cell count, of newborn's blood, 73
Relactation, 135–36
Relaxation, between contractions, importance of,
     24
Resources in Human Nuturing, International,
     136, 139
Rest
     after delivery, 99
     at home, 152
Resuscitation equipment, in delivery room, 85
Rh incompatibility, jaundice caused by, 73, 110
Rocking chair, need for, 179
Rubber pants, use of, 179

S

Safety pins, for diapering, 179
Salt intake, during pregnancy, 3, 6–7
Scalp, infant's, care of, 179
Scopolamine, dangers of, 56–57
Secobarbital (Seconal), dangers of, 56
Sensory experiences, baby's
     intrauterine, 15
     in isolette bed, 94–95
Separation, of mother and baby after birth, 39,
     76, 81, 93–95
Separation anxiety, in newborn, 94–95
Seracaine, dangers of, 56
Sex life
     during pregnancy, 20
     postpartum, 149, 173–74
Shaving, of pubic hair, 52
Siblings
     as helpers, 179–80
     reaction to new baby, 154
Silver nitrate, in newborn's eyes, 83
Skin-to-skin. *See* Physical contact
Sleeping arrangements, at home, 142, 180–81
Sleep patterns, of infant, 181

Smiling, by infant, 181
Smoking
    around baby, 154
    during pregnancy, 12
Society for the Protection of the Unborn through
    Nutrition (SPUN), 3
    diet of, 11, 19
    pregnancy hotline of, 10
Sodium. *See* Salt intake
Sodium bicarbonate, for newborn, 115
Sparine, dangers of, 56
Sparteine sulfate (Spartocin), dangers of, 57
Special Delivery, 41
Spherocytosis, congenital, jaundice caused by,
    110
SPUN. *See* Society for the Protection of the Un-
    born through Nutrition
Stomach, baby's, suctioning of, 85
Stress test, dangers of, 48–49
Sunbathing, of infant, 181
Sunlight, jaundice and, 109
Surfactant, in newborn's lungs, 72
Swelling. *See* Edema
Syntocinon, dangers of, 57
Syphilis, congenital, jaundice caused by, 110

T

Talwin, dangers of, 56
Temperature, infant's, taking of, 182
Tender Gift, The: Breastfeeding (Raphael), 138,
    161
Terror, in newborns, 94–95
Test(s)
amniocentesis, 49–50
    blood, 5–6, 61, 108
    intensive care, 116
    non-stress, 49
    oxytocin challenge, 48–49
Tetracaine, dangers of, 56
Thorazine, dangers of, 56
Thrush infection, in infant, 178, 183
Tobacco. *See* Smoking

Tocosamine, dangers of, 57
Touching: The Human Significance of the Skin
    (Montague), 15, 24, 144
Toxoplasmosis, congenital, jaundice caused by,
    110
Tranquilizers, dangers of, 56
Transfusion, in newborn, 97
    for jaundice, 109, 111
Trichloroethylene (TCE), dangers of, 57
Trilene, dangers of, 57
Trimar, dangers of, 57
Trimethylene, dangers of, 57
Twins, 183
    birth positions of, 25
    daily menu for, 8
    signs of, 25

U

Ultrasound, pros and cons of, 48
Umbilical cord. *See* Cord, umbilical
Umbilical hernia. *See* Hernia, umbilical
Urine, infant's, 183–84
Uterus, muscles of, 23–24

V

Vagina, self-examination of, 151
Valium, dangers of, 56
Vistaril, dangers of, 56
Vitamin E, for sore nipples, 133
Vitamin K, given to newborns, 96
    jaundice caused by, 98
Vomiting, with burp, 163
Vulva, infant's, care of, 184

W

Walking around
    during hospital stay, 99
    during labor, 53
    at home, postpartum, 184

X